**Urban Transportation
Technology**

Urban Transportation Technology

Thomas McGean

Lexington Books
D.C. Heath and Company
Lexington, Massachusetts
Toronto   London

Library of Congress Cataloging in Publication Data

McGean, Thomas.
    Urban transportation technology.

    Includes index.
    1. Urban transportation. I. Title.
TA1205.M25   629.04   75-10228
ISBN 0-669-99911-3

Copyright © 1976 by D.C. Heath and Company

Published simultaneously in Canada

Printed in the United States of America

International Standard Book Number: 0-669-99911-3

Library of Congress Catalog Card Number: 75-10228

To my wife Doris, in appreciation of her help and support

Contents

List of Figures

List of Tables

Preface

This book is intended to fill what appears to be an unmet need for an up-to-date text on urban transportation technology. By technology I refer to the engineering aspects of transportation hardware as opposed to the planning and design of systems for specific applications. The planning area is replete with numerous texts on demand models, origin destination studies, and so forth, but there does not appear to be a complementary source of information on the systems engineering tools for assessing hardware feasibility and performance, or for documenting the performance capabilities of modern existing and proposed hardware concepts. This book is intended to serve as an introduction to such hardware oriented technology.

It is important to emphasize that this book is not a text on the detailed design of transportation hardware. It is rather a transportation systems engineering text providing both rule of thumb performance capabilities for automobile, bus, rail, and new system technology, and some general engineering approaches suitable for estimating the performance of or for performing feasibility studies and parametric tradeoff analyses for any type of transit system.

The book is based upon the author's experience as a transportation systems engineer at the MITRE Corporation during which time he has analyzed the engineering characteristics and performance potentials of bus, rail, air cushion, and personal rapid transit systems as a consultant to the Urban Mass Transportation Administration. Most of the material has been developed as a result of teaching courses in urban transportation technology at both Howard and George Washington Universities.

The opportunity to prepare this material as a book was presented by the MITRE Corporation and Howard University who granted the author a half time appointment as the MITRE Visiting Lecturer in Transportation at Howard University for the year 1973-1974.

The material is designed to be presented in two parts. Chapters 1 through 7 deal with general systems engineering concepts, which should be of value to both the systems engineer and the urban planner. Topics include headway and capacity relationships, typical performance levels for different transportation systems, station design, and energy and environmental impacts. Chapters 8 through 12, which are primarily of interest to systems engineers, emphasize the technology of the vehicle. Topics include propulsion, braking, ride quality, and steering and switching concepts. These chapters should also be of help as a general introduction to the concepts of transportation vehicle design.

It is my hope that this book will prove of some value by assembling in one place the great variety of information on this subject that has been published in recent years as a result of government sponsored research and a general renaissance in transportation technology.

Acknowledgments

This book was made possible by support received jointly from the MITRE Corporation and Howard University in connection with a half time appointment to the faculty of the Howard University School of Engineering for the academic year 1973-74. Reed H. Winslow, as head of the Transportation Systems Planning Department at MITRE helped initiate the project and provided advice and guidance. Much of the information assembled in this book was acquired by the author during over five years as a member of the MITRE staff during which he was privileged to provide technical support to the Office of High Speed Ground Transportation and the Urban Mass Transportation Administration of the Department of Transportation.

At Howard University, Dr. M. Lucius Walker, Jr., at the time Associate Dean of the School of Engineering, initiated Howard's request to MITRE and provided constant encouragement despite the many obligations of his position. Dr. Charles Watkins, Head of the Mechanical Engineering Department to which the author was assigned, and Anthony Chambliss who, as his Graduate Assistant, helped with calculations and other arduous tasks, also deserve grateful appreciation.

Much of the chapter on stations is based upon the work of W.J. Roesler of the Johns Hopkins University Applied Physics Laboratory. Norman Lutkefedder, Manager Advanced Engineering Research Group of the National Highway Traffic Safety Administration, collaborated with me on the work on crash survivability research in chapter 4. Staff colleagues at MITRE also made major contributions. The figures and charts on energy consumption are mainly the work of John Lieb. Drs. Rodney Lay and William Fraize wrote portions of the chapter on propulsion systems. Jack Dais, now with the Bell Telephone Laboratories and formerly on the faculty of the University of Minnesota, made available his lecture notes, portions of which were incorporated into the chapter on energy. Finally, my thanks to C.L. Nelson, who prepared the illustrations, and to H.D. Tiller, who typed the final manuscript.

1 Introduction

The Urban Transportation Problem

Seventy-four percent of the population of the United States resided in the cities and their surrounding suburbs in 1970. By 1980 it is expected that 82 percent of the population will be living in urban areas.[1] This rapid urbanization of the United States has been accompanied by the phenomenal growth of the automobile from a toy of the rich around the turn of the century to the point (1970) that it was employed for 94 percent of all urban travel. Auto dependence and rapid urban growth are together at the root of today's urban transportation problem.

The urban transportation problem has numerous dimensions including congestion, lack of mobility for certain urban groups, adverse environmental, social, and economic impact, inadequate coordination and long range planning, and an inadequate level of safety.

Congestion

Perhaps the problem most obvious to those who must travel by automobile in our cities is that of congestion. Especially during the morning and evening rush hours, traffic is slowed to a crawl on major urban arteries. The solution of simply building additional freeways is being recognized as unsatisfactory. The commuter making his "trip to work" is the cause of most of the rush hour traffic and wooing him to mass transit is seen as a possible solution. Thus we have San Francisco, Washington, D. C., Baltimore, and Atlanta all building subway systems. An alternative to subways is the use of the existing freeway network in our cities for bus transit. The Shirley Highway, funneling traffic from Virginia's suburbs into the Pentagon and downtown Washington, has been chosen for a demonstration of the exclusive busway, in which a freeway lane is reserved for bus traffic only. This provides the bus with an exclusive right-of-way similar to that enjoyed by the subway or commuter train.[a] Free from auto congestion, the bus can then offer its riders time savings in exchange for the sacrifice of the door-to-door convenience of their automobiles. Riders apparently welcome the chance to take transit when it provides better service and the Shirley buses now carry over 24,000 daily passengers.[2]

[a] Carpools are currently also permitted to share the busway.

1

Lack of Mobility for Certain Urban Groups

For those who can drive, the automobile has introduced an era of unparalleled mobility. At the flick of a key, the entire country is at their fingertips. Social patterns have adapted themselves to the mobility characteristics of the automobile, resulting in drive-in movies, restaurants, and banks, and enormous shopping centers.

It is important to remember however, that only half of the American population is licensed to drive.[3] The remainder, comprising the young, the old, the poor, and the handicapped, must either rely upon a friend or family member with a license, or make do with what in most parts of the country is an inadequate mass transit system.

The vital role of the automobile as a source of mobility is reflected in the importance that young people attach to learning to drive and getting a car. Similarly, the elderly frequently try to keep their licenses long past the time when their physical capacity to drive safely has waned, fully aware that loss of the ability to drive will mean dependence on others for the basic necessities of living.

The growth of auto oriented suburbs has forced parents to spend a great deal of time ferrying their children to the many activities that, in a more compact urban environment, would be accessible by walking or by using mass transit.

The poor, especially in semirural outlying areas, lack transportation to obtain needed medical care. This has made inaccessible and ineffective many of the health services offered by our clinics.

The problem of mobility for these segments of our population is becoming critical and can be expected to receive increased attention in the years ahead.

Adverse Environmental, Social, and Economic Impact

The discovery in the 1950s that the smog in the Los Angeles basin was caused by a photochemical reaction involving sunlight and automobile exhaust made it clear that the atmosphere could no longer be considered an inexhaustible sink for effluent from transportation, power generation, and industrial sources. In recognition of this reality, a fragmented approach to regulation and control of environmental abuse began to emerge, first at the state level in California, and subsequently on a national scale.

In December of 1970, Congress formed the Environmental Protection Agency to permit coordinated and effective governmental action on behalf of the environment. The EPA was charged by Congress with enforcing stringent limits on automotive exhaust emissions. As a result the spark ignition engine, which has been synonomous with the automobile since its inception, began to sprout all manner of pipes, valves, and other contraptions and suffered significant deterioration in gasoline mileage. Fortunately this "band-aid" approach has been accompanied by longer range efforts involving the basic technology of prime movers. Automotive engineering magazines are currently replete with articles on Wankel engines, stratefied charge engines, Stirling engines, steam engines, and gas turbine engines. Even the electric car is getting renewed attention as battery technology advances.

The adverse impact of the automobile upon urban social structure has also received increasing attention. "Suburban sprawl" has become a part of the lexicon of sociologists and urban planners. The auto oriented society, because of its density and land use patterns, tends to lack suitable social centers where the young can congregate and the old can meet to talk. At the height of the era of highway construction, multiple lane freeways were sometimes permitted to carve up cities without adequate consideration of their effect upon local traffic patterns within the city or of their aesthetic impact. Structures that would stand for many generations were erected from standardized engineering specifications with little thought for harmonious site integration or impact upon the community.

Abuses of this sort eventually produced a counterreaction. It may be that the first sign of this reaction occured in San Francisco, where the citizens irate over the impact of freeway construction upon their city literally stopped the Embarcedero Freeway in midair. This led to the creation of the Bay Area Rapid Transit District and a successful public referendum in 1962 approving property tax levies in the Bay area to finance construction of the first subway in the United States to be built west of the Mississippi River.

Along with environmental and social impact, the economic impact of the automobile in urban areas has also come under closer scrutiny. Valuable downtown real estate is consumed by parking automobiles that stand idle throughout the day. In cities with populations of over a million, 14 percent of the total central business district ground area is devoted to parking.[4] Multilane highways also consume valuable tax producing urban land and incur high road maintenance costs. As congestion and noise deteriorate the quality of urban life, those with a choice flee to the suburbs, leaving a residue of disadvantaged behind to be supported by a dwindling economic base.

Inadequate Coordination and Long Range Planning

Many of these adverse impacts can be traced to a lack of proper coordination and planning of the urban transportation system. Transportation represents a mobility skeleton at the base of the growth of an urban area. As rivers and harbors were early forces in fostering the growth of our cities, so railroads, airports, and freeways determine urban growth and form today. While rivers and harbors were for the most part gifts of nature, freeways, railroads, and airports are the products of men. As such, they can either be forces for disintegration or forces for orderly growth and development depending on whether foresight or opportunism guides their creation. The considerable mass transit construction that will occur in the next decade creates what may be a unique opportunity to reshape the structure of our cities. Subways can be used to create high density corridors. New people movers can be used to integrate areas of related activities. Busways can be used to interconnect vital centers within the urban area.

Transportation systems thus provide tools by which urban planners and enlightened citizens can guide the development of the region without imposing a rigid design upon it. The transportation network provides a "skeleton" as it were, guiding, but not forcing the development of the area it serves. The noncoercive nature of the transportation network assures that the final form of the area will bear the imprint of numerous spontaneous decisions made by individual citizens. As a result, the intelligent use of transportation planning provides a middle road between the chaos of a laissez faire attitude and the sterility that is all too often the result of a totally planned effort.

Inadequate Level of Safety

The automotive death toll has become a serious national problem. In 1970, 53,816 Americans died in automobile accidents, over a third of them in urban areas.[5] This makes the automobile the nation's fourth killer, behind cardiovascular diseases, cancer, and pneumonia. Despite national concern with crime, more than three times as many Americans meet their death by automobile as are killed by homicide.[6]

In recognition of this problem, Congress established the National Highway Traffic Safety Administration (NHTSA) in 1970 to implement programs relating to the safety performance of motor vehicles and related equipment and motor vehicle drivers. NHTSA has implemented programs to reduce the occurrence and severity of highway crashes, improve postcrash survivability, reduce the economic losses in accidents, and provide various consumer information services. Motor vehicle safety standards are issued which prescribe levels of safety-related performance for all new vehicles sold in the United States.

Diversion of urban traffic to mass transit is another avenue to reduction of the automotive death toll. The urban fatality rate in 1970 was 2.2 per 100 million passenger miles traveled by automobile.[7] By comparison, fatalities on buses and subways run about 0.2 per 100 million passenger miles—making them over ten times safer.[8] Urban automobile accidents may be estimated to cost this nation some 1.6 billion dollars per year.[9] If even a portion of this traffic could be diverted to mass transit, the savings in both lives and dollars would be substantial.

Reliance on the Automobile

Table 1-1 taken from the 1972 National Transportation Report of the Department of Transportation indicates the extent of dependence on the automobile for transportation in urban areas. Taken together bus, rail transit, commuter rail, and taxicabs provide only six percent of our transportation services. For the remaining 94 percent we depend upon our automobiles.

The percentage of trips made by each "mode," such as auto, bus, or rail transit, is referred to as the "modal split." Table 1-1 provides modal split data on a national basis. The range of the total transit modal split runs from as low as one percent to as high as twenty percent in the larger cities.[10]

A basic problem for transportation planners is that of "diversion"—the change or potential change of ridership from one mode of travel to another or from one route to another. To improve the transit modal split it is necessary to divert traffic from the auto. A key element in such a diversion strategy will be the "choice riders," who choose transit freely even though they have a driver's license and an automobile is owned within their family. Since choice riders do have the option of using their automobiles, transit

Table 1-1
Urban Travel Statistics (passenger miles)

	1960 *million miles*	*Percent*	1970 *million miles*	*Percent*
Auto	423,300	88.4%	736,689	93.9
Bus	28,328	5.9	20,864	2.7
Rail transit	18,504	3.9	16,928	2.2
Commuter rail	4,600	1.0	4,600	0.6
Taxi	3,900	0.8	5,100	0.6

Source: "1972 National Transportation Report," U.S. Department of Transportation, Office of the Assistant Secretary for Policy and International Affairs, Washington, D.C., July 1972, page 189. Reprinted with permission.

must offer them a competitive service. Many planners feel that to stem the inexorable growth of the automobile, a direct appeal to this portion of the market is essential.

The Peaking Phenomena

Because of the large number of commuters spawned by the explosive growth of suburban areas, traffic patterns peak severely during the morning and evening rush hours. These are usually assumed to comprise the hours 7:00 to 9:00 A.M. and 4:30 to 6:30 P.M. Total traffic during this period of four hours typically exceeds the traffic carried during the entire remaining twenty hours of the day! Thus peak hour flow is often estimated at one eighth of the total daily traffic. Figure 1-1 shows typical trip distributions versus time of day for transit and automotive traffic.[11] The more severe peaking that occurs for transit is due to the greater proportion of transit trips that involve going to and from work. Half of all public transit trips are work oriented as opposed to only a quarter of all automotive trips. Transit's peaking problem is compounded since it is also heavily used by children going to school—15 to 20 percent of transit trips are school related.[12]

Peaking causes severe operating difficulties for transit systems. Adequate vehicles, drivers, and other personnel must be hired to handle the heavy rush hour demand. The rest of the day these capital and human resources are underutilized. Yet the capital costs must be written off on an annual basis, and the drivers must be paid for an eight hour day. If more off-peak ridership could be attracted, transit systems could make more efficient use of their system and decrease their cost per passenger mile. The use of the transit resource for goods movement during off-peak hours is also receiving considerable attention as a means of better utilizing equipment during slack hours.

Trip Orientation

The growth of the suburbs has lessened the dependence of metropolitan regions upon the traditional downtown area, or central business district (CBD) as it is often called. This has eliminated the traditional "many to one" nature of the trip to work, with diffuse origins in outlying areas all converging upon a fairly concentrated central business district. Instead we have a growing "many to many" type of trip pattern in which both the workers' homes and their places of work are scattered throughout the metropolitan area. Traditional transit systems can more easily serve well defined concentrated trip patterns, while the automobile is more successful

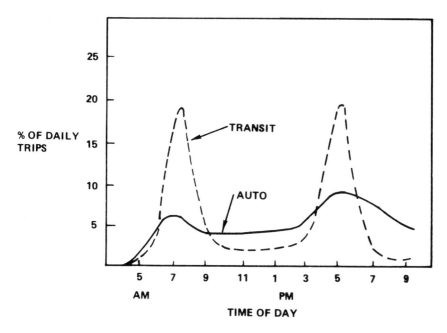

Figure 1-1. Typical Trip Distributions

in handling geographically dispersed origin-destination pairs. Thus 25 to 50 percent of all transit trips are CBD oriented as opposed to only 3 to 15 percent of auto trips.[13] This creates a vicious cycle in which increased auto use encourages a dispersed pattern of development which, since it is not well served by transit, encourages further increased use of the automobile.

Breaking this cycle will require either regional planning compatible with transit corridors, or the development of new transit systems which can effectively serve the "many to many" type of pattern that has evolved from reliance on the automobile. The use of personal rapid transit vehicles (PRT) providing a nonstop origin to destination trip has been proposed as one means of providing transit service competitive with the auto. Such vehicles would be summoned by the passenger pushing a button, much like an elevator, and are thus sometimes called "horizontal elevators." They would provide a private conveyance for each passenger or group of passengers and would bypass all intermediate stations, proceeding directly to the desired destination.

Trip Length

How long is the average urban trip? There is a strong relationship between the ease of using the transportation system, and the length of trip traveled. If it is necessary to walk several blocks and wait 15 minutes, the system will not be used for short trips. On the other hand, when it is just a matter of walking to the carport and turning a key, many short trips are taken. Thus automobile trips average three to four miles in length. Bus trips average 3 to 5 miles in length. Trips by rapid rail (the familiar subway or elevated rail systems) average 6 to 7 miles. And commuter rail systems, operating on regular railroad right-of-way from outlying suburban areas, average trip lengths of 10 to 17 miles.[14]

Components of the Urban Trip

The urban trip is the process of getting from the trip "origin" to the trip "destination." The total time involved in completing this process may be called the "portal to portal trip time." If the rider is fortunate enough to begin his trip at the train station with a train ready and waiting, and if his destination is one of the train stops further down the line, then his "travel time" will be identical with his "portal to portal trip time." Ordinarily he will not be so fortunate. He will begin his trip remote from the terminal, and his destination will similarly be some distance from the terminal at which he disembarks. He must thus spend some time getting to and from the terminals of the transit system. This time is referred to as "access time." One of the measures of the "Level of Service" or quality of a transit system is its accessibility. The larger the number of route miles and the closer together the stations are spaced, the greater will be the accessibility of the system.

When the rider arrives at the transit terminal he will then generally have to wait some time for the vehicle to arrive. This waiting time will of course depend upon the frequency of service, or how frequently vehicle arrivals are scheduled. On large subway systems during rush hour, trains arrive every two minutes. On the other hand, during slack hours commuter trains and buses may run as infrequently as once every hour.

Once the rider is on board the transit vehicle, the travel time will depend upon the speed of the vehicle, its acceleration and braking capability, and the number and duration of stops it must make enroute. Stops may be either scheduled stops to pick up and discharge passengers, or they may be caused by traffic congestion. In downtown areas the typical speed of a bus seldom exceeds ten miles per hour because of traffic congestion and frequent stops. Even rapid rail systems travelling at maximum speeds of 60 miles per hour, average only about 30 miles per hour if stops are accounted for. This average speed is usually referred to as the "schedule speed" and may be used directly to compute expected travel time. (Trip length divided by schedule speed equals expected travel time.) Finally, it may be neces-

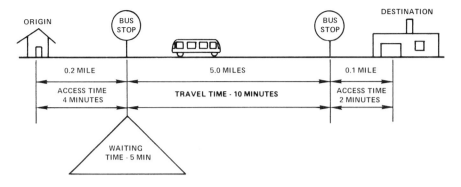

Figure 1-2. Trip Components

sary for the passenger to make a transfer in which case he will have to wait again for another vehicle to arrive.

Figure 1-2 shows a typical trip sequence indicating the various components. Typical times and distances have been included. Notice that actual travel time on the system is less than half of the portal to portal trip time. This is typical of the urban transit problem and explains the need for improved access and high frequency of service. For the example illustrated, a 72 percent reduction in travel time, (as might be obtained using a 150 mile per hour nonstop air cushion vehicle), would only reduce portal to portal trip time by 34 percent.[b] On the other hand, if true origin to destination transit service were available on demand, then even if travel time remained unchanged, the portal to portal trip time could be reduced by half. The private automobile very nearly approximates to this ideal of perfect accessibility and zero waiting time. Such service is often referred to as "demand actuated origin-destination service"—demand actuated because it is available at the request of the user; origin-destination because it very nearly approximates door to door service.

At present, no transit systems offer this type of service. In order to compete with the automobile the transit system—with inferior accessibility—must compensate by offering faster speeds for the vehicular portion of the trip. Unfortunately, the transit system has to stop to pick up and discharge passengers, and generally has poor acceleration capability, so it is inherently a slower system. If, like the bus, the transit system must also share the congested city streets with the auto, the situation is hopeless. Automobile travel must then be inevitably faster. Hope for conventional transit lies in freeing it from the congested street network. Rapid rail systems, traveling on their own grade-separated right-of-way, are free of highway traffic and can offer travel time savings during the rush hour

---

[b] Assumes acceleration and deceleration limited to 3 mph/sec.

despite poor accessibility.) Similarly, the Shirley Highway busway, by providing a private right-of-way to buses, is able to offer Virginia commuters typical savings of 10 to 30 minutes on their trip to downtown Washington.

Recently proposed personal rapid transit (PRT) systems attempt to match the demand actuated origin-destination service of the automobile by utilizing an extensive route structure and providing for service at the push of a button. Their ability reasonably to approximate the automobile's level of service at competitive costs has not yet been demonstrated.

Transit System Elements and Configurations

Functionally, any transit system must include certain basic elements in order to perform its mission. Typically these include:[15]

> *Terminals*. Places where passengers leave the transit system.
>
> *Vehicles*. Devices to confer mobility upon the passenger.
>
> *Way Links*. Paths on which the vehicles can move in space. Variously called highways, tracks, guideways, streets, etc., depending upon the mode.
>
> *Way Nodes or Interchanges*. Facilities that permit movement from one way link to another. (e.g., a freeway interchange).
>
> *Control System*. A set of devices, decision makers, and associated rules that provide for the safe, efficient, and rational operation of the system.
>
> *Right-of-way*. The land dedicated to way links, way interchanges, and terminals.
>
> *Support Facilities*. Maintenance, vehicle storage, personnel training centers, and other support facilities essential to operation of the system.

How these elements are combined determines the system configuration.

Figure 1-3 shows some typical configurations. In the simplest, known as a "shuttle" (Figure 1-3a), the terminals are located along a single guideway on which vehicles can travel in either direction. Use of the same guideway for travel in both directions limits the system to a single vehicle or train of vehicles. The most widely used shuttle system is the elevator. Other examples include the Seattle Monorail and the people mover at Tampa Airport.

By limiting traffic flow on the guideway to only one direction many vehicles can share its use. This leads to the loop configuration (Figure 1-3b) with stations located like beads on a necklace. This pure version of the loop

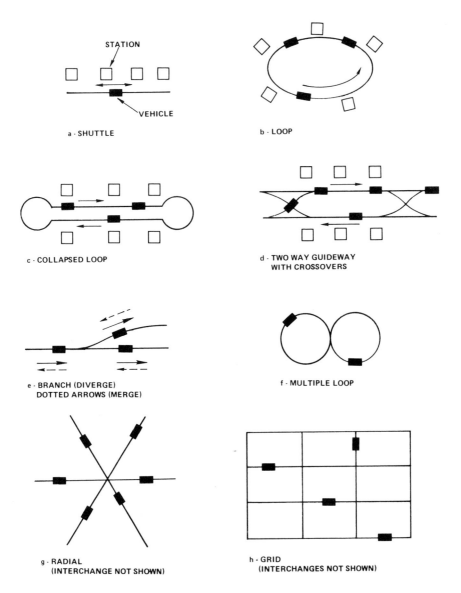

Figure 1-3. Transit System Configurations

is seldom seen except for race tracks or toy trains because it is necessary to traverse the entire loop to get to an adjacent terminal located counter to the direction of traffic flow. Instead the loop is usually collapsed into a two way guideway (Figure 1-3c and 1-3d). Figure 1-3c shows a simple collapsed loop with turnarounds at each end of the line. Vehicles only travel in one direction. The configuration of Figure 1-3d provides crossovers at each end so the vehicle can switch to the other guideway for the return trip. In this case, as for the shuttle, vehicles must be capable of travel in both directions. The two way link is typical of many commuter rail and rapid transit systems.

Provision of multiple interchanges makes possible a complete transit network providing vehicles with optional paths through the system. Figures 1-3e through 1-3h show typical networks including the branch, multiple loop, radial, and grid. The grid type network is the conceptual basis for much of our urban street network. It provides tremendous routing flexibility at the price of requiring a large number of interchanges.

It is the task of the transportation planner to combine the various modes and network configurations into a viable transportation system. In so doing he will often distinguish between the "line haul," "collection," and "distribution" functions. He makes this distinction because urban areas are usually not perfectly homogeneous, but instead consist of a number of readily identifiable "major activity centers," and lower density residential areas. Major activity centers include the central business district (CBD) as well as other primary trip generators such as large shopping centers, stadiums, and industrial parks.

It is efficient to use a collection system to gather passengers from low density residential areas to feed a line haul system. The line haul system provides a higher speed service with less frequent stops between major residential collection points and major activity centers. Within the major activity centers a distribution system is required, providing a lower speed service with more closely spaced terminals. Each of these systems has distinct characteristics:

Collection. Low population density, short trips, low speed, close station spacing.

Line Haul. High passenger flow rates, higher speeds, longer trips, longer station spacing.

Distribution. High passenger flow rates, low speeds, short trips, closely spaced stations.

Notes

1. "1972 National Transportation Report," U. S. Department of Transportation, Washington D.C., July 1972, page 189.

2. "Lindenwold Line and Shirley Busway: A Comparison," Vukan R. Vuchic and Richard M. Stanger, University of Pennsylvania, Report

presented to 52nd Annual Meeting of the Highway Research Board, Washington, D. C., January 25, 1973, page 24.

3. *1971 Automobile Facts and Figures*, Automobile Manufacturers Association, Detroit, page 45, and *Statistical Abstract of the U. S.*, 1971.

4. *Traffic Engineering Handbook*, 3rd Edition, edited by John Baerwald, Institute of Traffic Engineers, Washington, D. C., 1965, page 461.

5. "Fatal and Injury Accident Rates on Federal-Aid and Other Highway Systems," U. S. Department of Transportation, Federal Highway Administration, Washington, D. C., 1970, page 25.

6. *Statistical Abstract of U. S.*, 1971, page 61.

7. "Fatal and Injury Accident Rates," page 1 (and assuming an average auto occupancy of 1.4 persons).

8. National Highway Safety Board, (computerized records), Department of Transportation, Washington, D. C. (and assuming an average trip length of 5 miles).

9. Statistics from reference 5 on urban fatalities charged at the rate per accident of $89,000 as recommended by "Informational Report by Committee on Planning and Design Policies on Road User Benefit Analysis for Highway Improvements," American Association of State Highway Officials, Washington, D. C., 1960, page 143.

10. "1972 National Transportation Report," page 189.

11. Typical of data in *The Urban Transportation Problem*, J.R. Meyer, J.F. Kain, and M. Wohl, Harvard University Press, Cambridge, 1965, pages 92-95.

12. "1972 National Transportation Report," page 189.

13. Ibid., page 189.

14. Ibid., page 193.

15. Classification follows the general outline of "Modes of Transportation, Sources of Information on Urban Transportation," Report No. 2, August 1968, R. Soloman and J. Silien, American Society of Civil Engineers, New York, New York, page 6.

2 Capacity and Headway Considerations

The concepts of headway and capacity are very closely related. Together they determine in large measure the feasibility of almost any transportation system, be it a new freeway lane or a subway. System capacity should be adequate to satisfy passenger demand and to generate sufficient revenue to cover costs. Yet, capacity must not be increased to the point where safety is compromised. Much of the art of transportation system design involves the attempt to balance these conflicting requirements properly.

Volume and Headway

Formally the term volume may be defined as "the number of vehicles passing a fixed point on the guideway in a unit of time."[1]

Volume is closely related to headway, which is defined as the time interval between the arrival of the front of one vehicle and the arrival of the front of the following vehicle at a fixed point on the guideway.[2] The vehicles are moving along the same guideway or traffic lane and in the same direction. In other words, headway is the time noted by an observer, standing beside a traffic lane, and clocking the passage of each vehicle past him. An additional explanatory point involves cases where several vehicles are coupled into a train. In this case, headway refers to the time interval between the arrival of the front vehicle of successive *trains* past a fixed point on the guideway.

Some writers distinguish between the time headway, defined as above, and the distance headway which refers to the distance between the front of one vehicle and the front of the next vehicle.[3] To avoid confusion we will limit the term headway exclusively to the time distance between vehicles. The distance between the fronts of successive vehicles will be called "spacing."[4]

The "mean vehicle headway," denoted by the symbol h, is the average headway along a line. It is simply the reciprocal of the traffic volume on that line.[5]

Therefore:

$$V = 3600/h \qquad (2.1)$$

V = traffic volume—vehicles/hour

h = mean vehicle headway—seconds

Since it is not safe for vehicles to operate bumper to bumper at high speeds, there is invariably a "minimum allowable headway" which represents the shortest permissible time interval between the passage of two vehicles past a fixed reference point. We denote this headway as h_0. Theoretically, the maximum possible number of vehicles that can be transported by a single traffic lane will be the reciprocal of this minimum allowable headway. Thus we have:

$$V_m = 3600/h_0 \tag{2.2}$$

V_m = maximum possible (or theoretical) vehicular flow—vehicles per hour

h_0 = minimum allowable headway—seconds

We refer to V_m as the theoretical or nominal vehicular capacity.

Practical Vehicular Capacities

It is never possible to fill completely a traffic lane with vehicles all operating at the minimum allowable headway. For this reason, the practical or actual vehicular capacity of a guideway will always be less than the theoretical value. The ratio of practical to theoretical vehicular line capacity may be called the "guideway utilization factor," since it represents the efficiency with which vehicular traffic has been able to use the guideway.

Guideway utilization is always less than unity since space on the guideway must be set aside to permit merging of traffic, and since not all vehicles may be operating at the minimum allowable headway. Making use of a guideway utilization factor, the formula for actual vehicular capacity becomes:

$$V_a = \gamma V_m = 3600\gamma/h_0 \tag{2.3}$$

V_a = practical or actual vehicular capacity—vehicles/hour

γ = guideway utilization factor expressed as a ratio

The value of γ chosen should represent the guideway utilization achievable under maximum traffic conditions.

Passenger Capacity

In as much as the purpose of a transit system is to move people, the quantity of passengers being transported is ordinarily of more consequence than the vehicular flow. Consider first the relationship between theoretical passenger carrying capacity and the theoretical vehicular capacity:

$$Q_m = pNV_m = 3600pN/h_0 \qquad (2.4)$$

Q_m = theoretical or nominal line capacity—passenger/hour

p = maximum number of vehicles that can be joined into a train

N = maximum number of passengers each vehicle is designed to carry

Because of its greater importance, the term capacity, in this text, will always refer to passenger carrying capacity unless vehicular capacity is specifically mentioned.

Of course the actual capacity of a line will always be less than the theoretical or nominal value given by equation 2.4. Formally we define the practical or actual capacity of a single, one way traffic lane as the actual volume of passengers per hour which can be safely transported past a fixed point under normal operating conditions.

Just as it is not possible to utilize completely all the guideway space theoretically available for vehicles, so it may not always be possible to fill each vehicle completely with passengers. The ratio of the average vehicle occupancy to the occupancy level for which the vehicle was designed is called the "load factor." It is usually expressed as a percentage. Thus a 50 percent load factor refers to a vehicle that travels on the average at half its design capacity. During rush hour many transit systems carry more passengers than their design limit. In this case, load factor can exceed 100 percent.[6] The maximum number of passengers who can theoretically be squeezed into a vehicle is called its "crush load." Crush load sets the upper bound on load factor. The maximum load factor can never be more than 100 times the crush load divided by the design load. Needless to say, no one is very comfortable when a vehicle operates at this limit!

Since it is common for transit systems to be heavily loaded during rush hours, it is the usual practice when computing practical line capacity to assume 80-100 percent load factors for these vehicles. On the other hand, there is extensive evidence that the average automobile carries only about 1.2 persons during the rush hour. Therefore, highway capacity is generally computed on the basis of 1.2 persons per vehicle (including the driver), which represents a load factor of less than 25 percent.[7] This constitutes a bias against the automobile that should be kept in mind when capacity equations are compared. If car pooling could increase the average vehicle occupancy from 1.2 to 2.4 persons per vehicle, we could reduce rush hour congestion by 50 percent without spending a penny on new facilities!

From the foregoing discussion, it should be clear that practical or actual line capacity is related to theoretical line capacity by the load factor as well as by the guideway utilization factor. In terms of minimum allowable headway:[8]

$$Q_a = 36\sigma\gamma pN/h_0 \qquad (2.5)$$

Q_a = practical or actual line capacity—passengers/hour

σ = load factor expressed as percent

γ = guideway utilization factor expressed as a ratio

It is usual to use peak hour values for γ and σ in computing practical line capacity.

Equation 2.5 may be called the basic line capacity equation. An important systems implication of this simple formula is that line capacity can only be increased in five ways:

1. Increase the number of passengers carried by each vehicle.
2. Increase the length of trains.
3. Decrease the minimum allowable headway.
4. Improve the load factor.
5. Improve guideway utilization.

If either vehicle size or the number of vehicles connected into a train is increased, then the flexibility of the system is decreased. Each passenger must wait while the other passengers board and disembark. Each passenger must stop at the destinations of every other passenger. Travel time is necessarily increased. Frequency of service with the larger vehicles will be lower. The level of service is in short diminished. The great asset of the automobile is its freedom from these constraints.

Decreasing the headway tends to decrease the margin of safety with regard to vehicle collisions so that the limitation on short headway operation is passenger safety. An unforeseen stop by one vehicle should not involve following vehicles in a dangerous pile-up collision. If passenger loading is online, time must be allowed for the online loading operation.

The next several chapters will be devoted in large measure to analytical techniques for computing the minimum allowable headway and from it the line capacity of transit systems, making various assumptions concerning risk.

To increase line capacity, high load factors and guideway utilization would seem desirable. However, high load factors may mean an increased number of vehicle stops and a lower frequency of service, which are undesirable to the user. High guideway utilization may cause queues to form at merges or intersections. Studies indicate that guideway utilization of about two-thirds theoretical may typically be required to prevent such queuing.

Table 2-1
Typical Capacities and Headways for Transit Systems

System	Headway Seconds	Capacity Vehicles/Hour	Capacity Passengers/Hour
		for a single lane	
Automobile (1.2 passengers)			
City Street	4.5-6	600-800	720-960
Freeway	1.8-2.4	1500-2000	1800-2400
Transit Bus			
City Street	60	60	3000
Exclusive Busway*	6	600	30,000
Subway			
10 Car Train	120	30	30,000-60,000
Typical New Systems	10-20	180-360	1000-15,000

*Based on data from the exclusive bus lane on New Jersey I-495 between the New Jersey Turnpike and the Lincoln Tunnel.

Source: *Personal Rapid Transit,* Edited by J. Edward Anderson, J.L. Dais, W.L. Garrard, and A.L. Kornhauser, Institute of Technology, University of Minnesota, Dept. of Audio Visual Extension, Minneapolis, Minn., April, 1972.

Values for Typical Systems

Table 2-1 gives practical capacities in both vehicles per hour and passengers per hour for various transportation modes. Load factor is 100 percent except as noted. Headways given are mean headways between vehicles under capacity flow conditions.

Since the expression in equation 2.5 is proportional to vehicle occupancy, line capacity can always be increased in this fashion. This is why the subway, with relatively large headways, still has high capacity. The price is paid in frequency of service and travel time, with each passenger forced to stop at every destination enroute to his own. The tradeoffs between headway, vehicle occupancy, and line capacity are graphically portrayed in Figure 2-1. Notice that line capacity versus vehicle or train occupancy for a fixed headway will plot as a 45° line on a log/log plot since they are directly proportional to each other. Typical headway, line capacity, and vehicle or train occupancy ranges for bus, auto, and subway systems are indicated on the graph.

The very high capacities achievable with subway trains are far greater than are required by all but the very largest cities. Critics of rail transit claim it will encourage a high density corridor growth in order to generate

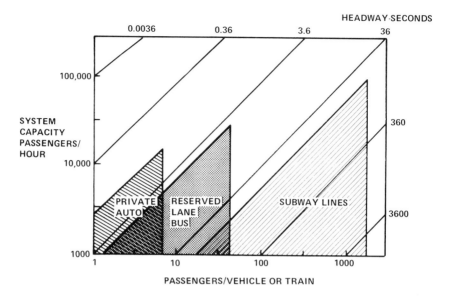

Figure 2-1. Typical Vehicle and System Capacities

support for the system. Autos, on the other hand promote a "sprawled out" fairly low density land use, for which they too have been criticized.

Spacing and Separation

"Spacing" may be defined as the distance between the front of a vehicle and the front of the vehicle immediately following it.[9] "Separation," on the other hand, refers to the distance between the *back* of a vehicle and the front of the vehicle immediately following it. "Separation" thus represents the distance *between* vehicles.[a] There is no unanimity in the transportation field on these definitions although an attempt has been made to follow common usage.

The relationships between spacing, separation, and headway are shown in Figure 2-2. Notice that separation plus vehicle length equals spacing. Spacing divided by vehicle speed equals headway.[10] Therefore the relation of separation to headway is given by:

$$h = \frac{s + pL}{v_0} \qquad (2.6)$$

v_0 = cruise speed—feet/second

---

[a] Separation is called "vehicular gap" in the *Highway Capacity Manual*. We have followed rail terminology (see, for example, "Good News for Commuters: Better and Faster Rapid Transit," Mayer Horn, *IEEE Spectrum*, February 1972, pages 55-61).

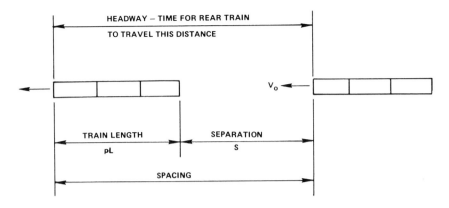

Figure 2-2. Relation between Spacing, Separation, and Headway

L = vehicle length—feet

s = separation—feet

p = number of vehicles in a train

That is, it takes h seconds for a vehicle traveling at a speed v_0 to travel a distance $s + pL$.

Obviously, the minimum allowable headway will depend on how small a separation is permitted between vehicles. This minimum allowable separation will be denoted s_0. Its specification will depend upon vehicle speed and deceleration capability, control system performance, reaction times, vehicle and guideway design considerations, weather conditions, and the degree of risk considered acceptable.

Safe Stopping Distance and K Factor

The term "safe stopping distance" is used to refer to the maximum distance required to stop a vehicle under worst case conditions. What do we mean by "worst case conditions"? Poor traction caused by a wet or icy road? Partial failure of the braking system? Stopping on a steep hill with a heavy tailwind? Grease or water on the brake linings? In fact, worst case conditions can mean all of these things together or it can mean none of them! The definition of the worst case conditions is a basic premise of system design that must be based upon operating environment, performance, safety, reliability, and cost considerations. In comparing the performance of different systems it is most important to see that they were designed to comparable constraints.

The traditional approach taken by railroad and rapid transit designers has been to compute safe stopping distance based upon a deceleration rate that experience has shown is generally achievable. A safety factor is then applied to the safe stopping distance in determining the minimum permissible train separation. Nonstandard conditions are ostensibly protected against by the safety factor. The safety factor, which has historically been denoted by the symbol K, has become known as the "K factor" and is a term that is invariably in evidence in discussions concerning headway. The K factor is defined as:

$$K = s_0/s_m \qquad (2.7)$$

$s_0 = $ minimum permissible train separation—feet

$s_m = $ safe stopping distance—feet

It is common in the train industry to use a value of K of 1.35 to 1.5 or a margin of safety of from 35 percent to 50 percent.[11] The following paragraph from *The New York Subway—Interborough Rapid Transit*[12] gives a good idea of the approach used in determining safe stopping distance and K factor. (The term overlap as used here is equivalent to our term "separation.")

The length of the overlap was given very careful consideration by the Interborough Rapid Transit Company, who instituted a series of tests of braking power of trains; from these and others made by the Pennsylvania Railroad Company curves were computed so as to determine the distance in which trains could be stopped at various rates of speed on a level track, with corrections for rising and falling grades up to 2 per cent. Speed curves were then plotted for the trains on the entire line, showing at each point the maximum possible speed with the gear ratio of the motors adopted. A joint consideration of the speeds, braking efforts, and profile of the road were then used to determine at each and every point on the line the minimum allowable distance between trains, so that the train in the rear could be stopped by the automatic application of the brakes before reaching a train which might be standing at a signal in advance; in other words the length of the overlap section was determined by the local conditions at each point.

In order to provide for adverse conditions the actual braking distances was [*sic*] increased by 50 per cent.; for example, the braking distance of a train moving 35 miles an hour is 465 feet, this would be increased 50 per cent and the overlap made not less than 697 feet.

The Brick Wall Stop

If vehicles are never spaced closer than the distance in which they are able to stop, ($K > 1.0$), then it should be possible for the trailing vehicle to stop safely even if the vehicle in front of it stops instantly. This has given rise to the concept of the brick wall stopping criteria: "In the worst case situation, the following vehicle must be able to stop even if the lead vehicle stops instantaneously, as it would if it struck a brick wall." Instantaneous deceleration is of course a physical impossibility, although there are conditions, such as a head-on collision, for which it is very nearly approximated. Ordinarily, the brick wall approach tends to be conservative from the standpoint of safety.

There are very good reasons why the brick wall criterion was adopted by the railroads. First, it is difficult, if not impossible, for a motorman to estimate accurately the speed of a train in front of him. Second, the automatic signalling systems used by railroads have no way of knowing the velocity of a vehicle occupying the section of track protected by a particular signal. Signal spacing must therefore be laid out on the assumption that the train is stopped.

As new automated transit systems have been proposed, operating at closer headways and using more sophisticated collision avoidance concepts, there has been a tendency to retain the concepts of "brick wall stop" and "K factor." This has perhaps caused a great deal of sometimes unnecessary controversy in recent years concerning achievable headways. However, even on the most modern systems, there are situations besides the head-on collision that might occur to approach closely a "brick wall" stop. These include:

1. Failure of the control system to detect a vehicle stopped on the guideway
2. Collision with a heavy obstacle on the guideway
3. Major suspension failure
4. Locking of the brakes
5. Thrust reversal of the propulsion motors
6. Vehicle collision with the guideway in a switch area
7. Two vehicles colliding at an intersection or merge
8. Vehicle attempt to traverse an improperly positioned switch

Short of a very careful failure analysis of the system, the conservative assumption of a brick wall stop still appears to be a useful engineering design criteria. Because of its history of successful use, the burden of proof will lie with those who propose less conservative criteria to demonstrate that safety is preserved. This represents an area where much research can be expected in the years ahead.

Stopping Distance for Constant Deceleration Braking

The simplest case for computation of stopping distance is that in which the

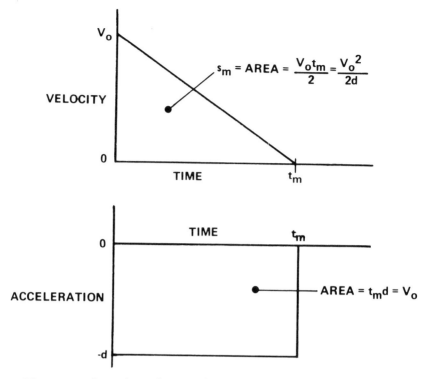

Figure 2-3. Stopping Distance for Constant Deceleration Braking

vehicle stops with a constant deceleration. Velocity and acceleration plots versus time are shown in Figure 2-3. From the area under the acceleration curve we obtain the time to stop. The area under the velocity curve represents the stopping distance. Thus:[13]

$$t_m = v_0/d \tag{2.8}$$

$$s_m = v_0^2/2d \tag{2.9}$$

$d =$ deceleration rate—feet/second

In terms of the K factor the minimum allowable separation is given by:

$$s_0 = Kv_0^2/2d \tag{2.10}$$

And the minimum allowable headway becomes:

$$h_0 = \frac{Kv_0}{2d} + \frac{pL}{v_0} \tag{2.11}$$

The theoretical capacity of such a system would be:

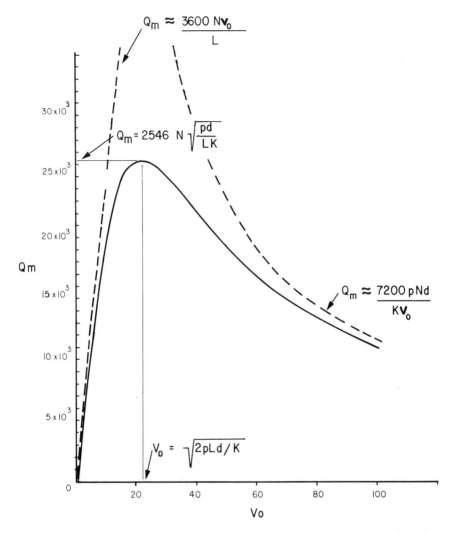

Figure 2-4. Brick Wall Stop Equations Assuming Constant Deceleration and No Reaction Time (Plotted for $L = 20$, $N = 14$, $p = 1$, $d = 16.1$, $K = 1.5$)

$$Q_m = \frac{3600pN}{\frac{Kv_0}{2d} + \frac{pL}{v_0}} \tag{2.12}$$

Equation 2.12 has been plotted in Figure 2-4 to show the effect of cruise speed upon line capacity. At high velocities the vehicle length becomes negligible and the capacity equation becomes:

$$Q_m = 7200pNd/Kv_0 \tag{2.13}$$

Notice that capacity decreases with increasing velocity. This is a key point. Any system using the brick wall type of stopping criteria to determine permissible headways will have difficulty maintaining high capacity at high vehicle speeds.

At low speeds, the physical space occupied by the vehicles predominates as v_0 approaches zero. Thus:

$$Q_m = 3600Nv_0/L \tag{2.14}$$

At low speeds the capacity also decreases, becoming as would be expected, zero at zero velocity.

Obviously there must be a maximum capacity, which can be determined by differentiating the capacity equation and setting it equal to zero. By noting that maximum capacity occurs at minimum headway we can differentiate the simpler expression for headway and set it equal to zero:

$$\frac{dh_0}{dv_0} = \frac{K}{2d} - \frac{pL}{v_0^2} = 0 \tag{2.15}$$

$$v_0 \text{ (maximum capacity)} = \sqrt{2pLd/K} \tag{2.16}$$

Thus minimum headway or maximum capacity occurs when the speed is equal to the square root of the product of twice the braking rate multiplied by the train length divided by any braking safety factor. The minimum allowable headway is found from substitution in equation 2.11 to be:

$$h_0 = \sqrt{2pLK/d} \tag{2.17}$$

The maximum theoretical capacity is then:

$$Q_m = 2546N \sqrt{pd/LK} \tag{2.18}$$

An interesting fact that is apparent from inspection of equation 2.15 is that maximum capacity and minimum headway occur when train separation $(Kv_0^2/2d)$ equals train length (pL). Thus the speed for maximum system through-put will be that for which the *minimum permissible separation is identical to the train length*. With 700 foot long trains the optimum separation would also be 700 feet.

Some Implications and Limitations

These simple equations tend to give a remarkably accurate picture of the qualitative characteristics of vehicle flow. The existence of an optimum speed predicted by equation 2.16 is observed to occur on both train systems and highways—even though highway traffic flow theory is currently based on a completely different theoretical approach. Experience verifies the predicted reduction in vehicular speed required to accommodate high traffic volumes. The equation suggests that as traffic builds up, vehicle speed will decrease until maximum traffic flow is reached at the speed $v_0 = \sqrt{2pLd/K}$. Any attempt to push additional traffic through will be self defeating—further reduction in vehicle speed only reduces traffic flow. The situation becomes unstable and a traffic jam is the result. (In the limit zero traffic flow at zero speed!) Besides this qualitative agreement with highway traffic behavior, these equations have served for years as the theoretical basis for the design of rapid transit and railroad block control systems, which have achieved an enviable safety record.

Nevertheless, there are some serious limitations. The deceleration value used must be an average value over the stopping period since the brakes can not actually be instantly applied or removed. Not only is such a sudden brake application physically unrealizable, but if achieved it would cause any standing passengers to lose their balance and be thrown to the floor.

Another limitation is the lack of any provision for system reaction time. Time is required to perceive the condition requiring a stop, and to command and then actuate the stopping mechanism.

Modified Brick Wall Stop Equations

The brick wall stop equations can be extended to account for the rate of application and removal of the brakes. To do so, we introduce the concept of "jerk." Jerk is defined as the rate of change of acceleration with time and is therefore the time derivative of acceleration. Figure 2-5 shows jerk, acceleration, and velocity profiles for what we may call a "trapezoidal deceleration profile."[14] In this profile jerk levels during both application and removal of braking are limited to a constant level j. The result is to increase or decrease deceleration linearly as a function of time up to or down from the desired level. The proper value of j is determined by passenger safety considerations and is heavily influenced by whether or not standees are permitted on the vehicle (see chapter 10).

Since the area under the jerk curve equals the deceleration:

$$t_1 = d/j \tag{2.19}$$

$$(t_3 - t_2) = d/j \tag{2.20}$$

where t_1, t_2, t_3 are as shown in Figure 2-5.

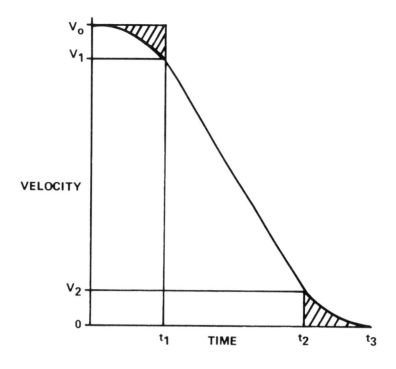

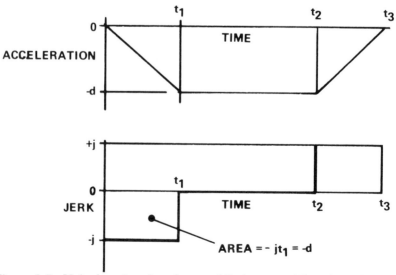

Figure 2-5. Velocity, Acceleration, and Jerk versus Time for a Trapezoidal Deceleration Pulse

Similarly the area under the acceleration curve can be used to compute the decrease in velocity:

$$v_1 = v_0 - dt_1/2 \tag{2.21}$$

$$v_2 = v_1 - d(t_2 - t_1) \tag{2.22}$$

$$0 = v_2 - d \frac{(t_3 - t_2)}{2} \tag{2.23}$$

Substituting the known values of time:

$$v_1 = v_0 - d^2/2j \tag{2.24}$$

$$v_2 = d^2/2j \tag{2.25}$$

By using these values for v_2 and v_1 in equation 2.22 we obtain:

$$t_2 - t_1 = (v_0/d - d/j) \tag{2.26}$$

The distance traveled is given by the area under the velocity diagram in Figure 2-5. Since the two shaded areas are equal by symmetry, the stopping distance is given by:

$$s_m = v_0 t_1 + \frac{(v_1 - v_2)(t_2 - t_1)}{2} + v_2(t_2 - t_1) \tag{2.27}$$

Substituting in known values for these parameters, one obtains after some algebraic manipulation the simple expression:

$$s_m = v_0^2/2d + v_0 d/2j \tag{2.28}$$

The effect of jerk is therefore to increase the safe stopping distance by an amount $v_0 d/2j$. Applying a safety factor of K, the minimum allowable headway (equation 2.11) would be increased by $Kd/2j$.

These equations assume a trapezoidal deceleration profile. With low permissible levels of jerk, it is possible that there may be no constant deceleration portion and the profile will appear as shown in Figure 2-6. This will occur only if $t_1 > t_2$ or from equations 2.19 and 2.26:

$$v_0 < d^2/j \tag{2.29}$$

For a purely jerk limited stopping profile of this type, the safe stopping distance may be readily verified to be given by:

$$s_m = \sqrt{v_0^3/j} \tag{2.30}$$

Consideration of the system reaction time will further improve the accuracy of the stopping distance computation. Assume the vehicle is traveling at a *constant* speed v_0 and that it takes t_r seconds between detection of the need to stop and the beginning of vehicle deceleration. In this case, the safe

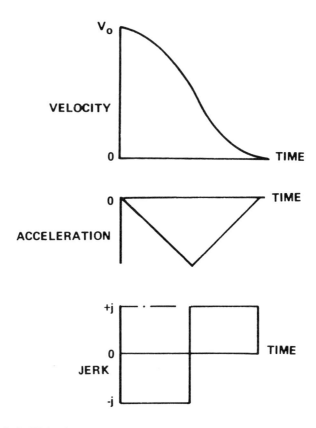

Figure 2-6. Velocity, Acceleration, and Jerk versus Time for a Triangular Deceleration Pulse

stopping distance will be increased by the amount $v_0 t_r$.[b] The safe stopping distance including effects of jerk and reaction time is therefore given by:

$$s_m = v_0 t_r + v_0^2/2d + v_0 d/2j \qquad (2.31)$$

Minimum allowable headway applying a safety factor of K becomes:

$$h_0 = K t_r + K v_0/2d + K d/2j + pL/v_0 \qquad (2.32)$$

Notice that the derivative of h_0 with respect to vehicle velocity is unchanged from the simpler expression ignoring jerk and reaction time (equa-

[b]This will be true *only* if the vehicle speed remains constant at v_0 throughout the reaction time. Should the vehicle be accelerating at the time the need to brake is first detected, this assumption will *not* be satisfied. (Such a condition might occur if the propulsion control system were to fail and command full forward thrust.) For operation at short headways, such possibilities should be considered in computing safe stopping distance (see chapter 4).

tion 2.11). This means the velocity at which maximum capacity occurs remains $\sqrt{2pLd/K}$ as before.

The theoretical capacity including jerk and reaction time is given by:

$$Q_m = \frac{3600pN}{Kt_r + \dfrac{Kv_0}{2d} + \dfrac{Kd}{2j} + \dfrac{pL}{v_0}} \qquad (2.33)$$

Capacities Using Non-Brick Wall Stopping Assumptions

Aside from historical precedent, there is no ironclad reason for the a priori assumption that a vehicle may stop instantly—as though it has struck a brick wall. There are of course numerous failure conditions that can produce high decelerations, but it may be possible to anticipate such failures in the design and preserve an adequate level of passenger safety. While all automatic transit systems presently operating follow the brick wall stopping criterion, there is considerable evidence that drivers of automobiles, trucks, and buses follow at shorter separations than it would require. This provides justification for the consideration of alternative stopping criteria. There are at least three others that have been seriously proposed for transit systems:

1. *Non-Brick Wall Stop*. The lead vehicle stops with finite, rather than brick wall deceleration.
2. *Constant Reaction Time*. Separation based solely upon a constant system reaction time. Assumes the following vehicle can duplicate any deceleration level experienced by the vehicle in front of it.
3. *Controlled Collision*. Vehicles are designed to be crash survivable and low speed collisions permitted under certain failure conditions.

The controlled collision approach is at the present time purely conceptual. It would utilize much of the progress in automotive crash survivability research to design transit vehicles that could safely impact one another without injury to the passengers. The result would be safe operation at much shorter headways—and therefore higher line capacities. This topic is addressed in chapter 4, which covers principles of close headway design. The other two non-brick wall stopping philosophies are discussed in the sections immediately following.

Non-Brick Wall Stop

In this approach we recognize that the lead vehicle can not stop in zero time. Therefore, the distance traveled by the failed car may be added to the initial vehicle separation to determine the distance available to stop the trailing vehicle. A safety factor k is applied to the stopping distance of the following vehicle in determining the minimum permissible separation. The relationship is shown in Figure 2-7:

$$s_0 = ks_m - s_f \tag{2.34}$$

$s_f = $ distance traveled by failed vehicle in stopping

$k = $ a safety factor[c]

Assuming the failed vehicle decelerates at a uniform rate d_f, it will travel a distance $v_0^2/2d_f$.

If the following vehicle stopping distance is given by equation 2.31, the minimum permissible separation will be:

$$s_0 = kv_0t_r + kv_0^2/2d + kv_0d/2j - v_0^2/2d_f \tag{2.35}$$

The theoretical capacity of a system designed to this criterion would be:

$$Q_m = \frac{3600pN}{kt_r + \dfrac{kv_0}{2d} + \dfrac{kd}{2j} - \dfrac{v_0}{2d_f} + \dfrac{pL}{v_0}} \tag{2.36}$$

There is some debate over what deceleration levels should be assumed. Unless the passengers are restrained by safety belts or air bags, the maximum deceleration of the trailing vehicle should probably not exceed 0.5 g or about 16 feet/second[2]. If standees are permitted on the vehicle, the maximum deceleration should be even lower. Depending on the cause of failure, the deceleration for the failed vehicle could be quite large—since it may not be under system control. Values might range from 1 g for a locked wheel skid to as high as 40 g for a serious collision.

If the failed vehicle deceleration is more than 4 or 5 times the deceleration permitted the trailing vehicle, then there will be little difference between equation 2.36 and the capacity obtained assuming a brick wall stop.

Constant Reaction Time

The State of Virginia advises its motorists to follow at a distance of no less than one car length for every ten miles per hour vehicle speed under ideal

---

[c] Notice that this safety factor is not the same as the brick wall K factor. They are related by the formula:

$$k = K + s_f/s_m$$

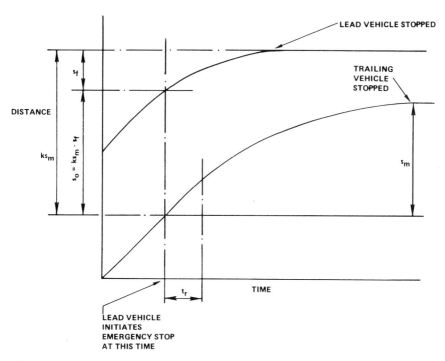

Figure 2-7. Relationships Governing a Non-Brick Wall Stop (ignores effects of overspeed)

conditions.[15] With wet pavement, the recommended separation is doubled. Minimum permissible separation following these guidelines may be represented by the formula:

$$s_0 = kLv_0/14.67 \qquad (2.37)$$

s_0 = separation—feet

v_0 = vehicle speed—feet/second

L = vehicle length—feet

k = 1.0—ideal
   2.0—wet pavement

From equation 2.6, the minimum allowable headway is simply:

$$h_0 = kL/14.67 + L/v_0 \qquad (2.38)$$

assuming p equals 1 for automobiles. The theoretical capacity of such a system is:

$$Q_m = \frac{3600N}{\dfrac{kL}{14.67} + \dfrac{L}{v_0}} \qquad (2.39)$$

Inspection of equation 2.36 will show that this criterion can be made identical to that for non-brick wall stopping with the assumption of equal deceleration and jerk rates for the failed car and the following car and a reaction time given by:

$$t_r = L/14.67 \qquad (2.40)$$

For a typical 18 foot automobile, t_r would be about 1.2 seconds. With wet pavement and a safety factor of two the effective reaction time is about 2.4 seconds.[d] Figure 2-8 plots the theoretical capacity given by equation 2.39 for such a constant reaction time criterion. At high speeds the term L/v_0 becomes negligible so the capacity becomes assymptotic to:

$$Q_m \text{ (high speeds)} = 52{,}800N/kL \qquad (2.41)$$

At low speeds, the L/v_0 term predominates and the capacity becomes linearly proportional to vehicle speed:

$$Q_m \text{ (low speeds)} = 3600Nv_0/L \qquad (2.42)$$

An important characteristic of this philosophy is that capacity is continually increasing with speed to the assymptotic value given by equation 2.41. Unlike the brick wall stop criterion, capacity does not decrease with speed. It must be emphasized that this model—based upon recommended following distances—does not agree with actual capacity-speed measurements made on automobile traffic. Such measurements *do* show reduced capacity at high speeds. (Actual highway capacity is treated in chapter 3). This is because drivers do not all follow at the same headway, and under congested conditions the conservative driver traveling slowly and at a large headway unduly influences system performance. Nevertheless capacities of the sort predicted by equation 2.39 might be approached by automatic control of vehicle spacing. This is one reason for the enthusiasm shown for automated highways where the separation of vehicles can be rigidly controlled. It could also be achieved by a personal rapid transit (PRT) vehicle operating with such a philosophy.

The key assumption, that the following vehicle can always safely decelerate at the same rate as the lead vehicle, will require very careful investigation to substantiate before such a strategy can be endorsed for public transit.

---

[d] For design purposes, the American Association of State Highway Officials assumes a driver perception, reaction and brake lag time of 2.5 seconds. This correlates very well with the results obtained from interpreting the Virginia recommendations.

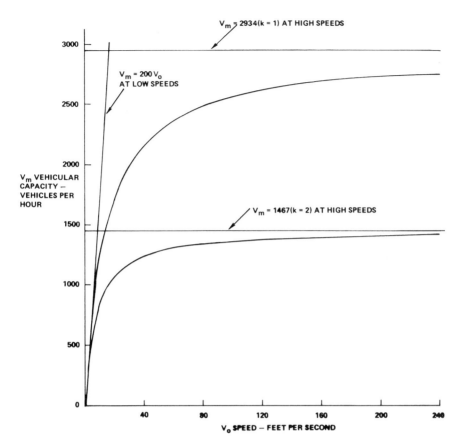

Figure 2-8. Virginia Highway Constant Reaction Time Equations for Vehicle Flow

Notes

1. Definition follows the general approach in the *Highway Capacity Manual*, Highway Research Board Special Report 87, Highway Research Board, Washington, D. C., 1965, page 16.

2. Ibid.

3. For example see *Headway and Switching Strategies for Automated Vehicular Ground Transportation Systems*, Michael B. Godfrey, PB173644, Massachusetts Institute of Technology, Cambridge, November 1, 1966, page IX.

4. This follows the procedure in the *Highway Capacity Manual*, page 16.

5. This follows the approach in the *Highway Capacity Manual*, page 51 (equation 3.3).

6. *The Urban Transportation Problem*, J.R. Meyer, J.F. Kain, and M. Wohl, Harvard University Press, Cambridge, 1965, page 195.

7. "Estimating Auto Occupancy—A Review of Methodology," U. S. Department of Transportation Federal Highway Administration, Government Printing Office, Washington, D. C., 1972.

8. The approach followed is similar to that in *Urban Rail Transit*, A.S. Lang and R.M. Soberman, Massachusetts Institute of Technology Press, Cambridge, 1964, page 61.

9. Definition follows the general approach in the *Highway Capacity Manual*, page 16.

10. *Highway Capacity Manual*, page 49 (equation 3.1).

11. *Urban Rail Transit*, page 118, and *The New York Subway–Interborough Rapid Transit*, Arno Press, New York, 1904, page 138.

12. *The New York Subway*, page 138.

13. *Headway and Switching Strategies*, page 23.

14. A more rigorous derivation is given in *Headway and Switching Strategies*, pages 25-27.

15. *Drivers Manual of Virginia*, Form O. L. 39, rev. July 1973, State of Virginia, Richmond, Virginia, page 48.

3   Practical Line Capacities

In practice, systems can only approach the theoretical capacities derived in chapter 2 because of unavoidable inefficiencies in vehicle and guideway utilization. Some vehicles travel empty or lightly loaded. Guideway space is wasted by uncertainties inherent in the regulation of vehicle spacing— and by the need to reserve space to permit vehicles to merge. This chapter considers some of the methods for computing capacity which are used in the design of actual transportation systems, including trains, subways, and automobile highways. While these methods are still "theoretical" in that not all inefficiencies are included, the representation will be more realistic than the basic approach of chapter 2.

Automobile Capacity

Automotive highway capacity depends on many variables or "traffic factors," which include traffic composition (the number of trucks and buses), lane distribution, and traffic interruptions. Because of their larger size and poorer acceleration and deceleration capability trucks decrease line capacity. On level terrain a truck is assumed equivalent to two to three cars.[1] On upgrades trucks have difficulty maintaining speed. For two lane highways in mountainous terrain this may result in a truck being equivalent to as many as ten cars in capacity computations.[2]

On multilane highways all lanes do not carry the same rates of flow. The left lanes can carry higher traffic volumes since the slower traffic tends to keep to the right hand lane. The left lanes are also free from the interfering effects of entrances and exits, most of which are on the right of freeways.

On a two lane highway, with one traffic lane for each direction, it is difficult to pass slower moving traffic safely. Provision of additional lanes therefore has a nonlinear effect on capacity. For example, a typical two lane highway may have a capacity of 1000 vehicles per hour per lane. Addition of a third lane will add 1500 vehicles per hour additional capacity.[3]

Interruptions in traffic flow may be caused by at grade intersections, toll gates, draw bridges, and railroad crossings. These interruptions force some or all of the vehicles to stop periodically, thereby impeding the highway's ability to carry traffic. Consecutive passenger vehicles stopped in line will rarely get under way at a faster rate than 1500 passenger cars per hour per lane. Since uninterrupted lane capacity can be as high as 2000 passenger cars per hour, the deleterious effect of stop and go traffic on line capacity is readily apparent.[4]

In general, traffic factors are accounted for by applying correction factors to the basic flow equations.[a] These flow equations relate vehicular capacity, average speed, and spacing.

Vehicular Flow Equations

The usual approach is to compute lane capacity based upon an empirically determined relationship between the average vehicle speed on the highway and the "density." "Density" is defined as the number of vehicles occupying a unit length of highway at a given instant.[5] In other words, if we snapped an aerial photograph of a highway and counted the number of vehicles in a mile length of a single lane, that would give the density of traffic on that lane in vehicles per mile. It should be readily apparent that density is merely the reciprocal of spacing and is given by the formula:

$$D_0 = \frac{5280}{s + L} \tag{3.1}$$

D_0 = density—cars/mile

s = separation—feet

L = length of automobile—(no training assumed for automobiles)

In 1934, B.D. Greenshields suggested that empirical studies of traffic flow data showed a linear relationship between density and vehicle average speed of the form:[6]

$$u = a - bD_0 \tag{3.2}$$

u = vehicle average speed—miles per hour

D_0 = density of vehicles per mile of guideway

a, b = constants

Greenshields's data gave values of 46 for a and 0.236 for b. Subsequent research has cast some doubt on whether the relationship is truly linear, but has not lessened its practical value. The linear assumption is still in wide

---

[a] In the case of grade intersections the effect is so great that a completely different approach is required.

use today although the values of a and b vary depending on the traffic conditions.

Since speed-density relationships are usually given in terms of the velocity in miles per hour, we have introduced a new symbol u, to avoid confusion with v_0 which has been used to denote the speed in feet per second. Except for this difference in units, the symbols may be used interchangeably so long as we remember that cruise speed for an automobile is a statistical number referring to the *average* vehicle cruise speed. (This distinction is necessary, since automobiles do not all travel at the same speed.)

Since density is simply the reciprocal of spacing, its relationship to headway may be obtained from equation 2.6 of chapter 2.

$$h = 5280/D_0v_0 \tag{3.3}$$

D_0 = density—vehicles/mile

v_0 = vehicle speed—feet/second

h = vehicle headway—seconds

By rearranging the basic Greenshields relationship between density and velocity and converting velocity to feet per second we obtain:

$$D_0 = \frac{a - 0.68v_0}{b} \tag{3.4}$$

The vehicle headway is then given by:

$$h = \frac{5280b}{av_0 - 0.68v_0^2} \tag{3.5}$$

The traffic volume in vehicles per hour is simply the reciprocal of the headway (equation 2.1 of chapter 2).

$$V = \frac{3600}{5280b} (av_0 - 0.68v_0^2) \tag{3.6}$$

Figure 3-1 shows the Greenshields speed versus density and volume versus speed relationships. Using typical values of a equals 40 and b equals 0.25:[7]

$$V = 109v_0 - 1.86v_0^2 \tag{3.7}$$

This volume versus speed relationship is a parabola whose maximum is readily found by differentiation of equation 3.7 to occur at 29.3 feet/second (20 mph). The maximum volume achieved at that speed is 1600 vehicles per hour. An obvious deficiency of this capacity formula is that at speeds above 40 miles/hour, the equation gives *negative* capacities. This is of course impossible and limits the range of validity.

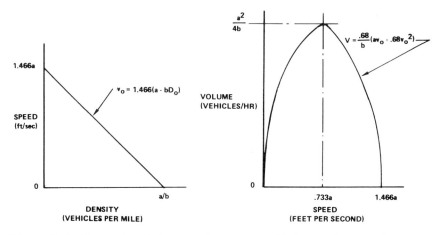

Figure 3-1. Greenshields's Density versus Volume Assumption and Resulting Volume versus Speed Relationship

It is worth noting that, like the constant deceleration braking—brick wall stop model in chapter 2, this formula gives a velocity for maximum capacity about which capacity declines as speed is either increased or decreased.

Comparison with Constant Reaction Time Model

At each speed, equation 3.7 purports to give the maximum practical traffic flow or V_a as it was denoted in chapter 2. It is interesting to compare this capacity with the theoretical vehicular capacity of a highway lane if every driver followed at the minimum separation recommended by highway officials. From chapter 2, equations 2.2 and 2.38, assuming ideal conditions ($k = 1$) and an 18 foot long automobile:

$$V_m = \frac{3600v_0}{1.227\, v_0 + 18} \tag{3.8}$$

The maximum value of equation 3.8 is 2934 vehicles per hour and is approached assymptotically at high speeds. The actual vehicular capacity (equation 3.7) reaches a maximum of 1600 vehicles per hour at a speed of 20 miles per hour. The ratio of V_a/V_m can be readily computed and represents the guideway utilization for the highway. Computation of γ will illustrate the poor efficiency obtained by the highway at high speeds. This is a major dilemma for the highway engineer. Reduced speed is the price that must be paid for increased line capacity—as any commuter is well aware!

Automatic Train Protection

Line capacities for subway and commuter rail systems are less than would be obtained based on the minimum separation because of limitations inherent in their train protection systems.

Train protection ordinarily refers to electromechanical signalling systems whose purpose is to guard against train collisions while permitting headways between trains as short as consistent with safe operation. Automatic train protection systems provide independent protection against collisions, without requiring any intervention by either a motorman or station operator. Most modern transit systems, including the Washington Metropolitan Area Transit Authority, Lindenwold line between Haddonfield and Philadelphia, and the Airtrans people mover at Dallas-Forth Worth Airport, base their collision avoidance upon traditional block signalling concepts. It is instructive to trace the history of these systems and analyze the theory of their operation.

History of Train Protection

There are two basic techniques used to keep trains apart. The earliest, known as "time spacing," is based on the principle that train separation can be regulated by controlling the time between the dispatch of trains. It is still widely used in the United States on lightly traveled railway lines. Trains run on the basis of timetable schedules—a minimum of five minutes apart. The problem with "time spacing" is that the schedule can be disrupted by an unplanned stop, which the crew of the following train may not learn about until it finds itself barrelling up behind the stopped train. To prevent such a disaster, a "flagman" is sent back a safe stopping distance behind a stopped vehicle to warn approaching trains.

Better protection is provided by using the "space interval" system in which at any given time a train has exclusive possession of a section or "block" of track. A "block" may be formally defined as a length of track that is controlled or protected by a signal at the entering end. A "block system" is a series of consecutive blocks. The block system separates trains in space rather than time. This is a more enforceable idea since the space cushion can not be affected by a schedule slippage.

In early systems, blocks were ordinarily the distance between stations—a matter of five to fifteen miles.[8] These systems employed "manual block control"—that is, the correct signal was determined and activated by the station operator. The operator would keep a complete record of the times of passage of trains which, in conjunction with the records kept by adjacent station operators, could be used to determine the condition of each block at all times—that is, whether it was empty or occupied. This condition would be displayed to oncoming trains by a signal placed at the entrance to the block and called the "home" signal. To provide advance notice to an oncoming train of whether it might be necessary to stop, another signal would sometimes be placed a safe stopping distance in front of the station. It was referred to as the "distant" signal.

The signal conveys an "indication" or instruction to the train by displaying an "aspect." "Aspect" refers to the signal state. Mechanically connected semaphores have three aspects depending on whether the flag is displayed vertically (proceed), horizontally (stop), or at a 45 degree angle (caution). If colored lights are used, the aspects are green (proceed), red (stop), and amber (caution).

With blocks five to fifteen miles long, giving exclusive possession of a block to a single train has a serious effect on line capacity. Obviously train headways would have to exceed thirty minutes with trains traveling thirty miles per hour and fifteen mile blocks. For this reason, a concept known as "permissive block signalling" is often employed. In permissive block signalling, the stop indication is treated like a full stop sign rather than a traffic light. In other words, instead of having to stop until the signal aspect changes, the engineer is permitted to enter the occupied block at reduced speed after coming to a complete stop. A flagman is used to advise the engineer in advance if a train is stopped ahead of him. Railroads in the United States commonly use permissive signalling on the mainline, but require absolute signalling whenever traffic from two lines merges together.

With the invention of the basic track circuit by Dr. William Robinson in 1872, it became possible to use the trains themselves to activate the signals automatically, instead of relying upon the station operator to keep a record of train location and display the proper signal aspects. This technique, known as automatic block signalling, not only eliminates the human element in setting signals, but by virtue of the "fail-safe" nature of the circuitry, virtually eliminates the hazard from any signal malfunction. "Fail-safe" means that any equipment failure will cause the signal to display an aspect that gives a safe indication. The track circuit consists of a relay connected to a battery through the steel rails (see Figure 3-2). Passage of a train over the rails shunts out the current below the value required to keep the relay energized. When the relay drops out, it indicates the block is occupied. The circuit is fail-safe with respect to broken rails, dead batteries, and loose connections, since any of them will result in dropping out the relay thus displaying a "block occupied" aspect. The circuit *will* give a false clear reading if the relay contacts should weld together. For this reason relays used in the circuits that control the signal state are defined as

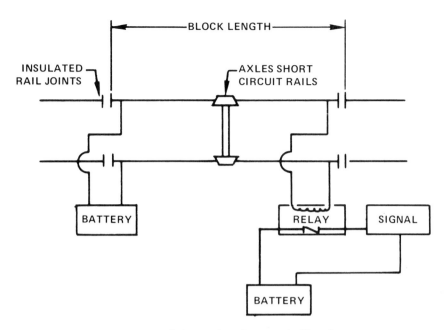

Figure 3-2. Schematic of a Track Circuit

"vital" components and are built to extremely high standards of reliability. The relay armature is mounted so that gravity will pull it to the de-energized position and all moving parts are sealed in glass. Contacts are of silver-impregnated graphite against silver—a combination that won't weld together even from such a high current overload as might occur if the system were struck by lightning. These relays are huge by telephone or electronics standards and typically cost about $200 apiece.

With the track circuit available to control the signals, the block may now be economically shortened to the limit imposed by the safe stopping distance.

Two Block Automatic Signalling

With block distance governed by the train's braking ability, it became logical to display the home and distant aspects in a single signal and employ what is known as "two block automatic signalling." The occupied block displays a red aspect, the block preceding it a yellow aspect, and all other blocks a green aspect. Automatic block signalling used in railroad systems is usually permissive—that is a train is permitted to enter an occupied block—first stopping and then proceeding prepared to stop short of a train

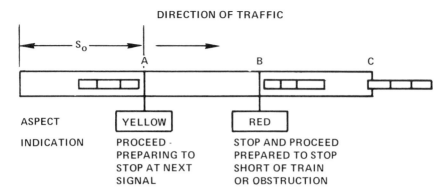

Figure 3-3. Two Block Automatic Signalling (permissive)

or obstruction. Figure 3-3 portrays the two block system. Notice that the two block system provides a "zone of protection" providing a yellow indication at least a stopping distance long. The worst case, which provides this stopping distance separation, occurs with the following vehicle at A and the lead vehicle at B in Figure 3-3. If trains are not to slow down, but instead maintain constant operation under a green aspect, they can not follow any closer than two blocks as is shown by the vehicles at A and C. Notice that this is the closest separation that can be guaranteed never to result in a restrictive aspect for vehicle A.

The headway required to maintain this "uninterrupted flow" of trains is thus given by:

$$h = \frac{2s_0 + pL}{v_0} \tag{3.9}$$

In other words, the train spacing should be two blocks plus the length of the train. The minimum permissible separation is given by equation 2.10 from chapter 2 as $Kv_0^2/2d$. Therefore the closest headway for uninterrupted operation will be:

$$h = Kv_0/d + pL/v_0 \tag{3.10}$$

(This headway can be used to compute the capacity of the line in trains/hour.)

The two block system is not foolproof—in particular it is prone to human abuse. The most notorious abuse is "riding the yellow." That is, instead of proceeding through the yellow with caution and prepared to stop, the engineer may assume that the vehicle in front of him is travelling at the same speed as he is. In that case the next signal he encounters will also display a yellow aspect and the engineer can continue without stopping.

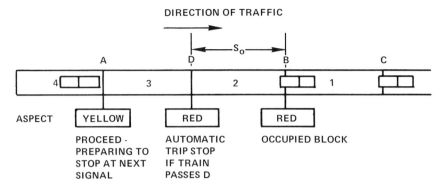

Figure 3-4. Three Block Clearing System

Sooner or later, however, the lead vehicle will turn out to be stopped at the entrance to the next block and the engineer will find himself with insufficient separation to stop without a collision.

Rapid Transit Train Protection

It is possible to eliminate human judgment from the train protection system by going to what is called a "three block clearing system." This approach is almost universally used on rapid transit systems. It includes a mechanical tripper in the track that is automatically moved into tripping position when the signal aspect is red. If the vehicle passes over the actuated tripper, it results in the application of the train emergency brakes. The three block system is best explained with reference to Figure 3-4.

Since the train in the occupied block might be stopped at B, the tripper must be located at D, a full block behind the occupied block. This results in the so-called "double red" indication system. Block 3 is reserved for a normal service stop. Block 2 is available for an emergency stop using the mechanical tripper in case the service stop was unsuccessful. There is a train somewhere in Block 1. The following vehicle, if it is to travel uninterrupted by restrictive signal aspects, must be no closer than Block 4. This system therefore requires a separation of at least three blocks to maintain uninterrupted flow. The equivalent headway is given by:

$$h = 3Kv_0/2d + pL/v_0 \qquad (3.11)$$

The headway must be further increased if there are stations on line in order to maintain an uninterrupted flow of vehicles. Lang and Soberman[9] show that for online stations, the average headway must be greater than:

$$h = T + \frac{pL}{v_0} + \frac{v_0}{2a} + \frac{(3K + 1)v_0}{2d} \tag{3.12}$$

$T =$ station stop time—seconds

$a =$ vehicle average acceleration to cruise speed—feet/second^2

The three block system is clearly much safer than the two block system but it also results in longer headways and reduced system capacity. Although widely used in rapid transit systems, it is seldom if ever found on mainline railroads.

Multiple Aspect Signalling

The normal three aspect signal system is limited to red, amber, and green, which means it can tell a train to stop, prepare to stop, or proceed. By using additional aspects it is possible to command the vehicle to reduce its speed but not necessarily stop. This provides additional flexibility for the system. In particular it permits slow moving trains, such as freight trains, to travel at closer headways than fast moving passenger trains while using the same signalling system. By reducing block size, it also permits shorter headway operation and increases line capacity. Multiple aspect signalling can be based either upon the railroad approach, which does not provide an additional block for emergency stopping—or on the rail transit approach in which an extra block is provided to permit a backup braking system to stop the vehicle. Since the rail transit approach is probably of more interest to the urban transportation planner or engineer, we will derive the equations assuming an extra block is provided for emergency stopping. By eliminating this block and following the same approach, the student should be readily able to obtain the equations that apply without this extra block.

Automatic block signalling, especially using multiple aspects, lends itself readily to the next step in train automation, automatic train operation (ATO). ATO regulates the speed of the vehicle without requiring intervention by the motorman. The approach is to transmit the signal aspect to a train propulsion control system as an electronic speed command. If speed has not been reduced to the command level by the next block, the vehicle is assumed "overspeed" and is put into irrevocable emergency braking. The speed command for one block thus becomes the speed limit for the next block. This approach is being used on many of the new automated rapid rail transit systems and was also used on the Airtrans system at Dallas-Fort Worth Airport.[10]

Figure 3-5 shows speed commands and speed limit for a multiple aspect block control system. The speed command is equivalent to the aspect

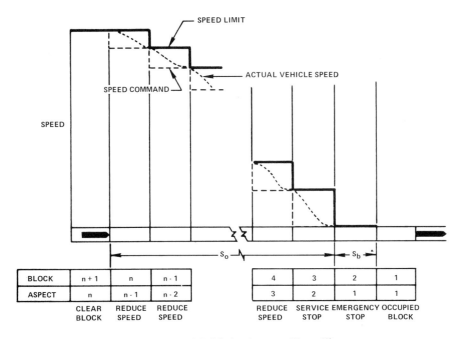

Figure 3-5. Multiple Aspect Signalling

displayed at the entrance to the block. The speed limit is the command for the adjacent less restrictive block.

The minimum permissible separation s_0 can be seen from Figure 3-5 to be composed of $(n - 2)$ blocks each of lengths s_b. Thus:

$$s_0 = Kv_0^2/2d = (n - 2)s_b \tag{3.13}$$

$s_b = Kv_0^2/(2(n - 2)d)$

$n = $ number of aspects

To assure uninterrupted flow, the separation must be equal to ns_b blocks. Substituting for s_b from equation 3.13 the headway for uninterrupted flow becomes:

$$h = \frac{nKv_0}{2(n - 2)d} + \frac{pL}{v_0} \tag{3.14}$$

Notice that for a three aspect system the equation reduces properly to equation 3.11.

The aspect displayed at the entrance to each block, or the speed command for the block if the system is under automatic control, must be sufficiently restrictive so that the vehicle can be brought to a complete stop without entering the extra emergency stop block. This requires:

$$v_i = v_0 \sqrt{\frac{i-3}{n-2}} \tag{3.15}$$

v_i = speed command for the ith block—feet/second (valid for $3 \leq i \leq n + 1$)

The maximum speed limit for each block which, if exceeded, should initiate irrevocable emergency braking, is the speed command for the adjacent less restrictive block. Therefore:

$$v_i^* = v_0 \sqrt{\frac{i-2}{n-2}} \tag{3.16}$$

v_i^* = speed limit for the ith block—feet/second (valid for $2 \leq i \leq n$)

Consider a five aspect system. The headway for uninterrupted flow is given by:

$$h = \frac{5Kv_0}{6d} + \frac{pL}{v_0} \tag{3.17}$$

The reduction in headway over a three aspect system is seen to be quite substantial (compare with equation 3.11).

The velocity in each block is given in Table 3-1.

Cab Signalling

Cab signalling is a method of displaying the signal aspect in the motorman's cab onboard the train instead of on a signal light at the entrance to the block. The aspect is transmitted to the train as an electronic signal that is sent down the track rails and picked up inductively by receiver coils hung from the train about six inches above the track. (Occasionally the signal may be sent through an auxiliary rail and resistively coupled to the train through sliding carbon brushes.)

The advantage of cab signalling is that it does not rely upon the sighting distance at which the motorman can see the signal. Changes in occupancy of the block ahead are immediately transmitted to the motorman, permitting him to take advantage of the fact the block ahead is clear without waiting until he can see the next signal.

Once cab signalling provided a means for supplying a speed command to the train from the signalling system, it was just a matter of time before this signal would be used to control directly the train propulsion system and automatic train operations would become possible. The Lindenwold line between Haddonfield and Philadelphia was the first application of this

Table 3-1
Velocity for a Five Aspect Signal System

Block	Speed Limit	Command Speed
6	v_0	v_0
5	v_0	0.82 v_0
4	0.82 v_0	0.58 v_0
3	0.58 v_0	0
2	0	0
1	0	0

concept to automatic train operation in the United States. Block signalling is thus not only important in its own right, but also as the basis for many systems of automatic train operation.

Maximum Capacity for Trains

The headways computed for block signalling systems were based on maintaining uninterrupted flow—that is, assuring that it would never be necessary for a train to encounter a restrictive signal under normal operation.

It is interesting to consider what flow can be obtained with a permissive system in which queues are allowed to form behind the stopped train. Consider a case where trains stop at online stations and other trains are permitted to queue up in back of the stopped trains. The rate at which trains can be processed through the station will depend on four factors:

1. Station dwell time
2. Time required to accelerate a stopped train from the queue to move it into the station
3. Time required to decelerate the train to a stop in the station
4. The reaction time between the departure of a train from the station and the movement of the following train from its position in the queue

Figure 3-6 shows trains queued up in a station. When train 1 leaves the station, train 2 must move a distance equal to the train length (pL) plus the clearance between the two stopped trains (c). Assuming equal acceleration and deceleration rates:

$$\frac{pL + c}{2} = \frac{at^2}{2} = \frac{dt^2}{2} \qquad (3.18)$$

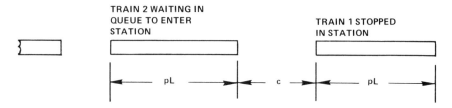

Figure 3-6. Situation with Trains Queued Up in Online Station

c = clearance between stopped trains—feet

p = number of cars in a train

L = length of each car—feet

a = average rate of acceleration—feet/second²

d = average rate of deceleration (assumed equal to a)

t = time for acceleration or deceleration phase—seconds

Solving equation 3.18 for t and recognizing that the total time for both acceleration and deceleration will be $2t$, the minimum headway between train arrivals is seen to be:

$$h_0 = T + t_r + 2 \sqrt{\frac{pL + c}{d}} \qquad (3.19)$$

T = station dwell time—seconds

t_r = reaction time—seconds

For a typical train the dwell time in the station might be thirty seconds. We can allow another three seconds reaction time. If ten 72 foot long cars compose the train, the clearance between trains is nine feet, and the average deceleration and acceleration is 4 feet/second², then the minimum headway from equation 3.19 is one minute. The system can process sixty trains in an hour. Using a three block clearing system, the closest headway to maintain uninterrupted flow may be obtained from equation 3.12. Assuming a 45 mph cruise speed and K equal to 1.5, the headway is 94.5 seconds, or over a minute and a half. In other words, a fifty percent increase in line capacity can be obtained by using a permissive signalling system and forming station queues.

This practice is known in the rapid transit industry as "keying through," since the motorman must turn a key to defeat the automatic emergency brake tripper. After a spate of mishaps in 1970, the New York Transit Authority was advised to prohibit keying through, adopting in effect an absolute signalling system.[11] Other systems still use the permissive approach.

Notes

1. *Traffic Engineering Handbook*, 3rd edition. John E. Baerwald, Institute of Traffic Engineers, Washington, D. C., 1965, pages 186-194.

2. Ibid.

3. Ibid.

4. Ibid.

5. *Highway Capacity Manual*, Highway Research Board Special Report 87, Highway Research Board, Washington, D. C., 1965, pages 66-70 and 88-110.

6. *Traffic System Analysis for Engineers and Planners*, M. Wohl and B.V. Martin, McGraw-Hill Book Company, New York, 1967, pages 322-338.

7. *Introduction to Highway Transportation Engineering*, edited by D.G. Capelle, D.E. Cleveland, and W.W. Rankin, Institute of Traffic Engineers, Arlington, Virginia, 1968, pages 26-27.

8. "All About Signals," John Armstrong, reprinted from *Trains*, Kalmbach Publishing Company, June and July 1957, pages 3-26.

9. *Urban Rail Transit*, A.S. Lang and R.M. Soberman, Massachusetts Institute of Technology Press, Cambridge, 1964, pages 116-124.

10. "Automated Personal Transit Control Systems," Peter M. Kirk, American Society of Mechanical Engineers 73 ICT-41, Intersociety Conference on Transportation, Denver, Colorado, September 23-27, 1973.

11. "Report of the Panel Appointed to Study the Safety of Train Operations on the Subway System on the New York City Transit Authority," Robins, Kekonius, and Paterson, November 13, 1970 (unpublished document under the auspices of the Institute for Rapid Transit).

4 Close Headway Operations

Research into the concept of personal rapid transit (PRT) has caused considerable expansion of our understanding of the close headway operation of automated transit systems. This chapter considers three aspects of this. First, a general discussion is presented of the approaches being taken towards close headway command and control. Since close headways increase the risk of accidents, the next section discusses the design of transit vehicles for crash survivability, covering much recent research by the National Highway Traffic Safety Administration concerning the collision survivability of automobiles. Equations are derived permitting estimation of collision severity for various conditions of lead vehicle and trailing vehicle deceleration. The final section treats some of the real tolerances and variables that act to increase safe headways beyond the theoretical values derived in chapter 3. Factors considered include vehicle overspeed, position error, braking tolerance, the effect of line speed changes, and the effect of grades.

Control System Technology

Control systems can be distinguished in several ways. In terms of system function, control is usually divided between collision avoidance, which prevents collisions of vehicles; vehicle control, which provides acceleration and deceleration, station stops, speed control, and similar functions usually associated with a motorman on a nonautomated system; and system management, which addresses the problems of routing vehicles properly throughout the system and monitoring system status. Figure 4-1 breaks down command and control in this system-functional manner.

In terms of hardware elements, a control system may be broken down into sensors, data processors, command generators, actuators, and communication links. Such a breakdown is also indicated in Figure 4-1.

Sensors and detectors are used to provide information on the status of the system. Information typically required might include vehicle position and velocity, switch position, door position, and failure alarms. Sensor elements in common use may be excited by magnetic and electric field effects, or by heat, light, or physical contact. In addition sensors may obtain information from acoustic or electromagnetic signal reflection (sonar and radar devices).

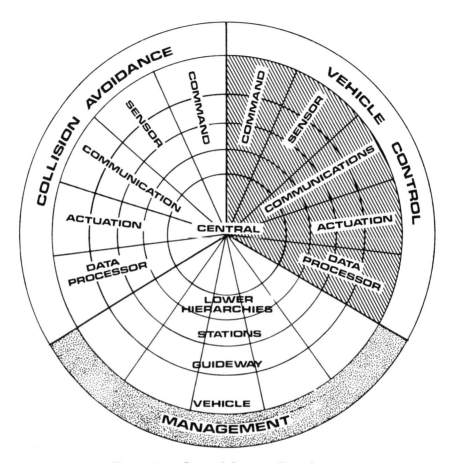

Figure 4-1. Control System Functions

Magnetic field effects are utilized by inducive loop antennas which detect the magnetic field from a buried cable in the guideway. Antennas can also be used to detect the field from permanent magnets used as position markers along the route. Permanent magnets may also be used to excite reed relay switches. Electric field effects are used by capacitive sensors. Photocells and IR detectors are examples of the use of light and heat energy respectively. A mechanical tripper is a widely used example of excitation by physical contact.

Data from the sensors is transmitted via a communication link to a data processor. The processed information is relayed to the command generator where the appropriate response is decided upon and a suitable command issued. In many cases the command element involves human intervention. In that case an elaborate communication link is required between the data processor, usually a computer, and the human decision maker. This link involves information displays utilizing cathode ray tubes and large screen situation displays to transmit information across the man-machine interface. In other cases, such as that of a hardwired block safety system, the command generating function is determined by the response of vital relays permanently wired into a switching network so that both data processing and command generation are combined in a single element involving no manual control.

The appropriate command, once generated, must be transmitted to an actuating element that is able to execute the command by modifying the state of the system. The actuator might change the voltage of a propulsion motor, it might move a switch into a different position, or it might apply the emergency brakes if the command generator has detected a potentially unsafe condition. System response is then detected by the sensors and transmitted back to the data processor. Figure 4-2 illustrates the cyclical nature of this functional characterization of a control system.

The physical location of these functions provides another means of classification. The data processing and command functions may be located at a control center for the entire system or perhaps at a control center occupying a lower position in a control hierarchy. Alternatively, these functions could be located in the station, on board the vehicle, or in the guideway.

There is less flexibility with regard to the actuation and sensing equipment. The actuation equipment must be located where the appropriate response is required. Thus a brake actuator or switch must be located either on the vehicle or in the guideway. Propulsion actuation would normally be in the vehicle. However, for an air propelled vehicle (e.g., Uniflo) the propulsion control may be in the guideway, while for a cable car it could even be in a central control location. Similarly, sensors must be in proximity to that which is being monitored. Despite these restrictions there is a definite, if limited, flexibility in the location of both the actuation and sensing equipment.

The location of the communication links, on the other hand, is completely determined by the location of the other functions. Communication links may be required between the data processing and command functions, between the command and actuation functions, and between the sensing and the data processing functions. Communication is thus the means for linking up functions located in different hierarchical positions. It connects the central control with station, guideway, and vehicle control elements. Some systems tend to have the major information located centrally. This creates an inflexible system that tends to fail in a very ungraceful fashion. At the other end of the spectrum are systems in which control functions are primarily on board the individual vehicle—our

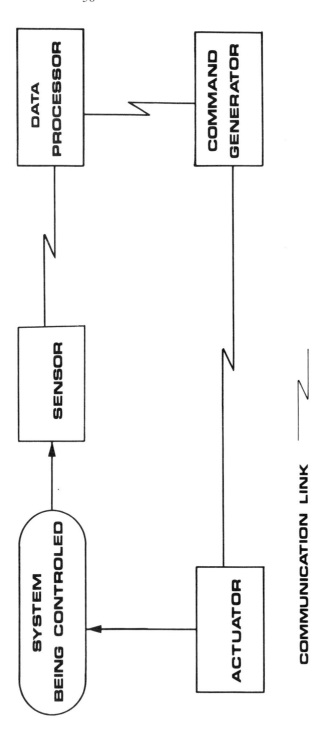

Figure 4-2. Hardware Elements of a Command and Control System

present automobile network is a prime example. Flexibility is outstanding but system management is poor. It is difficult to relay information to optimize use of the system since a central source of information on system status is unavailable and no central communication to the vehicle exists. Between these extremes lie numerous proposals for command and control concepts for modern rapid transit systems.

Still another way by which control systems are frequently classified is in terms of the system entropy—or, in communications terminology, the amount of information available to operate the system. Rail transit systems use a simple block system that provides no velocity information and position information to a fineness no greater than the block length. Each block must be long enough to enable a train to stop in a single block under worst-case conditions. High speed rail systems generally use a multiple block system with civil speed limits for each block depending upon track conditions and the distance from an occupied block. Such a system could provide maximum velocity information and position information to a fineness equal to the block length if it were incorporated into an automatic control system. Since it is not necessary for a vehicle to stop within a single block, the block length can be smaller than for the rail transit system.

Finally, if we imagine the block size gradually diminishing to zero, continuous position information becomes available. Depending upon how much differentiation such data will stand without generating excessive noise, the same data can also provide velocity, acceleration, and jerk information for each vehicle. At its limit we have a system in which position, velocity, and perhaps even acceleration and jerk can be known for each vehicle in the system at all times to a specified level of accuracy.

The greedier we are for precise vehicle information, then the higher the data rate, the larger the communications bandwidth for each vehicle, and the closer the spacing between location sensors on the guideway must be. In return, the higher level of information permits closer headway operation. It is generally agreed that near continuous position and velocity information on all vehicles is essential for any control system for close headway personal rapid transit.

Control systems capable of approximating a state of continuous position and velocity information have been categorized into several types. Synchronous systems are those in which each vehicle is assigned a slot in an imaginary "string of beads" that progresses in lock step through the system. Actual vehicle speed is controlled to maintain this position synchronism. Thus, the time for any vehicle to go between two fixed points is constant. Trip times may be readily computed at central control and all intersection conflicts resolved by forward projection of the system status prior to releasing a vehicle from the station. In theory, the system management is clean and simple—in practice, many problems arise.

A failure anywhere in a synchronous system will propagate throughout the entire system. If a vehicle fails, other vehicles cannot be routed around the failure since the routing change will introduce intersection conflicts into the system. Similarly, a vehicle berth at the destination cannot be guaranteed since passenger boarding times and vehicle departure rates are not known in advance. If the station is blocked, there is no way to reroute the vehicle that is refused admission without generating conflicts. Thus, any unplanned failure causes the immediate shutdown of the entire network which is rigidly tied together under an inflexible central control.

To avoid such problems, the concept of local intersection control has been proposed in conjunction with synchronous operations. Aerospace Corporation, an advocate of this approach, calls it "quasi-synchronous."[1] In this technique vehicles still travel in synchronism throughout the system. However, conflict-free merges are not guaranteed before launching a vehicle. Instead, each intersection is provided with its own local "traffic cop" to regulate merges. Its options include permitting vehicles to slip slots or refusing their request to merge. In the latter case, central control simply selects a new route to reach the desired location. By keeping line density below a saturation level, acceptable miss rates can probably be achieved. Such a system is far more flexible and permits a single link with a disabled vehicle to be isolated from the rest of the system and dynamic rerouting of vehicles enroute to their destination. Trip times are no longer determinate, however, and cannot be computed in advance.

The most flexible of all position and velocity control systems is a proximity-type system. In such a system no synchronism is established between vehicles. Vehicle gaps are random and limited only by a minimum headway between vehicles, which varies as a function of vehicle speed. Operation is much like an automotive highway except that position and velocity information for all vehicles is known centrally, so optimum routing information can be provided and traffic management significantly improved. At intersections, queues may be permitted to develop if necessary in the same fashion as at traffic lights. Random gaps are not quite as efficient for headway maintenance as the synchronous slots, since fractions of a safe headway distance exist that cannot be filled by vehicles.

The random approach is not as clean from the point of view of the central controller and may lead to somewhat reduced guideway utilization. But it does provide enormous flexibility, including the ability to reduce speeds at particular areas and times, such as on steep hills or during bad weather. Much current discussion centers on quasi-synchronous systems. However, a pure synchronous system was developed at Morgantown, West Virginia, by Bendix under subcontract to Boeing. And, on the other hand, a working proximity-type system was demonstrated by General Railway Signal on the Rohr Monocab system at TRANSPO. Because of its rigidity, it is likely that no pure synchronous system will ever be used in a large network application.

The central question concerning control systems—and one generating considerable controversy— is that of risk. At the conservative end of the spectrum, some suggest the system should be designed to be fail-safe under all conditions, including an instantaneous or brickwall stop of any vehicle on the guideway. Their claim is that current train control systems are designed to such a standard. This, however, is not the case. A recent collision in Chicago between an Illinois Central Gulf Highliner commuter train and an older commuter car showed that train control systems are not completely fail-safe by design.[2] In general, train control systems rely heavily upon driver judgment.

In fact the completely fail-safe system never has and probably never will exist. We approximate it based upon implicit risk assumptions as to what is necessary to provide adequate safety.

An alternative to fail-safe design is redundant design, in which system operation is assured in the event of single failures or critical multiple failures by the use of redundancy. The use of four engines on a jet plane or a dual master cylinder in an automobile are examples. A problem with redundant design is failure detection. If the system continues to operate after the first failure, sooner or later it will fail again. This time there will be no redundancy! Thus, it is necessary to have a proper maintenance and repair system if redundant design is used. Such an approach has been quite successful in the aircraft industry—however, it means significantly higher maintenance costs than are typical for the transit industry.

Implicit in non-fail-safe design is the acceptance of risk, and thus it becomes prudent to design for crash survivability and to establish emergency procedures. This has been the practice for years in the aircraft industry and is now being accepted by the auto industry. The transit industry is also moving towards design for crash survivability.

Design for Crash Survivability

The transit industry is accustomed to thinking in terms of maximum deceleration levels of perhaps 0.5 g, or even less if standees are involved. Auto braking rates are similarly usually less than 0.5 g. However, in the event of a collision, far higher values of deceleration occur and can be safely tolerated by the passenger under certain conditions. To emphasize this point, let us review the results from three examples in which human volunteers were subjected to severe impact decelerations.[a]

[a] The material in this section is taken from "Application of Automotive Crash Survivability Research to Close Headway PRT Systems" by T.J. McGean and N.W. Lutkefedder, Report

On June 1, 1951, Dr. John Paul Stapp (for whom the annual Stapp Car Crash Conference is named) was seated on a decelerator and restrained by an Air Force harness with lap and shoulder belts, at Edwards Air Force Base, Muroc, California. He experienced a head deceleration of 45 g's during a velocity change of 120 mph within 0.228 seconds.[3]

Stunt man Ross Collins, under contract to General Motors Research Laboratories, dove from heights as high as 57 feet, landing on a 3-foot-thick polyurethane foam-filled mattress at speeds up to 40 mph. Collins experienced head decelerations of up to 48 g's.[4]

The National Highway Traffic Safety Administration (NHTSA) has concluded a series of human volunteer tests at Holloman Air Force Base, Alamogordo, New Mexico.[5] The tests involve simulated vehicle crashes to evaluate the effectiveness of inflatable restraints commonly known as "air bags." Sled deceleration reached 19.3 g's on impact from 30 mph. No injury or discomfort was experienced by the volunteer who was not restrained by lap or shoulder belts, but was protected by an air bag. His head and chest decelerations were 39 and 49 g's respectively.

Now certainly these professionals who were in especially good health cannot be considered typical subjects for determining allowable deceleration rates, but they do indicate the enormous capability for punishment inherent in the human body.

A very important part of NHTSA's efforts is that of issuing and regulating motor vehicle safety standards (MVSS).[6] The standard that is most relevant to crash survivability is MVSS 208—"Occupant Crash Protection."[7] The intent of the standard's head injury criterion is to set limits on the acceleration exposure of the head that reflect the available biomechanical data in terms that can be satisfactorily measured by a test dummy. Other injury criteria within this standard include the acceptable dummy chest accelerations and femur force levels. In addition to specifying injury criteria, MVSS 208 establishes general requirements for dummy sizes, occupant restraint configurations, test conditions, and data recording procedures.

As published on November 3, 1970,[8] MVSS 208 specified a head acceleration level of 70 g's that could not be exceeded for a cumulative duration of more than 3 milliseconds, and a maximum peak acceleration of 90 g's. As amended on March 10, 1971,[9] the MVSS 208 criterion for head injury was changed to the SAE Severity Index system originally developed by C.W. Gadd and published as SAE Information Report J885a.[10] The Severity Index is computed by taking the head acceleration at each instantaneous point during the crash event, raising it to the 2.5 power and integrating over the entire time interval as shown by:

No. 73 ICT-52. Presented to the Intersociety Conference on Transportation in Denver, Colorado, September 23-27, 1973.

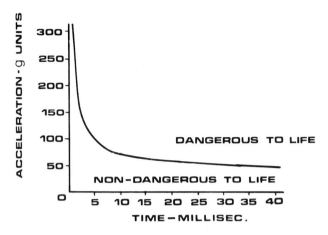

Source: "Human Tolerance to Impact Conditions as Related to Motor Vehicle Design—SAE J885a," Society of Automotive Engineers Information Report, approved March 1964, revised October 1966. Reprinted with permission.

Figure 4-3. Impact Tolerance for the Human Brain in Forehead Impacts Against Plane, Unyielding Surfaces.

$$SI = \int a^n \, dt \tag{4.1}$$

SI = Severity Index

a = resultant acceleration expressed in multiples of g

n = weighting factor of 2.5

t = time

The acceptable index level established in the standard, as amended, was 1000 on the basis of data from injury tolerance research, including head injury tolerance studies at Wayne State University (Figure 4-3). The curve in Figure 4-3 shows the upper limit on head accelerations that are non-dangerous to life. SAE J885a also specifies a maximum head acceleration level (distributed loading) of 80 g's and that for the thigh-hip complex (load applied through knees) of 35 g's to prevent death or serious injury (Table 4-1).

As amended on June 23, 1972,[11] MVSS 208 incorporated a new head injury criterion (*HIC*), which was based on average acceleration and is expressed as:

$$HIC = \left[\frac{1}{t_2 - t_1} \int_{t_1}^{t_2} a \, dt \right]^{2.5} (t_2 - t_1) \tag{4.2}$$

Table 4-1
Human Tolerance to Impact Conditions—Experimentally Determined Levels of Impact, Producing Minor to Moderate Injury (Response Function)

Body Area Impacted	Minimum Contact Area square inches	Effective Weight pounds	Peak Force pounds	Peak g	Severity Index Limit	Conditions Used to Obtain Tolerance Data
Face* (localized loading)	4	15	600	40	400	Smooth, collapsible, padded surface, with accelerometers mounted on bone opposite impact
Face* (distributed loading)	15	15	1,200	80	1,000	Smooth collapsible, padded surface, with accelerometers mounted on bone opposite impact
Throat	2		150**		—	Force distributed with deforming pad
Brain (skull)	3	15	1,500	100	1,000	Various surfaces with accelerometers mounted as with "face"
Chest	30	75	1,500	—	—	Load cell mounted to comfortable chest contact surface
Side Above Pelvis, Below Ribs	10	75	Maximum dynamic prorusion into subject area of 1.25 in.			
Knee-Thigh-Hip Complex (load applied through knees)	3	40	1,400	35	—	Load cell mounted to comfortable knee contact surface

*Below eyebrows.
**This is considered to be a reasonable value in the opinion of biomechanics investigators, based on the strength of similar human structure throughout the body. The number may be modified as better data is gathered.

Source: "Human Tolerance to Impact Conditions as Related to Motor Vehicle Design—SAE J885a," Society of Automotive Engineers Information Report, approved March 1964, revised October 1966. Reprinted with permission.

where a is resultant acceleration expressed in g's and t_1 and t_2 are any two points in time during the crash. The times t_1 and t_2 are chosen to maximize the function throughout the impact. The product (*HIC*) shall not exceed 1000.

In summary, then, it is seen that short duration deceleration levels of the occupant in the order of 35 g's would be acceptable in a collision. However, these levels could be maintained only if no standees were allowed, passengers were properly restrained, impacts from packages or sharp edges were prevented, and the structural integrity of the occupant compartment were assured.

What Can Be Achieved with Present Survivability Technology?

Figure 4-4 shows an approximate cumulative percent distribution of fatalities and injuries for passenger cars with respect to equivalent barrier frontal speeds. It can be seen that the equivalent test speeds associated with frontal collision injuries are approximately 7 mph lower than those for frontal fatalities. Also from the curve, it is seen that about 38 percent of the deaths and 64 percent of the injuries fall below an equivalent barrier speed of 30 mph.[12]

Table 4-2 gives the results of an analysis of 25,000 injury causing accidents recorded in the Automotive Crash Injury Research (ACIR) files of the Calspan Corporation. "The most interesting finding from the analysis of these statistics was a showing that although frontal collisions are the most frequent accidents, side collisions and rollovers are by far the most dangerous, as measured both by the extent of hazardous damages to the automobile and the actual occurrence of severe or fatal injury to the driver."[13]

How does the structure of present automobiles perform in protecting occupants from dangerous levels of deceleration? Based on the results of approximately 100 automobile crash tests, it appears that current full-size automobiles are capable of keeping the deceleration of an adequately restrained body in the passenger compartment within tolerable limits in a frontal collision with a fixed object at impact speeds of up to 35 mph. In a side collision with a tree or a utility pole, impacts are survivable up to about 10 mph, and in a side collision with a similar sized vehicle, impacts are survivable at closing speeds up to about 25 mph.[14]

Figure 4-5 shows typical acceleration levels for the passenger compartment and dummy occupant head for frontal collisions of automobiles with a rigid barrier at various test speeds. Reference maximum deceleration levels to avoid serious injury, as specified in NHTSA's Experimental

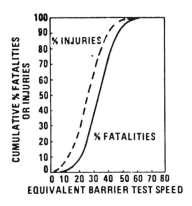

Source: "Application of Automotive Crash Survivability Research to Close Headway PRT Systems," by T.J. McGean and N.W. Lutkefedder, Report No. 73-ICT-52 presented to the Intersociety Conference on Transportation in Denver, Colorado, September 23-27, 1973. Reprinted with permission.

Figure 4-4. Distribution of Deaths and Injuries for Passenger Cars

Table 4-2
Accident Distribution

Auto Accidents	Percent of all auto accidents in sample	Percent that produced dangerous or fatal injuries to the driver
Frontal	59%	9.6%
Rear	7	4.5
Side	13	16
Rollover	21	17

Source: "Crashworthiness of Automobiles," P.M. Miller, *Scientific American*, Vol. 228, No. 2, February 1973, page 80.

Safety Vehicle (ESV) Program, are also shown.[15] The test data (from actual collision runs performed in the USA, Germany, France, Italy, and Japan) tend to bear out the high survivability potential at 30 mph.[16]

In interpreting such data, it must be understood that a head-on collision between two equal mass vehicles (with equal energy management characteristics), each traveling at speed v, is essentially equivalent to a frontal collision with a rigid barrier of a single vehicle traveling at speed v. Likewise, a front-to-rear collision of two vehicles with a closing speed of v is equivalent to collision with a rigid barrier at one-half the speed v (assuming equal energy dissipation). Thus, a 30 mph impact of a vehicle with a stationary vehicle is equivalent to a 15 mph impact with a rigid barrier in

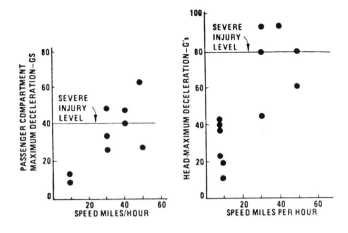

Source: "Application of Automotive Crash Survivability Research to Close Headway PRT Systems," by T.J. McGean and N.W. Lutkefedder, Report No. 73-ICT-52 presented to the Intersociety Conference on Transportation in Denver, Colorado, September 23-27, 1973. Reprinted with permission.

Figure 4-5. Acceleration Levels for Frontal Impact with a Rigid Barrier

Table 4-3
Relationships of Vehicle Impact Speeds

Vehicle/Vehicle Collision	Speed at which one vehicle must impact a rigid barrier to produce the same energy dissipation as vehicle/vehicle collision
Head-on collision of equal mass vehicles each at speed v	v
Rear-end collision at closing speed v, one vehicle stopped but free to roll	$0.5\ v$
Rear-end collision at closing speed v one vehicle stopped but *not* free to move	$0.7\ v$

terms of accident severity (assuming the stopped vehicle is not braked and is free to move). Unfortunately, it is probably necessary to assume that the stopped vehicle has seized brakes or for some other reason may not be free to move. In the latter case, calculations indicate that collision severity would be approximately equal to that produced by impacting a rigid barrier at 70 percent of the 30 mph speed or about 21 mph. These relationships are summarized in Table 4-3.

Design Strategies to Improve Survivability

Let us now consider the basic design strategies which, when integrated, can be used to improve passenger safety.

Increase Impact Deflection and Decrease Peak G Levels. Current production automotive designs, as can be seen in Figure 4-6 have a deceleration versus displacement curve that follows a ramp function at 5 g's per foot. Significant improvement in performance could be achieved by a better approximation to a square wave pulse.

The most efficient use of distance to stop an object within a specified acceleration limit is a constant or "square wave" acceleration. this consists of an instantaneous increase from zero to the maximum tolerance acceleration, constant velocity decay at the maximum acceleration level until the motion stops, at which time the acceleration drops immediately to zero.

Maintain Integrity of Passenger Compartment. While increased structural deflection is useful in decreasing the peak g's involved in the collision, it will do no good if collapse of the passenger compartment crushes the passenger. The approach must thus involve embedding a rigid passenger capsule within the vehicle structure. It is important that this passenger compartment be inviolate. No intrusion should occur; i.e., no other parts of the vehicle should be pushed into the passenger compartment by the force of the collision. Also, collapse of the compartment itself should be minimized to prevent the passenger from being crushed within the structure.

Occupant protection in side impacts presents special problems because of the short distance between the occupant and the impact surface. This lack of distance renders ineffective most systems used for protection in frontal impacts. Studies indicate a need to stiffen door pillars and add cross members to stiffen laterally the frame under the passenger compartment.[17] Stiffened occupant compartments rigidly coupled to a reinforced frame, and crushable foam energy-absorbing systems, are also effective in minimizing severity of side impacts.[18]

Avoid or Minimize Secondary Impacts. Within the passenger compartment, the passenger must be protected from "secondary" impacts by proper stowage of carry-on packages and by appropriate restraints to prevent his being thrown out of his seat. The most well-known occupant restraint systems are the now ubiquitous lap belts and shoulder belts. Analysis of accidents involving 14,261 occupants showed that failure to use seat belts increased the risk of immediate death or severe injury by 100

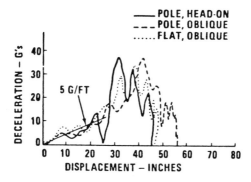

Source: "Application of Automotive Crash Survivability Research to Close Headway PRT Systems," by T.J. McGean and N.W. Lutkefedder, Report No. 73-ICT-52 presented to the Intersociety Conference on Transportation in Denver, Colorado, September 23-27, 1973. Reprinted with permission.

Figure 4-6. Comparison of Occupant Compartment Acceleration from a 38-MPH Crash

percent.[19] For all practical purposes, use of seat belts prevented ejection. This effect was estimated to account for about one-quarter of the foregoing risk differentials. The remaining three-quarters of the risk differentials are attributed to the effect of the seat belt in: (a) preventing injury entirely and (b) alleviating injury sustained within the vehicle. Seat belts have been found especially useful in cases of side collisions. Unfortunately, only 30 percent of Americans use the lap belt and only 6 percent use the more effective lap and shoulder belt combination.

For this reason, considerable attention is currently being given to "passive" restraint systems that do not require any action on the part of the motorist. This approach has focused mainly on the air bag and passive belt concepts.[20]

There are other factors besides proper passenger restraints that must be considered in preventing secondary impacts. No sharp objects must be present in the passenger compartment. Surfaces should be padded and free from protrusions. Window materials should have high impact resistance and should not shatter into dangerously sharp fragments.[21]

For a personal rapid transit (PRT) vehicle, the question of avoiding secondary impacts is a major concern. If seat belts are to be used, it will probably be necessary to prevent vehicle departure from the station if the belts are not fastened. How to handle proper restraint of children and babies is especially perplexing.[22] Packages will probably require a safe underseat storage space, although it is not clear how passengers will be discouraged from placing such objects on a handy vacant seat. Commercial airlines have successfully obtained passenger cooperation with the use of seat belts and safe package storage, but their success is mainly attributable to careful surveillance by the stewardesses. It is inherent in the PRT concept that personal surveillance will not be available; however, closed circuit TV monitoring of the passenger compartment is conceivable and would also help protect the system against vandalism and crimes of assault.

Prevent Derailment. Automotive accident statistics indicate a high potential for passenger injury in the event the vehicle rolls over. Similarly, many serious train accidents involve derailment. Thus, for passenger safety, any transit system should have a high level of lateral stability. Stability should be sufficient to prevent a merge collision from causing the derailment of one of the vehicles. Bumper surfaces should be located so as to produce minimal overturning moments when struck

Consider Post Crash Factors. Survival during the crash phase of an accident is not sufficient to assure passenger safety.[23] A few of the important postcrash problems are the following:

1. Escape worthiness
2. Flammability of materials
3. Fire protection/fire control
4. Toxic and noxious gases
5. Emergency communications
6. Egress of the disabled
7. Emergency rescue vehicles and techniques
8. Electrical fires
9. Escape and rescue tools
10. Survival and aid kits

This list is concerned with three basic areas: (a) prevention and control of fires, (b) safe egress or rescue of the passenger, and (c) providing proper emergency first aid. Safe passenger evacuation must be designed into the transit vehicle and not added as an afterthought. Otherwise, it may be found that it is not possible to locate properly the required emergency exits. Questions of safe passenger evacuation are especially serious if the system design does not lend itself to providing safe passenger access to the guideway. Integral with provision for emergency evacuation, procedures are required to assure that guideway electrical power is turned off. Communications between passengers and the control center should be provided so passengers may be given proper instructions.

According to a German study involving 10,271 accidents with passenger injuries, while fire occurred in only 0.2 percent of the accidents, 20 percent of those accidents involved fatalities.[24] Thus, automobile fires, though infrequent, are serious when they occur. Electrified systems do not have the fire hazard inherent in the gasoline carried by automobiles. But, high voltage electric power systems, if one can judge by rail experience, represent a serious potential fire hazard, especially with the presence of flammable materials.[25]

NHTSA has established Motor Vehicle Safety Standards for flammability of materials and for emergency evacuation exits from public conveyances.[26] The latter standard establishes minimum requirements for bus window retention and release to reduce the likelihood of passenger ejection in accidents and enhance passenger exit in emergencies.

Calculation of Collision Impact

If collisions are to be possible for an automated transit system, we should be able to determine the conditions under which they may occur. The most obvious case will be where a vehicle stops so quickly that the following vehicles are unable to react in time. What could cause such a rapid deceleration of the lead vehicle? Some of the possibilities along with estimated rates of deceleration are listed in Table 4-4.

To analyze the situation we assume such a failure causes a sudden deceleration of the lead vehicle (car one) at a rate d_1. The following vehicle (car two) is separated from the lead vehicle by a distance s_0. We assume that after a reaction time t_r, the following vehicle stops at his maximum safe braking rate d_2. There are three distinct possibilities for the fate of car two:

1. If car two is very close to car one, he will collide before he has even begun to decelerate.
2. If car two is further back he will have a chance to begin decelerating before he hits car one.
3. If the separation satisfies the non-brick wall stop equations (chapter 2 equation 2.35) no collision will occur.

For both cases 1 and 2 there are two possible states for vehicle one:

a. Vehicle one may be decelerating at the time of impact.
b. Vehicle one may have already stopped at the time of impact.

There are thus five different conditions for which collision equations are required. Denoting parameters for car one with the subscript 1 and parameters for car two with the subscript 2, the equations for each of the five cases are listed below, where:

$$v = \text{vehicle velocity}$$

Table 4-4
High Deceleration Failure Modes

Vehicle hits heavy obstacle on guideway	1-20 g
Collision with undetected vehicle stopped on guideway	30-40 g
Accidental thrust reversal	1 g
Collapse of guideway	∞ g
Switch improperly positioned	0.5-10 g
Collision with switch frog (loss of lateral guidance)	10-40 g
Collision with another vehicle (pileup situation)	10-40 g
Damaged pavement	0.5-1 g
Damaged lateral guidance surface	1-2 g
Crossing collision	10-40 g
Merge collision	10-40 g
Emergency brakes inadvertently applied	0.5-1 g
Parking brake inadvertently applied	0.5 g
Wheel bearings freeze	0.25 g
Major suspension failure	1 g
Loss of a wheel	0.25-0.5 g
Bearing failure in propulsion motor	0.5 g
Lockup of clutch or transmission	0.5 g
Lockup of differential	0.5 g
Derailment—vehicle tips over	1-2 g
Vehicle hits station (excessive roll)	2-40 g
Vehicle hits snubber at end of track	1-2 g

s = vehicle position

d = vehicle deceleration

t = time from beginning of car one deceleration

t_c = time at which collision occurs

Δv = relative collision velocity at time of impact

Case 1: car 1 stopping, car 2 at cruise speed

Limits
$$\sqrt{2s_0/d_1} \leq t_r \leq v_0/d_1$$

$$t_c = \sqrt{2s_0/d_1} \tag{4.3}$$

$$\Delta v = \sqrt{2s_0 d_1} \tag{4.4}$$

Case 2: car 1 stopped, car 2 at cruise speed

Limits
$$\sqrt{2s_0/d_1} \leq t_r \text{ and } v_0/d_1 < t_r$$

$$t_c = s_0/v_0 + v_0/2d_1 \tag{4.5}$$

$$\Delta v = v_0 \tag{4.6}$$

Case 3: car 1 stopped, car 2 stopping

Limits $\quad\quad\quad\quad t_r < \sqrt{2s_0/d_1} \text{ and } t_r \le v_0/d_1$

$$t_c = \frac{\Delta v - d_2 t_r}{d_1 - d_2} \tag{4.7}$$

$$\Delta v = \sqrt{2(d_1 - d_2)s_0 + d_1 d_2 t_r^2} \tag{4.8}$$

Case 4: car 1 stopping, car 2 stopped

Limits $\quad\quad\quad\quad v_0/d_1 < t_r < \sqrt{2s_0/d_1}$

$$t_c = (v_0 - \Delta v)/d_2 + t_r \tag{4.9}$$

$$\Delta v = \sqrt{v_0^2(1 - (d_2/d_1)) + 2d_2(v_0 t_r - s_0)} \tag{4.10}$$

Case 5: no collision

Limits $\quad\quad\quad\quad s_0 > v_0^2/2d_2 - v_0^2/2d_1 + v_0 t_r$

$$\Delta v = 0 \tag{4.11}$$

The collision velocity Δv may be converted to an equivalent brick wall collision velocity by using momentum and energy relationships. For equal weight vehicles and an assumed inelastic collision, the energy dissipated in the collision may be readily found. From conservation of momentum:

$$v_1 + v_2 = 2v_f \tag{4.12}$$

$v_f =$ final speed of vehicles after inelastic collision

The energy E dissipated in the collision is then:

$$E = \frac{mv_1^2}{2} + \frac{mv_2^2}{2} - \frac{2m}{2}\left(\frac{v_1 + v_2}{2}\right)^2 \tag{4.13}$$

$m =$ mass of one vehicle

Simplifying:

$$E = m\left(\frac{v_1 - v_2}{2}\right)^2 = m\left(\frac{\Delta v}{2}\right)^2 \tag{4.14}$$

Assuming each vehicle receives half of the collision energy:

$$E \text{ per vehicle} = m\Delta v^2/8 \tag{4.15}$$

In a brick wall stop from a speed v_b, a vehicle dissipates:

$$E_b = mv_b^2/2 \tag{4.16}$$

The equivalent speed at which a vehicle must impact a rigid brick wall to dissipate the same energy as the actual collision is therefore:

$$v_b = 0.5 \, \Delta v \qquad (4.17)$$

v_b = equivalent brick wall impact speed

The rigid barrier speed is just half of Δv and is a useful index of collision severity. Figures 4-7 and 4-8 plot v_b for various values of s_0 and d_2. The failed vehicle deceleration in all cases is 1 g and the initial speed 15 mph.

Headway Analysis for Actual Conditions

Up to this point, all of our headway analyses have assumed the trailing vehicle to be cruising at a constant speed at the time that some failure caused either a brick wall or a high deceleration rate stop of the vehicle in front of it.

It is possible, however, that the trailing vehicle might be accelerating at the time, or that its velocity might be somewhat higher than cruise speed. It might not be precisely located where the control system believes it to be. The braking system may not deliver precisely the design deceleration rate. It is for these reasons that a so-called "K factor" greater than one was historically used in rail transit. In modern, close headway applications it is desirable to estimate these effects analytically, instead of applying a nominal safety factor.

As an example of such an analysis consider the situation shown in Figure 4-9.[27] This illustrates a vehicle overspeed condition. The vehicle is initially traveling at a speed v_0. At time t equals zero the motor "runs away" accelerating the vehicle at a rate a_0. When velocity reaches v_*, the overspeed detection system recognizes the problem and calls for an emergency stop. After a reaction time t_r, a jerk limited emergency stop is executed with jerk j and deceleration d.

Kinematic analysis reveals the following relationships:

$$t_a = \frac{v_* - v_0}{a_0} \qquad (4.18)$$

$$v_a = v_*$$

$$s_a = \frac{v_*^2}{2a_0} - \frac{v_0^2}{2a_0}$$

$$t_b = t_a + t_r \qquad (4.19)$$

$$v_b = v_* + a_0 t_r$$

$$s_b = \frac{v_*^2}{2a_0} - \frac{v_0^2}{2a_0} + v_* t_r + \frac{a_0 t_r^2}{2}$$

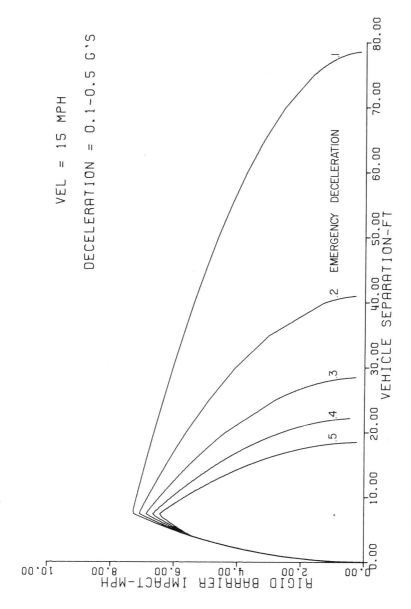

Figure 4-7. Collision Velocity versus Initial Vehicle Separation for Various Trailing Vehicle Deceleration Rates

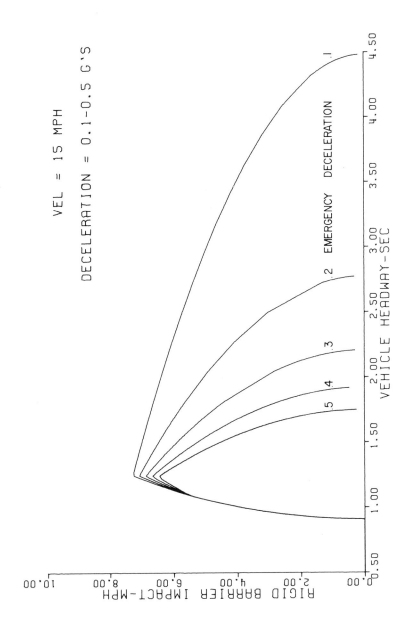

Figure 4-8. Collision Velocity versus Initial Vehicle Headway for Various Trailing Vehicle Deceleration Rates

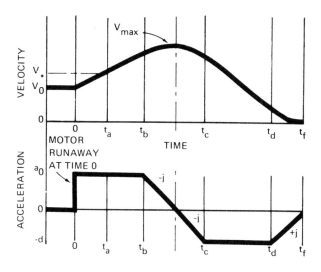

Figure 4-9. The Runaway Motor Problem

$$t_c = t_b + \frac{a_0 + d}{j} \tag{4.20}$$

$$v_c = v_b + a_0^2/2j - d^2/2j$$

$$s_c = s_b + \frac{v_b a_0}{j} + \frac{v_b d}{j} + \frac{a_0^3}{3j^2} + \frac{a_0^2 d}{2j^2} - \frac{d^3}{6j^2}$$

$$t_d = t_c + v_c/d - d/2j \tag{4.21}$$

$$v_d = d^2/2j$$

$$s_d = s_c + \left(\frac{v_c}{d} - \frac{d}{2j}\right)\left(\frac{v_c}{2} + \frac{d^2}{4j}\right)$$

$$t_f = t_d + d/j \tag{4.22}$$

$$v_f = 0$$

$$s_f = s_d + d^3/6j^2$$

s = distance

v = velocity

t = time at the locations indicated in Figure 4-9

These equations are valid only if the maximum velocity reached is greater than d^2/j (otherwise there will be no constant deceleration phase).

Solution of these equations gives the stopping distance s_m as:

$$s_m = \frac{v_*^2}{2a_0} - \frac{v_0^2}{2a_0} + v_* t_r + \frac{a_0 t_r^2}{2} + \frac{a_0^2}{j^2}\left(\frac{a_0}{3} + \frac{d}{4} + \frac{a_0^2}{8d}\right)$$

$$+ (v_* + a_0 t_r)\left(\frac{a_0}{j} + \frac{d}{2j} + \frac{a_0^2}{2jd} + \frac{v_*}{2d} + \frac{a_0 t_r}{2d}\right) \tag{4.23}$$

Assuming vehicles of length L, with a position error per vehicle of $\Delta s/2$, the headway for a brick wall stop is given by:

$$h_0 = \frac{s_m + L + \Delta s}{v_0} \tag{4.24}$$

In the case of a non-brick wall stop, the stopping distance is reduced by the factor δ, where:

$$\delta = v_0^2/2a_1 \tag{4.25}$$

Here, a_1 is the deceleration rate of the lead vehicle. We have assumed a locked-wheel skid with a pavement skid number of unity for worst case stopping. Assuming a 5 percent downhill grade, this yields a deceleration rate of 0.95 g.

The headway equation becomes:

$$h_0 = \frac{s_m + L + \Delta s}{v_0} - \frac{v_0}{2a_1} \tag{4.26}$$

Open and Closed Loop Braking Levels

The maximum braking rate is that set by passenger safety. For standees, braking is often limited to 0.25 g and jerk to 0.1 g/second. For unrestrained seated passengers, higher levels of up to 11 feet/second² are not considered alarming and up to 0.5 g is probably acceptable. However, available traction for wet pavement is limited to 0.36 g at 30 mph according to the *Traffic Engineering Handbook*.[28] Therefore, unless nonskid brakes are used, about 0.35 g is the upper limit for seated passengers. Jerk is less important for seated passengers—0.4 g/second is acceptable for an emergency maneuver. Most PRT systems now operating (including those at TRANSPO and Morgantown) use open loop emergency brakes that are not modulated to account for changing conditions. The most common type simply applies a fixed force to the braking surfaces. Such a brake is susceptible to variations in brake lining coefficient, mass of the vehicle (whether crush loaded or empty), and head and tail winds. Furthermore, if 0.25 g is the maximum deceleration force the passenger can tolerate, it must be re-

Table 4-5
Braking Analysis

	Open Loop		Closed Loop	
	Standees	*Seated*	*Standees*	*Seated*
Comfort Limit	0.25 g	0.35 g	0.25 g	0.35 g
Lining Variation (μ = 0.3-0.4)	0.06 g	0.09 g	DNA	DNA
Load Variation (full/empty = 4/3)	0.05 g	0.06 g	DNA	DNA
Wind Variation (30 mph winds)	0.015 g	0.015 g	DNA	DNA
Control Tolerance ($\pm$10 percent)	DNA	DNA	0.05 g	0.07 g
Grade Effect (5 percent grades)	0.05 g	0.05 g	0.05 g	0.05 g
Net Minimum g	0.075 g	0.135 g	0.15 g	0.23 g
Assumed Jerk	0.1 g/second	0.4 g/second	0.1 g/second	0.4 g/second

DNA: does not apply

membered that when traveling at constant speed on a 5 percent downhill grade he will receive a 0.05 g longitudinal force. The kinematic deceleration allowable is thus only 0.2g.

If closed loop brakes are used, lining variation, load variation, and winds can be compensated for. There will still be grade effects and a control tolerance. At present we know of no existing closed loop PRT emergency brake, although the development of such a brake is certainly desirable. Table 4-5 shows typical degradation in open and closed loop braking performance due to the above factors.

It is possible to compute braking system degradation for open loop braking from the following equation:

$$\ddot{x}_{min} = \frac{\mu_{min}}{\mu_{max}} \frac{W_{min}}{W_{max}} A_{max} - \frac{g\,\mu_{min}}{\mu_{max}W_{max}} F_H - \frac{g\,F_T}{W_{max}} - g \sin \theta \qquad (4.27)$$

$\ddot{x}$ = minimum guaranteed deceleration

A_{max} = maximum deceleration received by the passenger under worst case conditions

W_{min} = empty weight

W_{max} = gross weight

μ_{min} = minimum brake lining friction coefficient

μ_{max} = maximum brake lining friction coefficient

g = gravity constant

F_H = worst case headwind

F_T = worst case tailwind

θ = grade angle—worst case down grade

To illustrate typical achievable headways, computations have been performed assuming both a brick wall stop of the lead vehicle and a one g stop. Other conditions were as follows:

1. Wind speed — 30 mph and 60 mph
2. Reaction time — 1/2 second
3. Maximum overspeed at detection — 10 percent
4. Vehicle length — 20 feet
5. Total position error (2 vehicles) — 2 feet
6. Overspeed acceleration — 0.1 g

Jerk and deceleration rates used were those derived in Table 4-5 for standing and seated passengers with open and closed loop brake systems. Results are shown in Figures 4-10 to 4-12.

Closed loop emergency braking systems allow headways of 7 seconds for all seated passengers. With standees, 10 seconds is required. (Values are for 40 mph cruise speed).

If brick wall stopping criteria are abandoned in favor of 1.0 g lead vehicle deceleration, headway reduction is less than one second. This does not seem worth the institutional risk involved in breaking with tradition.

For open loop braking in 30 mph winds, the minimum headway is 9 seconds for seated passengers and 17 seconds for standees (at 40 mph cruise speed). With winds of 60 mph, the values would be over 30 seconds for standees and 13 seconds for seated passengers.

Headway Compression–The Effect of Speed Change Maneuvers

Speed change maneuvers can affect the required separation between vehicles if the brick wall stop criteria is to be satisfied throughout the maneuver. The specific case in which a following vehicle tends to catch up with a vehicle in front of it that is executing a reduced speed command may be called "headway compression."

Headway compression is caused whenever vehicles slow down. If it is possible for two vehicles that are one headway apart both to enter the same

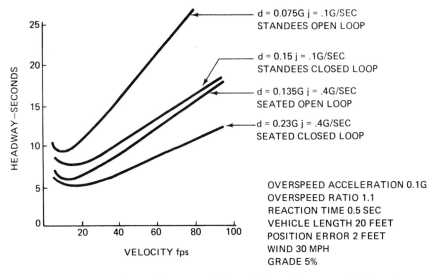

Figure 4-10. Headways Computed from Motor Overspeed Equations

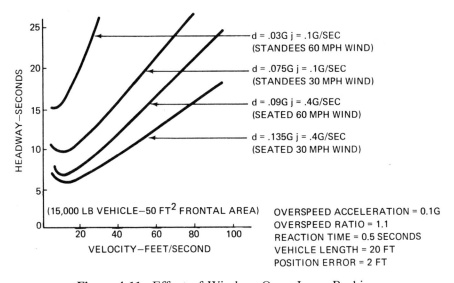

Figure 4-11. Effect of Wind on Open Loop Braking

station lane, headway compression must be considered on the station lane. In this case, the total velocity differential is equal to v, since the vehicles are assumed to stop at the stations. This problem can be eliminated by routing consecutive vehicles into different parallel station lanes but this adds the additional expense of two parallel lanes.

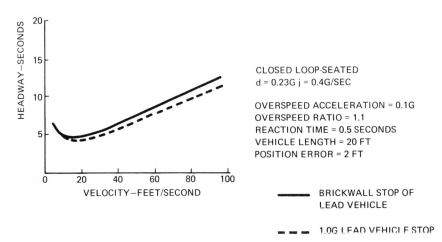

Figure 4-12. One g Lead Vehicle Stop Compared to Brick Wall Lead Vehicle Stop

In addition, vehicle speed reductions may occur on the mainline. These can also cause headway compression. Figure 4-13 illustrates how headway compression occurs.

The initial separation between vehicles at the line speed v_0 is assumed to be s_0. Under service operation it is assumed in this analysis that a speed change command is given at a specific location along the guideway. When a vehicle reaches such a location it begins decelerating at a rate d_s, the average service deceleration rate. The next vehicle must travel a distance equal to s_0 plus the vehicle length L before it begins to also decelerate. During this time, which is precisely equal to one headway h, the lead vehicle is slowing down while the trailing vehicle is not. This leads to a headway compression.

If the lead vehicle is noted by the subscript 1 and the trailing vehicle by the subscript 2, the equations for velocity and distance are given by:

For the lead vehicle:

for
$$0 < t \ \le \ \frac{v_0 - v_f}{d_s}:$$

$$s_1 = v_0 t - (1/2)d_s t^2 \tag{4.28}$$

For
$$\frac{v_0 - v_f}{d_s} < t:$$

$$s_1 = \frac{(v_0 - v_f)^2}{2d_s} + v_f t \tag{4.29}$$

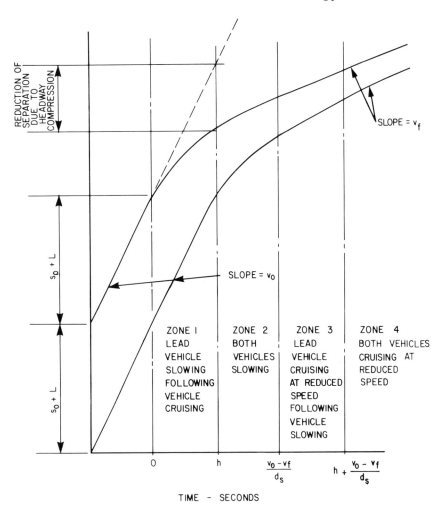

Figure 4-13. Headway Compression

t = time in seconds measured from zero when the lead vehicle begins decelerating

v_f = final speed to which vehicles are decelerating

s_1 = distance traveled by the lead vehicle with respect to its location at time $t = 0$

For the trailing vehicle:

For $0 < t < h$:

$$s_2 = v_0 t \qquad (4.30)$$

$$v_2 = v_0 \tag{4.31}$$

For $h < t$:

$$s_2 = v_0 t - (1/2)d_s(t - h)^2 \tag{4.32}$$

$$v_2 = v_0 - d_s(t - h) \tag{4.33}$$

s_2 = distance traveled by the trailing vehicle with respect to its location at time $t = 0$

The actual separation s between vehicles at any time t is given by:

$$s = s_0 + s_1 - s_2 \tag{4.34}$$

However, the required separation between vehicles to satisfy the brick wall stop criteria is given by computing s_m using either equation 4.23 from this chapter or the trapezoidal stopping distance equation (equation 2.31 of chapter 2).

When t equals 0, the required separation as given by these equations may be denoted s_{m0}. For steady state operation of the two vehicles, the initial separation s_0 should be set equal to s_{m0}. However, if vehicle speeds change so as to produce headway compression, the actual separation s becomes less than the minimum permissible separation during the maneuver. Since one has no way a priori of knowing where in the speed change maneuver the critical vehicle separation will occur, one solution is to compute the actual separation between vehicles s throughout the maneuver. The analysis can be simplified by assuming that the critical separation always occurs at $t = h$ seconds and that $0 \le h \le (v_0 - v_f)/d_s$. In this case when t equals h seconds:

$$s_2 - s_1 = (1/2)d_s h^2 \tag{4.35}$$

Therefore, from equation 4.34:

$$s = s_0 - (1/2)d_s h^2 \tag{4.36}$$

Now if we are to satisfy the safe headway criteria at $t = h$ seconds, the separation s must be equal to s_m. But, since v_2 equals v_0 for $t = h$ seconds, s_m equals s_{m0}. Making use of this and substituting for s from equation 4.36 we obtain:

$$s_0 = s_{m0} + (1/2)d_s h^2 \tag{4.37}$$

Now, substituting s_0 from equation 4.37 into equation 2.6:

$$hv_0 - L = s_{m0} + (1/2)d_s h^2 \tag{4.38}$$

(p has been assumed equal to one.)

Equation 4.38 is a quadratic directly soluble for h:

$$h = \frac{v_0}{d_s} - \sqrt{\left(\frac{v_0}{d_s}\right)^2 - \frac{2(s_{m0} + L)}{d_s}} \qquad (4.39)$$

The minus sign will turn out to be appropriate from physical considerations.

Computer analysis verifies the correctness of the assumption that headway is critical when $t = h$ for typical values of interest to designers. Therefore equation 4.39 becomes a useful simplification in many practical cases.

Notes

1. Munson, A.U., et al., "Quasi-synchronous Control of High Capacity PRT Networks," in *Personal Rapid Transit*, edited by J.E. Anderson, J.L. Dais, W.L. Garrard, and A.L. Kornhauser, Institute of Technology, University of Minnesota, Department of Audio Visual Extension, Minneapolis, April 1972.

2. "U.S. Probing Cars in Train Disaster," *The Evening Star and Daily News*, Washington, D.C., October 31, 1972.

3. "Tolerance to Abrupt Deceleration," J.P. Stapp, *Collected Papers on Aviation Medicine,* Butterworth Scientific Publications, London, 1955, pages 126, 136, 161.

4. "Thoracic Tolerance to Whole-Body Deceleration," H.J. Mertz and C.W. Gadd, Proceedings of Fifteenth Stapp Car Crash Conference, Society of Automotive Engineers, New York, 1972, page 135.

5. "Impact Biodynamics and Protection Systems Studies," Interim Report, National Highway Traffic Safety Administration, Washington, D.C., contract DOT-HS-017-1-017, NHTSA Docket 69-7: "Occupant Crash Protection," General Reference No. 195, submitted November 1972.

6. "Program Plan for Motor Vehicle Safety Standards," NHTSA Publication DOT-HS-820-163, Washington, D.C., October 1971.

7. "Occupant Crash Protection—Passenger Cars, Multipurpose Passenger Vehicles, Trucks and Buses," "Motor Vehicle Safety Standard" 208, NHTSA, Washington, D.C., January 1, 1972 (as amended).

8. "Notice 7, NHTSA Docket 69-7: Occupant Crash Protection," Federal Register, Vol. 35, No. 214, Washington, D.C., November 3, 1970, pages 16927-16931.

9. "Notice 9, NHTSA Docket 69-7: Occupant Crash Protection," Federal Register, Vol. 36, no. 47, Washington, D.C., March 10, 1971, pages 4600-4606.

10. "Human Tolerance to Impact Conditions as Related to Motor Vehicle Design—SAE J885a," Society of Automotive Engineers, Information Report, Society of Automotive Engineers, Warrendale, Pennsylvania, revised October 1966.

11. "Notice 19, NHTSA Docket 69-7: Occupant Crash Protection," Federal Register, Vol. 37, No. 122, Washington, D.C., June 23, 1972, page 12393.

12. "Passive Protection at 50 Miles Per Hour," NHTSA Publication DOT-HS-210-197, Washington, D.C., June 1972.

13. "Crashworthiness of Automobiles," P.M. Miller, *Scientific American*, Vol. 228, No. 2, New York, New York, February 1973, page 80.

14. "Basic Research in Automobile Crashworthiness," Final Report, NHTSA Contract FH-11-6918, Calspan Corporation (then Cornell Aeronautical Laboratory, Inc.), Buffalo, New York, 1971; "Basic Research in Crashworthiness II," Final Report, NHTSA Contract FH-11-7622, Calspan Corporation, Buffalo, New York, 1973; "Underride/Override of Automobile Front Structures in Intervehicular Collisions," Final Report, NHTSA Contract FH-11-7317, Calspan Corporation, Buffalo, New York, 1971; and "Preliminary Vehicle Tests—Inflatable Occupant Restraint Systems," Final Report, NHTSA Contract FH-11-7622, Calspan Corporation, Buffalo, New York, 1971.

15. "United States Experimental Safety Vehicle Program Status," A.J. Slechter, *Report on the Third International Technical Conference on Experimental Safety Vehicles*, NHTSA Publication DOT-HS-820-217, Washington, D.C., June 1972, pages 2-282.

16. "Crashworthiness of Automobiles," loc. cit. Also, Bohers, S., "Criterion Programs and Progress Report," pages 2-28, 29, 32, 33, 34; Montabone, O., "The Fiat Technical Presentation," pages 2-167; Brumm, K., "Opel's Concept for a Safety Vehicle of the Lower Weight Car Class," pages 2-194; Fiala, E., "Experimental Safety Volkswagen," pages 2-211; Sugiura, H., "Occupant Protection of 1,500 Pound Experimental Safety Vehicle," pages 2-251; and all selected papers from *Report on the Third International Technical Conference on Experimental Safety Vehicles*, NHTSA Publication DOT-HS-820-217, Washington, D.C., June 1972. And lastly, "Basic Research in Crashworthiness II—Low Speed Impact Tests of Unmodified Vehicles," NHTSA Publication DOT-HS-800-684, Washington, D.C., January 1972, pages 5, 14, 33.

17. "Basic Research in Crashworthiness II," Final Report.

18. "Side Impact Crashworthiness of Full-Size Hardtop Automobiles," Final Report, NHTSA Contract DOT-HS-046-1-209, Dynamic Science, Inc., October 1972.

19. "Efficacy of Seat Belts in Injury and Noninjury Crashes, in Rural Utah," Calspan Corporation, Calspan Report No. VJ-2721-R3, Buffalo, New York, May 1969.

20. Selected Papers on Occupant Restraint Developments, *Report on the Third International Technical Conference on Experimental Safety Vehicles,* NHTSA Publication DOT-HS-820-217, Washington, D.C., June 1972; "Alternate Passive Occupant Restraint Development," Final Report, NHTSA Contract DOT-HS-220-2-375, Beta Industries, Inc., January 1973; "Impact Biodynamics of Driver and Passenger Protection Systems," Final Report, NHTSA Contract DOT-HS-063-1-081IA, U.S. Naval Air Development Center, scheduled for completion in December 1973; "Inflatable Occupant Restraint Systems for Rear Seat Occupants," Final Report, NHTSA Contract DOT-HS-053-1-168, Calspan Corporation, Buffalo, New York, February 1972; and "Advanced Inflatable Occupant Restraint Development," Final Report, NHTSA Contract DOT-HS-053-2-280, Calspan Coporporation, Buffalo, New York, scheduled for completion in October 1973.

21. "Glazing Materials—Passenger Cars, Multipurpose Passenger Vehicles, Motorcycles, Trucks and Buses," "Motor Vehicle Safety Standard" 205, NHTSA, Washington, D.C., January 1, 1968.

22. "Child Restraint Development," Final Report, NHTSA Contract DOT-HS-031-1-180, University of Michigan, Highway Safety Research Institute, Ann Arbor, September 1972.

23. "Escape Worthiness of Vehicles and Occupant Survival," Final Report, NHTSA Contract FH-11-7303, University of Oklahoma Research Institute, Norman, December 1970; "Escape Worthiness of Vehicles for Occupant Survival and Crashes," Final Report, NHTSA Contract FH-11-7512, University of Oklahoma Research Institute, Norman, July 1972.

24. "Interior Safety of Automobiles," K. Langwieder, *Report on the Third International Technical Conference on Experimental Safety Vehicles,* NHTSA Publication DOT-HS-820-217, Washington, D.C., June 1972, pages 2-218.

25. McGean, T.J., "Rapid Rail Research Requirements," Preprint No. 1464, Joint ASCE and ASME Transportation Engineering Meeting, Seattle, Washington, July 26-30, 1971.

26. "Flammability of Interior Materials—Passenger Cars, Multipurpose Passenger Vehicles, Trucks and Buses," Motor Vehicle Safety Standard 302, NHTSA, Washington, D.C., September 1, 1972; and "Bus Window Retention and Release," Motor Vehicle Safety Standard 217, NHTSA, Washington, D.C., September 1, 1973.

27. McGean, T.J., "Headway Limitations for Short-Term People

Mover Programs'" in *Personal Rapid Transit II,* edited by J.E. Anderson, University of Minnesota, Minneapolis, 1974.

28. *Traffic Engineering Handbook,* 3rd edition, edited by John E. Baerwold, Institute of Traffic Engineering, Washington, D.C., 1965.

5 Station Operations

The station or terminal is an essential element in the transportation system. The station represents the interface between the transportation system and the city at large and is the place where passengers enter and leave the system. Taken in total the station complex accomplishes several functions:

1. It provides a means for passengers to board the transit system.
2. It provides a comfortable and weather protected place to wait for the vehicle to arrive.
3. It provides information aids to assist the passenger in the proper use of the system.
4. It provides a means of collecting fares from the passengers.
5. Under certain cases it may provide storage space for transit vehicles not in use.

This chapter will limit itself to the problems of vehicle and passenger flow, represented by items 1 and 5. Specifically, we shall be concerned with provision of adequate vehicle berths to service the station demand, and with the interaction between station design and level of service as reflected in passenger waiting time and vehicle queues.

Online Stations

For conventional train and subway systems the problem of station design is quite straightforward. The platform length must exceed pL, the length of the longest train. The product of door width times the number of doors on one side of a rapid transit car is typically 15 to 25 percent of the length of the car.[1] Platforms can be located either on the center strip between the two tracks or on either side of the tracks. The side location facilitates ready passenger access, but requires duplication of station facilities on each side of the tracks. Location on the center strip permits a single facility to serve both tracks but requires under or overpasses for passenger access. Platform widths for side stations range from 8 feet for low density locations to 12 feet for stations with high demand levels. For central platforms, widths range from 15 to 30 feet.[2]

Under congested conditions, the minimum area occupied by passengers is about 1.5 square feet per person. Unavoidable contact with strangers will occur at area occupancies less than 2.75 square feet per person. 3.5 square feet per person is required for the area to be considered uncrowded. In general for queues at loading areas of station platforms, the preferred area occupancy should be at least five square feet of platform per person. (This follows Fruin.[3] The Institute for Rapid Transit[4] more conservatively recommends providing eight square feet per person for platform areas.) Assuming a seventy foot long subway car could be expected to discharge up to 100 persons at a busy station, the holding area required would be 500 feet. This requires a platform width of 7.1 feet. Since people tend to stay at least 18 inches from walls or platform edges, the platform width should be about ten feet. Typically rush hour trains might consist of ten cars and arrive once every two minutes. Using the above example, this implies that 1000 persons must be dispersed from the station area in the two minutes before arrival of the next train. The passenger circulation system must be able to handle up to 30,000 passengers per hour. Since a walkway has a maximum capacity of 1500 persons/hour per foot of width, sufficient walkways must be available exiting the system to provide a total width of at least twenty feet.

For lower patronage stations, the flow is usually constrained by the requirement to be able to completely evacuate a train under emergency conditions. The Institute for Rapid Transit recommends exits be sized to permit such evacuation at any station within four minutes. This will typically require an aggregate exit width of at least fifteen feet, regardless of station patronage levels.

Table 5-1 presents data on walkways and other pedestrian conveyors frequently used in stations. It is usual in transit practice to use crush values, because of the severe peaking phenomenon during rush hour. Lower values are recommended for more comfortable conditions or if two way flow is expected. This information can be used to estimate the passenger handling requirement for a station under known conditions of peak demand.

The vehicular processing rate for online stations was calculated in chapter 3 for both permissive and absolute signalling strategies (see equations 3.12 and 3.19). For rapid transit systems, typical vehicle flows would be thirty trains per hour for absolute signalling—with vehicles required to stop and remain stopped for a red aspect. If permissive signalling is used the throughput can be approximately doubled.

Offline Stations

To eliminate delays caused by frequent stops, many new transit concepts

Table 5-1
Pedestrian Conveyor Performance

System	Capacity passengers/hour	Width feet	Speed feet/minute
Walkway	600	(per foot width)	250
	1500	(per foot width)	maximum flow under crush conditions
Escalator	3750	2	90
	5025	2	120
Moving walk	3600	2	120
Stairs	1000-1200	(per foot width)	maximum flow under crush conditions

Source: *Pedestrian Planning and Design*, John J. Fruin, Ph.D., Metropolitan Association of Urban Designers and Environmental Planners, Inc., New York, 1971.

propose the use of offline stations. This permits mainline traffic to bypass stations at which a stop is not required. Such techniques are applicable to both origin destination service, as proposed for personal rapid transit systems, and for a skip stop type of scheduled service. In the latter service, vehicles are scheduled to serve a particular set of stops on the route. Some vehicles may offer point to point express service—others might stop at alternate stations.

Concepts using offline stations frequently also involve close headway mainline operation, since trains are no longer blocking the mainline while loading and unloading passengers. Frequently acceleration and deceleration is also performed off line, leaving all vehicles on the mainline free to maintain a constant cruise speed at all times. The "Airtrans" system recently installed at the Dallas-Fort Worth regional airport is a good example of a modern transit system with offline stations. Trains are designed to operate at headways of less than twenty seconds. With large numbers of vehicles operating at close headways, the problem of processing vehicles in the station becomes significant. This processing may be divided into several distinct activities:

1. Vehicle deceleration from cruise speed
2. Passenger unloading
3. Passenger loading
4. Insertion back into the mainline
5. Movement of vehicles in and out of station storage

It is possible for queues to develop where vehicles must wait during the loading, unloading, and insertion operations. These operations thus require holding areas for waiting vehicles. To prevent the queue from becoming unacceptably long, it may be necessary to provide more than one servicing area so that simultaneous processing of more than one vehicle is possible. Problems that can cause excessive vehicle processing time include:

1. Excessive queues for an available loading or unloading facility
2. Excessive dwell time while loading or unloading
3. Delay at the dock while waiting for a downstream vehicle to complete loading or unloading
4. Delay while waiting to merge

Passenger delays will of course be caused by any of these conditions that delay vehicle processing. In addition, passengers can be delayed by the following other problems:

1. Passenger arrival rate too high for available facilities—i.e. formation of passenger queues
2. Inadequate supply of vehicles
3. Problems in matching passenger and vehicle destinations

From the passenger's point of view, these various processing problems can cause three distinct types of delays:

1. Waiting in the station for the vehicle to arrive
2. Waiting in line to board the vehicle
3. Waiting on board the vehicle before station departure or mainline merge

It is also possible under extreme demand conditions for the passenger to have to wait to enter the station itself.

Offline Station Flow Analysis

Figure 5-1 shows the flow relationships into and out of an offline station connected to the mainline by single merge and diverge lanes. The station itself may contain multiple loading and unloading facilities and holding areas, but only one lane is available for entrance or exit from the main line. A storage area is provided from which vehicles may be requisitioned or dispatched in response to station requirements. The average or steady state flow on each branch is shown in Figure 5-1. Symbols are defined below:

$V_m^* =$ theoretical mainline capacity—vehicles per second

$V^* =$ actual vehicle flow on mainline just upstream of entrance to station—vehicles per second

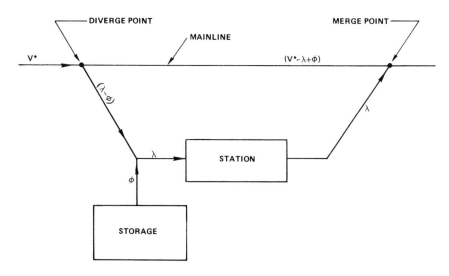

Figure 5-1. Station Flows

λ = average departure rate of vehicles from the station— vehicles per second

ϕ = average rate of vehicles entering station from storage—vehicles per second

Notice that vehicle flow rates have been expressed in vehicles per second instead of vehicles per hour as was the case when line capacity was discussed. This will make the subsequent analysis clearer and is typical of station studies in the literature. An asterisk has been appended to the expressions for mainline flow to distinguish them from similar symbols in earlier chapters expressed in vehicles per hour. Notice also that flow *from* the storage area is assumed positive. V_m^*, V^*, λ, and ϕ must be understood to represent average values of vehicle flow taken over a long enough time interval that random fluctuations have been filtered out. Nonrandom variation caused by changes in demand with time of day or station location do effect V_m^*, V^*, etc.

Over a period of time, the difference between the arrival rate and departure rate can only be supplied by the flow out of or into storage. Thus the number of vehicles leaving the mainline to enter the station will be $\lambda - \phi$. The departure of vehicles from the mainline at a rate of $\lambda - \phi$ creates additional room on the mainline by reducing the mainline traffic density. As a result the mainline traffic density just upstream of the station merge point is only $V^* - \lambda + \phi$. The maximum possible rate at which vehicles can be inserted onto the mainline from the station would be that which causes 100 percent of line capacity or a flow of V_m^*. Thus:

$$\lambda \leq V_m^* - V^* + \lambda - \phi$$

$$\phi \leq V_m^* - V^* \tag{5.1}$$

Notice that the expression is independent of λ and relates only to the rate at which vehicles are removed from storage. This is because each vehicle leaving the mainline to enter the station creates a space on the mainline into which a vehicle leaving the station may be inserted. In the steady state we thus have inherent equilibrium between station arrivals and departures which is upset only by the flow of vehicles into or out of storage. This storage flow must not be so large that the theoretical vehicular flow rate on the mainline is exceeded—a requirement that is met provided the storage flow satisfies equation 5.1.

What all of this means is that, unless a large number of vehicles are being transferred to the station from storage, the merge problem is inherently stable. Queues may develop but they will be stable queues of finite length regardless of the vehicle arrival rate, assuming of course that equation 5.1 is satisfied. Studies have shown that the insertion queue generally need not be any longer than the total number of berthing areas in the station providing that the mainline flow downstream of the station does not exceed 85 percent of the theoretical maximum—V_m^*. The major problem is thus not insertion queues, but rather delays in processing vehicles within the station itself caused by the time required to load and discharge passengers.

We next turn our attention to this problem. Before we do, notice that the station arrival rate is equal to the sum of the mainline departure rate $\lambda - \phi$, and the flow from storage ϕ. The station arrival rate, on the average, is thus identical to the station departure rate λ. We will make use of this in the presentation that follows.

Station Flow Stability

The preceding relationships assumed the station itself could process whatever number of vehicles λ arrive in it from the mainline and from storage. In this section we will consider the requirements for stable station queues following the approach of Roesler and his associates at the Johns Hopkins Applied Physics Laboratories.[5] We assume docks or berths in the station capable of servicing one vehicle at a time. Both loading and unloading are performed at the same berth. The station has a total of j berths located on m parallel spurs with n berths on each spur. ($j = mn$). The physical arrangement can vary from one in which all j berths are on a single spur ($n = j$, $m = 1$) to one in which there are j spurs each with but a single berth ($n = 1$, $m = j$). Typical configurations are shown in Figure 5-2.

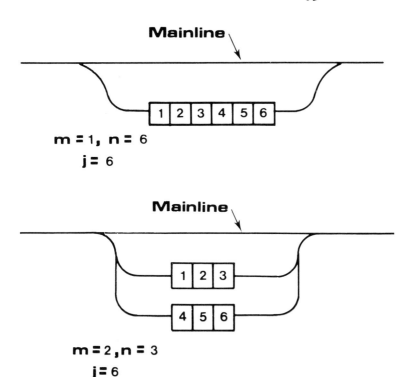

Figure 5-2. Typical Series/Parallel Berthing Arrangement

For a net arrival rate in the station (from both mainline *and* storage) of λ, vehicles arrive once every $1/\lambda$ seconds. We assume the arrival rate is uniform at this rate. This will be optimum from the point of view of utilization of station berths. Any short term irregularities in vehicle arrival rate will decrease berth utilization and cause increases in waiting times. The results of the steady state approach will tell us the absolute minimum number of berths required to prevent the formation of queues that grow to infinite length over time. (To provide reasonable queue lengths, some additional spare berths are required to handle fluctuations causing short term increases in vehicle arrival rates.)

The time to process a vehicle in the station is assumed to include movement of the vehicle from any queue into the station berth as well as passenger loading and unloading times.[a] We define this time as T_p. The berth processing rate is then:

$$\mu = 1/T_p \tag{5.2}$$

---

[a] In other words, we assume vehicle acceleration/deceleration time is either negligible or has been incorporated along with the dwell time into the processing time T_p.

If no delays are to occur for a system with a single berth it is clear that the arrival rate must not exceed the processing rate. By similar reasoning, if there are m parallel spurs each with one dock, the condition to prevent delays causing the formation of infinite queues will be:

$$\lambda \leq m\mu \tag{5.3}$$

For example, if vehicles arrive every ten seconds and it takes thirty seconds to service them, then at least three parallel docks are required. Table 5-2 illustrates this three parallel dock case.

Dock occupancy is indicated as a function of time assuming an empty system at time zero and a uniform arrival rate of one vehicle every ten seconds. After 30 seconds the vehicle departs from the berth. Vehicles are lettered consecutively in their order of arrival and shown in the appropriate berth for a 30 second period. Notice that once flow is established, docks are occupied 100 percent of the time. Any temporary increase in arrival rate will thus cause a queue to form in the station area. Any permanent or nonrandom increase in the arrival rate will cause an infinite queue to develop.

Let us next consider the case in which the berths are connected in series as shown at the top of Figure 5-2. An arriving vehicle can occupy any empty berth it wishes *unless* the empty berth is blocked by an occupied berth upstream of it. In this case it will be delayed. Such delays are inevitable for any case in which more than one berth is occupied at the same time. Thus the condition for no delays is:

$$\lambda/\mu \leq 1 \tag{5.4}$$

This is the same as the condition for no delays with only a single dock in series. It implies that the provision of more than one dock in series must result in additional processing delay. However it need not result in the formation of infinite queues. In fact an infinite queue will not develop for a set of series berths providing:

$$\lambda/\mu \leq n \tag{5.5}$$

This is similar to the constraint for parallel berths as given by equation 5.3. Within the range $1 \leq \lambda/\mu \leq n$, the series berth provides an increased throughput over a single berth but at the expense of causing additional vehicle delays. These delays are caused by the fact that an empty slot at the downstream side of the station loading area can not be accessed until all loading areas upstream are also cleared. In effect, it is necessary to *batch load* for series berths. The cause of these delays can be appreciated by considering the case when λ/μ is equal to n, the number of docks. This you will recall, gives the maximum possible throughput without formation of infinite queues. In this case vehicles arrive every $1/\lambda$ seconds and it takes

Table 5-2
Dock Occupancy for Three Parallel Docks
(Letters signify vehicles in their order of arrival.)
$\lambda = 0.1$, $\mu = 0.033$

Time (seconds)	0	10	20	30	40	50	60	70	80	90
Berth 1	A	A	A	D	D	D	G	G	G	
Berth 2		B	B	B	E	E	E	H	H	
Berth 3			C	C	C	F	F	F	I	

T_p equals n/λ seconds to process them. If vehicles are moved directly into the series berths, the first vehicle will be ready to leave after n/λ seconds. Entrance into this empty berth will be blocked until all upstream berths are also cleared. This will take an additional $(n - 1)/\lambda$ seconds. During this time a queue of $n - 1$ vehicles will form behind the last berth. When all berths are clear, this queue can be moved forward enmasse into the n vacant berths and the process continued. In this way the λ arrival rate can be processed with n docks and a processing time per dock of n/λ. The first vehicle delayed in the queue must wait $(n - 1)/\lambda$ seconds. The nth vehicle arrives at the queue just as it is being moved en masse into the berths and thus waits zero seconds. The average wait in the queue is therefore $(n - 1)/2\lambda$ seconds. The longest queue caused by holding the vehicles until a group is available to fill all n docks at once is $n - 1$ vehicles long.

This explanation can be clarified by considering a concrete example. Take a case with six berths in series. The arrival rate is one vehicle every 5 seconds. The processing rate is one vehicle every thirty seconds. Dock occupancy is shown in Table 5-3 along with queue formation. Vehicle A takes the farthest downstream berth and berths are filled consecutively until vehicle F occupies the sixth berth. From this point on vehicles G through K must queue up until F is processed. With vehicle F departing, all six berths are available and can immediately be occupied by vehicles G through L. Since these vehicles are batch loaded, they all leave at once during which time another five vehicle queue has grown. Vehicles G, M, and S experience the maximum delay of 25 seconds. Vehicles L and R experience no delay at all. The average delay is 25 + 20 + 15 + 10 + 5 + 0 equals 12.5 seconds. (Check and verify that these results satisfy the general equations.) Notice that once the flow is established all berths are 100 percent utilized. Thus any increase in the arrival rate must cause formation of an unbounded queue.

Next consider the same series berthing condition but with λ/μ less than n. The first vehicle enters the dock at time $t = 0$ and departs at time T_p. The nth vehicle enters the dock at time $(n - 1)/\lambda$ and leaves at time $(n - 1)/\lambda + $

Table 5-3

Series Berth Occupancy as a Function of Time (Letters refer to vehicles in their order of arrival)

$\lambda = 0.2$, $\mu = 0.033$, $n = 6$, $m = 1$, $j = 6$

Time (seconds)	0	10	20	30	40	50	60	70	80	90	100	110
BERTH 1	A	A	A	A			G	G	G	M	M	M
BERTH 2		B	B	B	B	B	H	H	H	N	N	N
BERTH 3			C	C	C	C	I	I	I	O	O	O
BERTH 4			D	D	D	D	J	J	J	P	P	P
BERTH 5			E	E	E	E	K	K	K	Q	Q	Q
BERTH 6				F	F	F	L	L	L	R	R	R
QUEUE 1					G	G	M	M	M	S	S	S
QUEUE 2					H	H		N	N		T	T
QUEUE 3						I		O	O		U	U
QUEUE 4						J			P			V
QUEUE 5						K			Q			W

T_p. During the time T_p between the arrival and departure of the nth vehicle, a queue builds up equal to $T_p\lambda - 1$ vehicles.[b] At time $(n-1)/\lambda + T_p$, the entire set of berths is once again clear and $T_p\lambda$ vehicles move into the n slots (the $T_p\lambda - 1$ vehicles in the queue plus one vehicle that has zero waiting time). An additional $n - T_p\lambda$ vehicles are processed without delay to fill the remaining vacant berths. (With $\lambda/\mu < n$ the queue is insufficient to fill all n berths.) Then another queue of $T_p\lambda - 1$ vehicles is formed. Notice that $n - T_p\lambda$ vehicles have a zero wait while $T_p\lambda$ vehicles have a wait ranging from zero to a maximum of $(T_p\lambda - 1)/\lambda$ seconds. The average wait is thus:

$$T_a = \frac{\left(\dfrac{T_p\lambda - 1}{2\lambda}\right)T_p\lambda}{n} = \frac{\lambda}{2n\mu}\left(\frac{1}{\mu} - \frac{1}{\lambda}\right) \tag{5.6}$$

The maximum wait is:

$$T_m = \frac{T_p\lambda - 1}{\lambda} = \frac{1}{\mu} - \frac{1}{\lambda} \tag{5.7}$$

And the maximum queue length is:

$$q = T_p\lambda - 1 = \frac{\lambda - \mu}{\mu} \tag{5.8}$$

Notice that for $\lambda/\mu = n$, the above equations degenerate to the expressions derived for that special case. Thus equations 5.6, 5.7, and 5.8 may be extended to $\lambda/\mu \leq n$.

Combined Series and Parallel Operation

We have seen thus far that both series and parallel berths can process the same number of vehicles, namely:

$$\lambda = m\mu \text{ or } n\mu \tag{5.9}$$

The advantage of parallel docks is that under steady flow conditions vehicles experience no delay other than the actual processing time. For series berths an additional delay is caused by the necessity to store up n vehicles and then process them in batches. Unfortunately, parallel berths generally require more guideway and switching than series berths so the series arrangement, although less efficient, is often preferable. To optimize the efficiency, parallel berths can be used in combination with series berths. With series berths we need to be able to do something with the vehicles while the first group of n is being processed. With only a series berthing

[b]The $T_p\lambda$ vehicle arrives just as the berths are cleared and thus has a zero wait. It is therefore not counted as part of the queue.

arrangement these waiting vehicles formed queues. With parallel berths, they can be diverted into an adjacent parallel spur. No delay will occur so long as one spur can be emptied before the last available berth on all the other spurs has been taken. This means that the processing time must be less than the time from the arrival of the last vehicle in spur 1 to the time of the arrival of the last vehicle in spur m. In terms of λ and μ:

$$\lambda/\mu \leq (m - 1)n + 1 \qquad (5.10)$$

The maximum processing capacity for m parallel spurs with n series berths occurs when the same length queue is permitted to develop behind each series queue as if it did not have any parallel brothers. In this case we do have delays, but no infinite queues develop. Since each set of series berths has the same capacity as if it were operating by itself, and since there are m such sets of series berths, the relationship for maximum flow without infinite queues is simply:

$$\lambda/\mu = mn \qquad (5.11)$$

Any steady state arrival rate in excess of that satisfying equation 5.11 will cause unbounded queues to develop. Finite queues develop within the limits of equations 5.10 and 5.11. Thus for stable queues:

$$[(m - 1)n + 1] \leq \lambda/\mu \leq mn \qquad (5.12)$$

Effect of Randomness on Station Flow

Up to this point we have assumed deterministic arrival rates and processing times. In a scheduled operation these may be reasonable assumptions. However, in a demand actuated system arrivals are more likely to be completely random. Processing times can also vary due to differences in passenger dexterity, number of persons boarding, and the need to maneuver suitcases or packages. To assess the effect of randomness on station capacity, consider a simple single berth model. For random arrivals, it is usual to assume a Poisson distribution of the form:[6]

$$P(x) = \frac{(\lambda t)^x e^{-\lambda t}}{x!} \qquad (5.13)$$

$P(x)$ = probability of exactly x vehicles arriving in a time interval t

λ = the mean arrival rate—vehicles per second

The service time distribution will be continuous rather than discrete. It is usual to represent completely random service times by the exponential distribution:

$$p(t) = \mu e^{-\mu t} \qquad (5.14)$$

$p(t)$ = the probability density function for the service time t

μ = the mean servicing rate—vehicles per second

So long as λ is less than μ, infinite queues will not develop. However, because of the random nature of the arrival rate and processing time, occasionally temporary queues will develop. Using the above assumptions for the arrival and processing distributions, the probability of having more than r units in the system is given by:[7]

$$P(k > r) = \rho^{(r+1)} \qquad (5.15)$$

k = the number of vehicles in the system

ρ is defined as the utilization factor. For a single berth case ρ equals λ/μ.

Equation 5-15 thus gives us the probability that we will never need to provide for more than r vehicles in the system at one time. Figure 5-3 plots the maximum number of vehicles that must be provided for in the system as a function of the system utilization if we are to have a 99 percent probability of accommodating all arriving vehicles. This is equivalent to a station "miss rate" of 1 percent. It is obvious that to keep vehicle queue requirements reasonable, the utilization should be below 70 percent.

Multiple Berths

Analysis of random effects for multiple parallel and series berths is best performed using computer simulation. A study by Dais and York[8] of series berthing indicates that the upstream queue should be about twice as long as the number of the series station berths. To obtain 1 percent miss rates, throughput was kept to 60 to 75 percent of the theoretical maximum. Experience shows these are reasonable "rule of thumb" estimates for preliminary station sizing although it is of course essential to simulate properly any proposed station arrangement before its final adoption.

Effects of Offline Stations on Waiting Time

The purpose of offline stations is to permit vehicles to bypass intermediate stations and proceed more quickly to their destination. A side effect of the bypassing of stations is that fewer vehicles stop at each station, hence increasing the waiting time between vehicle arrivals.

To assess this trade off, consider a simple loop system. Vehicles oper-

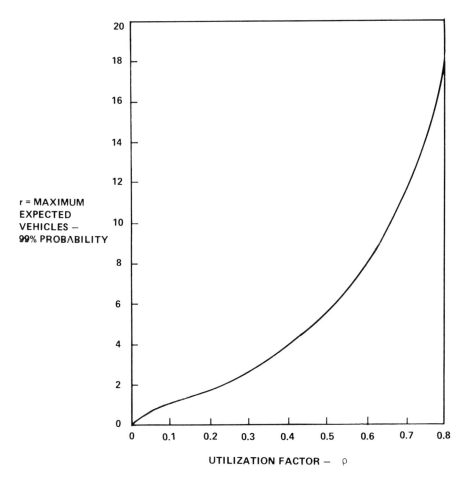

Figure 5-3. Number of Vehicles Station Must Be Designed for as a Function of Utilization Factor

ate on the loop at an average headway of h seconds. If every vehicle stops at every station and passengers arrive at random intervals, the average waiting time will be equal to half the headway. This is the case for a typical online scheduled transit system such as a subway.

Now consider the case where each vehicle serves only a single origin destination pair (e.g., nonstop origin destination service). Assume all origin destination pairs are equally likely so vehicles are dispatched at equal intervals to all stations. It can be shown that the percentage of vehicles approaching a station on the mainline that will have the station as their destination is given by:

$$p = 2/N \qquad (5.16)$$

p = fraction of vehicles destined for station

N = number of stations

Thus with only two stations all vehicles approaching a station enter it, while with six stations only a third of the approaching vehicles enter the station. The time between arrival of vehicles in a station is thus equal to $Nh/2$. Since passengers are going to $N - 1$ destinations, the time between dispatch of vehicles to the same destination is given by $N(N - 1)h/2$ seconds. The average waiting time is equal to half this or:

$$\text{Waiting Time} = N(N - 1)h/4 \qquad (5.17)$$

This result was first derived by Anderson and Sher in an excellent study of the waiting time problem.[9] To get a feel for the impact of waiting time on the passenger's level of service, consider a simple ten station loop. As one alternative, vehicles operate on line at 120 second intervals. The other alternative is to operate at 15 second headways with offline stations and origin destination service. Assume that 30 seconds is lost each time a station stop is made. Since the average passenger makes 4 intermediate stops, he saves 120 seconds by travelling nonstop. His waiting time, however is only 60 seconds for the online system versus 337.5 seconds for the offline system. Thus on the average the trip takes 157.5 seconds *longer* on the offline system than with the simpler online system.

This is a major limitation of offline stations. Unless headways are very short, the reduced frequency of vehicle arrivals increases the waiting time more than the nonstop service reduces the travel time. Since it is common to assume waiting time is twice as objectionable to the patron as travel time, the trade off is even less favorable to the offline station than the above analysis suggests.

Notes

1. A.S. Lang and R.M. Soberman, *Urban Rail Transit*, Massachusetts Institute of Technology Press, Cambridge, 1964, page 50.

2. Ibid., page 31.

3. *Pedestrian Planning and Design,* John J. Fruin, PhD., Metropolitan Association of Urban Designers and Environmental Planners, Inc., New York, 1971, page 64.

4. *Guidelines and Principles for Design of Rapid Transit Facilities,* Institute for Rapid Transit, Washington, D. C., May 1973.

5. "Operating Strategies for Demand-Actuated ACGV Systems," W.J. Roesler, M.C. Waddell, B.M. Ford, and E.A. Davis, APL-JHU

CP004/TPR 019, Vol. 11, Johns Hopkins Applied Physics Laboratory, Silver Springs, Maryland, March 1972, pages 175-197.

6. *Introduction to Elementary Queuing Theory and Telephonic Traffic,* Petr Gechman, The Golem Press, Boulder, Colorado, 1968, page 35, equation 1, and page 36, equation 4.

7. *System Engineering Handbook,* R. Machol, W. Tanner, and S. Alexander, McGraw-Hill Book Company, New York, 1965, pages 28-29.

8. "Platoon Operated Stations for Quasi-Synchronous Personal Rapid Transit Networks," Jack L. Dais and Harold C. York, *Transportation Research,* Vol. 8, Pergamon Press, 1974, London, pages 63-70.

9. "Analysis and Simulation of Small Vehicle, Offline Station, Demand Responsive Transit System," P. Anderson and N. Sher, Honeywell Report 7203-3001, Honeywell Systems and Research Division, Minneapolis, Minnesota, January 1973.

6

Engineering Considerations of Right-of-Way

Transportation consumes over a third of the land in urban areas.[1] Typically, this land is a net consumer rather than generator of tax revenues. Urban transportation systems, to be economical, should make minimal demands upon the valuable urban land resource.

Flexibility in routing is one way a transportation system can reduce its demand for scarce land. Routing flexibility means the ability to climb steep hills and turn tight corners so that expensive condemnations to obtain perfectly straight and level right-of-way are not required, and so that space required for stations, interchanges, and maintenance facilities can be kept to a minimum. Propulsion and braking capability and suspension design are therefore major determinants of the right-of-way costs of urban transit systems. High vehicle speeds, because of the demands they place upon propulsion, braking, and suspension systems, reduce routing flexibility and increase the costs of right-of-way.

The use of elevated or underground construction are also methods of reducing right-of-way requirements. Elevated systems tend to intrude upon the urban environment unless they are very aesthetically implemented. For this reason elevated systems generate high public resistance. Underground systems create congestion problems during construction and cost on the average of three times as much as elevated systems. The desire to provide a grade separated exclusive right-of-way for transit systems to avoid interference from automotive traffic is a major deterrent to at-grade construction. Expensive underpasses or overpasses are required for automotive traffic to prevent the guideway from partitioning the city.

In short, as seems usual for all aspects of the transportation problem, right-of-way location has no easy answer. It calls for imagination, careful planning, sensitivity both to the environment and to the feelings of the public, and prodigious quantities of that cardinal virtue patience. Some additional room to maneuver can be obtained in two ways:

1. operate at as low a speed as is consistent with good service.
2. take advantage of improvements in vehicle systems such as suspension, propulsion, and braking.

The use of low speeds not only reduces guideway required for stations and interchanges but it reduces the noise level significantly. Noise tends to

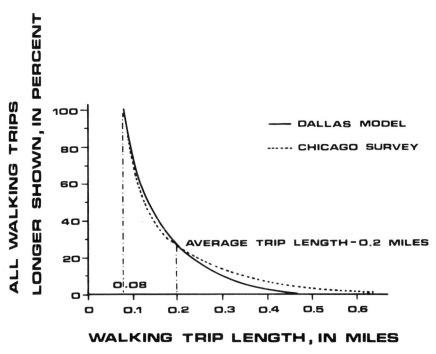

Source: Reprinted from "Future Urban Transportation Systems, Descriptions, Evaluations and Programs," PB178265, Stanford Research Institute, Menlo Park, California, March 1968, page 98.

Figure 6-1. Walking Distances in the Center City

increase as the cube of speed;[2] thus a low speed system will be far more acceptable. In addition the lower speeds reduce dynamic loads, thereby lightening both the vehicle and the guideway structure. This reduces both costs and intrusiveness. Improved suspension can make possible cheaper guideway construction, and can permit sharper radius curves to be negotiated without passenger discomfort. A good suspension will also result in a quieter ride. Propulsion and braking systems can reduce the required acceleration and stopping lane lengths.

Properly applied in this fashion instead of in a mindless quest for higher speeds and power, technology can be a friend of the environment, resulting in cheaper, quieter, and less intrusive transportation systems.

Station Spacing

Station spacing is heavily constrained by the conflicting requirements of

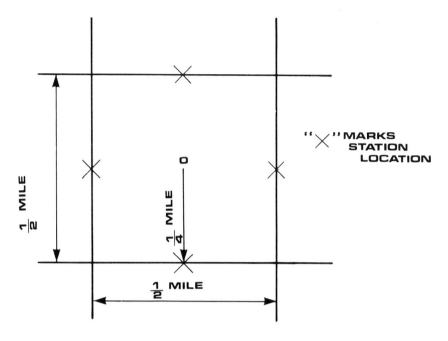

Figure 6-2. Hypothetical One Half Mile Grid

providing adequate passenger access on the one hand, and the intractable laws of physics and economics on the other.

Figure 6-1 shows walking distances in the center city for Dallas and Chicago.[3] It tends to support the generally held view that people are unwilling to walk much farther than a quarter of a mile. Consider a hypothetical transit system built along a half mild grid with stations at the midpoints (Figure 6-2). For such a system, the longest walk from point o satisfies the quarter mile criterion. Any larger spacing will cause significant loss of patronage due to access problems. On the other hand, the station and guideway requirements for such a grid would be prodigious. Even assuming that the lines only provide for one way travel such a system requires 8 stations and four miles of mainline track per square mile. To install such a system in the city of New York would require over 2500 stations and nearly 1300 miles of mainline guideway. (This does not include guideway for stations and intersections.) By contrast the New York City Transit system, which is by far the largest in the United States, has only 481 stations and 720 miles of one way track.

It is generally not economically feasible to install such a fine-grained network, but we should not forget that access is one of the key advantages that cause people to use their automobiles. Aside from the costs, there are significant engineering problems that limit station spacing which we shall now address.

Schedule Speed

"Schedule speed" may be obtained by dividing the distance between two stations by the difference between the timetable arrival times for each of them. In other words, it is the average speed that can be maintained between stations taking account of dwell time in the stations, time to accelerate and brake, and any reduced speed zones. For transit systems with online stations (e.g., subways), schedule speed is constrained by the need to stop at every station and by the time required to accelerate and decelerate into the station. Consider a hypothetical situation in which the train leaves the station, accelerates at a constant rate a up to its cruise speed, and cruises until it must begin decelerating into the next station. It then decelerates at a constant rate d and remains stopped in the station for a dwell time T. The situation is portrayed in Figure 6-3. The time required to accelerate to cruise speed will be v_0/a and the time to decelerate into the station will be v_0/d. The total distance consumed by acceleration and deceleration will be given by $v_0^2/2a + v_0^2/2d$. The distance spent in the cruise mode is therefore:

$$s_c = s_t - \frac{v_0^2}{2a} - \frac{v_0^2}{2d} \qquad (6.1)$$

s_t = distance between two adjacent stations—feet

s_c = distance at cruise speed—feet

The time at cruise speed is then:

$$t_c = \frac{s_t}{v_0} - \frac{v_0}{2a} - \frac{v_0}{2d} \qquad (6.2)$$

The total time taken from the departure from one station to the departure from the next station will be the sum of the time to accelerate, the time at cruise speed, the time to decelerate, and the station dwell time:

$$T_0 = T + \frac{v_0}{a} + \frac{v_0}{d} + t_c \qquad (6.3)$$

The schedule speed is therefore:

$$v_s = \frac{s_t}{\dfrac{s_t}{v_0} + \dfrac{v_0}{2a} + \dfrac{v_0}{2d} + T} \qquad (6.4)$$

v_s = schedule speed—feet per second

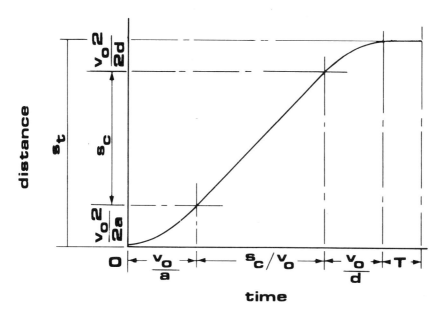

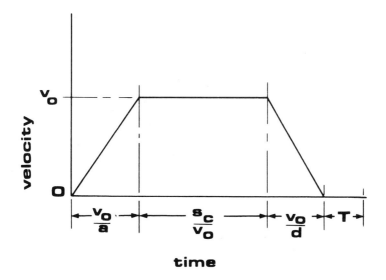

Figure 6-3. Schedule Speed Relationships

It is interesting to determine the maximum possible schedule speed that can be achieved with a given station spacing. This is achieved by eliminating the cruise phase and spending all the time traveling between stations either accelerating or decelerating. In other words t_c equals zero. Thus, from equation 6.3:

$$v_{sm} = \frac{s_t}{T + \dfrac{v_0}{a} + \dfrac{v_0}{d}} \tag{6.5}$$

But,

$$s_t = \frac{v_0^2}{2a} + \frac{v_0^2}{2d} \tag{6.6}$$

Therefore:

$$v_0 = \sqrt{\frac{s_t}{1/2a + 1/2d}} \tag{6.7}$$

Substituting in equation 6.5 and simplifying:

$$v_{sm} = \frac{s_t}{T + \sqrt{2s_t\left(\dfrac{1}{a} + \dfrac{1}{d}\right)}} \tag{6.8}$$

v_{sm} = maximum achievable schedule speed—feet per second

For equal acceleration and deceleration and negligible station dwell time equation 6.8 simplifies to:

$$v_{sm} = (1/2)\sqrt{as_t} \tag{6.9}$$

Therefore the maximum achievable schedule speed is proportional to the square root of both the spacing and the acceleration. Figure 6-4 plots equation 6.8 for equal acceleration and deceleration rates of 0.1 g and station dwell times of zero and 20 seconds. Notice that for half mile station spacings the schedule speed with a 20 second dwell time is only about 25 mph. For this reason alone, it is desirable that online systems have station spacings of one to two miles. Online stations not only severely limit headways, but they also limit achievable schedule speed and thus station spacing.

Schedule Speed Equations with Jerk

It is also possible to derive the schedule speed equations for trapezoidal

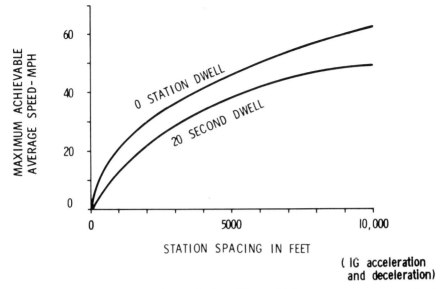

Figure 6-4. Station Spacing Relationship (vehicles stop at every station)

acceleration and deceleration profiles limited by a constant jerk j. In that case, following the same procedure:

$$v_s = \frac{s_t}{\dfrac{s_t}{v_0} + \dfrac{a}{2j} + \dfrac{v_0}{2a} + \dfrac{d}{2j} + \dfrac{v_0}{2d} + T} \qquad (6.10)$$

The maximum achievable schedule speed if there is no cruise phase at all is given by:

$$v_{sm} = \frac{s_t}{\dfrac{v_0}{a} + \dfrac{a}{j} + \dfrac{v_0}{d} + \dfrac{d}{j} + T} \qquad (6.11)$$

In equation 6.11, v_0 represents the maximum speed achieved during the acceleration phase prior to the start of braking. To determine the value of v_0 we make use of the fact that the entire distance between stations is taken up by acceleration and braking:

$$s_t = \frac{v_0 a}{2j} + \frac{v_0^2}{2a} + \frac{v_0 d}{2j} + \frac{v_0^2}{2d} \qquad (6.12)$$

If the acceleration and deceleration levels are equal in magnitude (e.g., $a = d$), substitution of equation 6.12 in equation 6.11 will yield after some simplification:

$$v_{sm} = \frac{s_t}{\dfrac{a}{j} + \sqrt{\left(\dfrac{a}{j}\right)^2 + \dfrac{4s_t}{a} + T}} \tag{6.13}$$

It is worthwhile to complete the derivation of equations 6.10 through 6.13 as an exercise.

Design of Curves

To minimize right-of-way requirements and obtain maximum routing flexibility we would like to use the tightest radius turns possible. Unfortunately, the minimum turn radius at a given speed is limited by passenger comfort, suspension characteristics, and safety. It is instructive to consider a typical banked highway turn as shown in Figure 6-5.

The highway is banked at an angle β. The centrifugal force caused by turning the vehicle about a radius R_0 feet is given by:

$$C_f = Wv_0^2/gR_0 \tag{6.14}$$

v_0 = speed of vehicle—feet per second

R_0 = turn radius—feet

W = vehicle weight—pounds

g = gravity constant—32.2 feet/second²

By summing forces in a direction perpendicular to the road surface (the y direction in Figure 6-5), the normal force exerted by the road surface reaction on the vehicle tires is found to be:

$$N = W \cos \beta + (Wv_0^2/gR_0)\sin \beta \tag{6.15}$$

β = superelevation angle—degrees

N = normal force—pounds

Summation of forces in a direction parallel to the road surface (the x direction in Figure 6-5), shows that the component of centrifugal force parallel to the road surface is resisted both by a lateral tire side friction and by a portion of the vehicle weight. The lateral tire side friction force is assumed equal to the product of the normal force times a coefficient of friction f. Thus:

$$W \sin \beta + fN = (Wv_0^2/gR_0)\cos \beta \tag{6.16}$$

By substituting for the normal force as given in equation 6.15 we obtain:

$$\tan \beta + f = (v_0^2/gR_0)(1 - f \tan \beta) \tag{6.17}$$

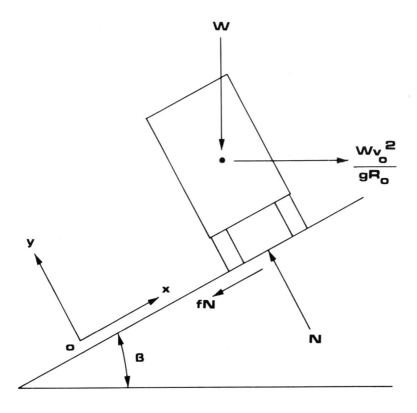

Figure 6-5. Superelevated Curve Design

It is usual to define $\tan \beta$ as the highway superelevation e expressed in feet per foot of guideway width. Substituting e for $\tan \beta$ we can solve for the minimum safe curve radius at a given speed v_0.

$$R_0 = \frac{v_0^2}{g} \frac{(1 - ef)}{(e + f)} \tag{6.18}$$

Typical values of f range from 0.16 at 30 mph to 0.12 at 70 miles per hour. Superelevation e is generally limited to less than 0.10 feet/foot width.[4] Otherwise a stopped car might slide down the incline if the road were icy. For this range of values, the product ef is negligible and equation 6.18 simplifies to the familiar curve design equation:

$$R_0 = \frac{v_0^2}{g(e + f)} \tag{6.19}$$

Minimum Curve Speed

To prevent the vehicle from sliding down the hill, the minimum velocity must be greater than:

$$v = \sqrt{\frac{gR_0(e - f)}{1 + ef}} \tag{6.20}$$

The vehicle will slide down the hill only if the superelevation is greater than the available lateral tire friction force can hold against. In this case, a minimal amount of centrifugal force is required as given by equation 6.20. Equation 6.20 is readily obtained by recognizing that for incipient sliding downhill the tire side friction acts in the opposite direction from that in the case when excessive centrifugal force is causing the vehicle to go out of control. In other words equation 6.20 is obtained simply by reversing the sign of the tire friction force in equation 6.18. It is not good practice to require a minimum vehicle speed on a curve to prevent sliding down the curve. The usual practice is to design so that vehicles may stop on the curve without sliding, even if the roadway is icy. In this case it is necessary that the tire friction force be always greater than the superelevation or:

$$f \geq e \tag{6.21}$$

It is this relationship that generally limits superelevation of highway curves to no greater than 0.1 feet per foot width.

Effect of Winds

Most highway manuals do not consider the effect of sidewinds upon curve design. Presumably the effect is accounted for by a conservative selection of the tire scrubbing force. However, if it is desired to include wind effects in the curve design equations, the sidewind force divided by the vehicle weight can be simply subtracted from the friction factor in equation 6.19.

Passenger Comfort on Turns

In many cases, turn radius will be dictated not by available tire friction but by consideration of the passenger's comfort. In the absence of wind forces, the forces on the passenger are identical to those on the vehicle. Accordingly the resultant lateral force on the passenger is the same as the lateral tire force, or solving equation 6.18 for f:

$$f_p = \frac{v_0^2/gR_0 - e}{1 + ev_0^2/gR_0} \tag{6.22}$$

f_p = lateral force per pound mass acting on the passenger

The superelevation that should be used in this expression corresponds to the superelevation of the floor of the passenger compartment. Since most suspensions permit a certain amount of vehicle roll, this will be less than the guideway superelevation for an overhung suspension, with the passenger compartment above the guideway. (It would be more than the guideway superelevation for an underhung suspension where the passenger compartment is below the guideway.)

f_p will be the lateral acceleration read by an accelerometer placed on the floor of the passenger compartment with its axis perpendicular to the longitudinal axis of the vehicle. For this reason, it is frequently referred to as the "lateral acceleration" even though it includes the gravity component e as well as the lateral component of the centrifugal acceleration. It is usual to limit the lateral acceleration as given by f_p to no more than 0.1 g, based upon considerations of passenger comfort on turns.

For most actual cases the term ev_0^2/gR_0 will be second order and equation 6.22 may be approximated by:

$$f_p = v_0^2/gR_0 - e \tag{6.23}$$

Vehicle Tipping

The previous equations have assumed the vehicle itself does not tip over under these loads. This should be verified by a summation of the moments on the vehicle. Such an analysis requires knowledge of the vehicle track, location of the vehicle center of gravity, and location of any lateral guidance wheels. As such it is more a question of vehicle design than of guideway layout. The question of vehicle stability is dealt with in chapter 12, which treats vehicle steering and guidance.

Superelevation Deficiency

Fully counteracting centrifugal force by superelevation whenever possible is objectionable since it results in all but the most gradual curves being superelevated to the practical maximum slope of 0.10. On the other hand, requiring the maximum allowable friction on all curves is similarly unwise since it reduces the margin of safety for vehicles taking the corner at speeds in excess of the design speed. Highway practice is to take out all of the centrifugal force obtained at 75 percent of the design speed by superelevation and rely upon lateral friction for the remainder.[5] Thus curves on a highway with an assumed design speed of sixty miles per hour would be superelevated to compensate for the centrifugal force developed at 45 mph except where this required a superelevation in excess of the 0.10 limit. The additional centrifugal force would be reacted by lateral forces. The additional superelevation required so there would be no lateral force at the design speed is referred to as the "superelevation deficiency."

Spiral Transitions

It is desirable to enter a curve gradually so there is not an immediate change in the centrifugal acceleration level. The rate of change of lateral acceleration, commonly called the lateral jerk, is usually limited to 2 feet/second[3] in the design of highway curves. The planner and systems engineer require a feel for the space required by spiral transitions and how it is affected by vehicle speed. The theory presented in this chapter follows the approach commonly used in highway design as outlined in Barrett's *Transition Curves for Highways*. This is essentially the same as the technique used for design of railroad curves as outlined by the American Railway Engineering Association.

Figure 6-6 shows a transition spiral from a straight section of guideway to a constant radius curve of radius R_0. The centrifugal acceleration at any point on the spiral transition is given by:

$$a = v_0^2/R \tag{6.24}$$

v_0 = vehicle speed through the curve—feet/second

R = local radius of curvature—feet

Notice we are assuming the vehicle proceeds through the curve at a constant speed v_0. A transition spiral is required that accomplishes the transition with a constant level of jerk j. Since the vehicle speed is constant throughout the curve:

$$\frac{da}{ds} = \frac{da}{dt}\frac{dt}{ds} = \frac{j}{v_0} \tag{6.25}$$

Notice that the radius of curvature is infinite at the entrance to the spiral where the guideway is straight. Thus a, equals zero when s equals zero. Furthermore, since both j and v_0 are constant throughout the spiral, integration of equation 6.25 gives simply:

$$a = js/v_0 \tag{6.26}$$

In other words, the acceleration increases linearly with distance along the spiral arc. By combining equations 6.24 and 6.26 we obtain the relationship between the local radius of curvature and the distance along the spiral:

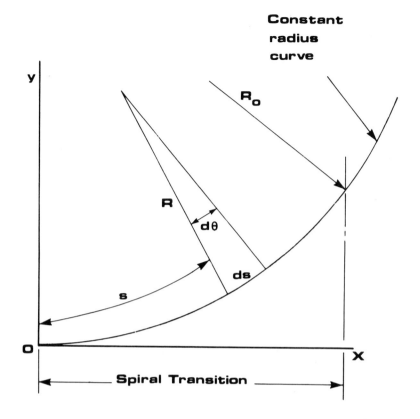

Figure 6-6. Layout of a Transition Spiral

$$s = v_0^3/jR \qquad (6.27)$$

The length of spiral required to accomplish the transition from straight track to a curvature R_0 may be obtained by setting R equal to R_0 in equation 6.27.

$$L_s = v_0^3/jR_0 \qquad (6.28)$$

L_s = total length of spiral transition—feet

Combination of equations 6.27 and 6.28 leads to the further relationship:

$$R = \frac{R_0 L_s}{s} \qquad (6.29)$$

In other words the radius decreases inversely with distance along the arc.

It is usual in highway engineering to define the "degree of curvature" D_c as the central angle subtended by an arc of 100 feet measured along the centerline of the highway. In mathematical terms:

$$D_c = d\theta^*/ds^* \tag{6.30}$$

$\theta^* =$ curve angle—degrees

$s^* =$ curve length—hundreds of feet

Notice from Figure 6-6 that:

$$R \, d\theta = ds \tag{6.31}$$

$R =$ local radius of curvature—feet

$\theta =$ curve angle—radians

$s =$ curve length—feet

Now θ equals $\theta^*\pi/180$ and s equals $100 \, s^*$. Therefore direct substitution in equation 6.31 yields the following expression for D_c.

$$D_c = \frac{d\theta^*}{ds^*} = \frac{18000}{\pi R} \tag{6.32}$$

Substituting for R from equation 6.29 we obtain the following integral expression for θ^*:

$$\theta^* = \frac{18000}{\pi R_0 L_s} \int_{s=0}^{L_s} s \, ds^* = \frac{180}{\pi R_0 L_s} \int_{s=0}^{L_s} s \, ds \tag{6.33}$$

Integrating with respect to s and recognizing from equation 6.28 that L_s equals $v_0^3/(jR_0)$:

$$\theta^* = \frac{90L_s}{\pi R_0} = \frac{90v_0^3}{\pi j R_0^2} \tag{6.34}$$

Equation 6.34 gives the number of degrees of the curve that are taken up by the entrance spiral. Since there is also an exit spiral, the number of degrees at a constant radius R_0 for a curve of Δ degrees will be:

$$\theta_c = \Delta - 2\theta^* = \Delta - \frac{180v_0^3}{\pi j R_0^2} \tag{6.35}$$

$\Delta =$ total curve angle—degrees

$\theta_c =$ angle subtended by constant radius portion of curve—degrees

Accordingly, the length of the constant radius portion of the curve will be:

$$L_c = \frac{\pi}{180} R_0 \theta_c = \frac{\pi R_0 \Delta}{180} - \frac{v_0^3}{R_0 j} = \frac{\pi R_0 \Delta}{180} - L_s \qquad (6.36)$$

The total length of the curve will be:

$$L_t = L_c + 2L_s = \pi R_0 \Delta / 180 + L_s \qquad (6.37)$$

Thus the use of a spiral transition increases the curve length by a total of L_s or $v_0^3/(R_0 j)$ feet over the length that would be required without transitions.

Turn Radii for Actual Systems

It is important to have an idea of the radii of curvature encountered on actual transportation systems. Table 6-1 gives curve radii for typical applications.

Space Requirements for Offline Stations

A major disadvantage of offline stations is the substantial amount of additional guideway which they require. This guideway is required for four purposes:

1. To switch off the mainline and make an "s" turn onto a parallel siding
2. To decelerate the vehicle to a stop
3. To accelerate back to mainline speed
4. To switch back onto the mainline making another "s" turn from the parallel station lane

Vehicle Clearance Considerations

Vehicle deceleration can not begin until the diverging vehicle is completely clear of the main line, if constant speeds at minimum permissible headways are to be maintained on the mainline. Figure 6-7 illustrates the situation. One approach that has been assumed by investigators constructs an "s" curve out of four transition spirals as shown in Figure 6-8. The initial reaction is often that only two spirals would be sufficient to make the "s" curve. This, however, would lead to an instantaneous change in curvature from convex to concave at the midpoint of the "s" curve, leading to an infinite value for jerk. When the curve is constructed of four transition spirals, the first decreases the curve radius from infinity at the entrance to the curve, to the minimum radius as dictated by allowable lateral acceleration. The next spiral increases the radius back to infinity accomplishing

118

Table 6-1
Curve Radii for Transportation Systems

Application	Minimum Radius* feet
Auto[a]	
30 mph	210-270
40 mph	400-510
50 mph	640-830
60 mph	960-1260
Subway[b]	
minimum on existing systems	85-90
minimum recommended to prevent wheel screech	350-500
Bicycle[c]	
10 mph speed	14
Auto[d]	
Minimum turn circle**	40 (diameter)
Bus[e]	
Minimum turn circle**	74.5 (diameter)

[a]From *Traffic Engineering Handbook*, 3rd edition, edited by John E. Baerwold, Institute of Traffic Engineers, Washington, D. C., 1965, page 613.

[b]From "Research Requirements Survey of the Rapid Rail Industry," T.J. McGean, Mitre Corp., McLean Va., PB204438, June 17, 1971, pages 37-38.

[c]From "Planning Criteria for Bikeways," Vincent R. DeSimone, P.E., A.S.C.E., National Transportation Engineering Meeting, Milwaukee, Wisc., July 17-21, 1972, pages 15-16.

[d]From *The Observers Book of Automobiles*, compiled by the Olyslager Organization. Fred Warne and Co., New York, 1970.

[e]From "Transit Coaches" (brochure), GMC Truck and Coach Division, Pontiac, Michigan, December 1967.

*Measured to centerline of turn.

**Minimum distance between two parallel curbs in which the car can negotiate a U turn without backing up.

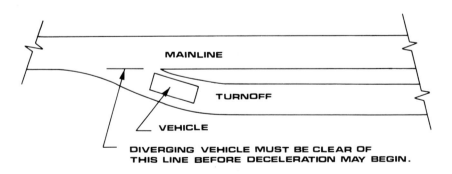

Figure 6-7. Clearance Required for Turnoff

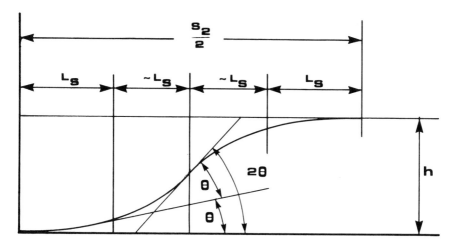

Figure 6-8. Arrangement of Four Spiral Transitions into an "S" Curve for a Station Lane

a total rotation of the guideway angle of 2θ, or twice the spiral angle for a single transition. The next spiral again reduces the radius of curvature from infinity back to the minimum as dictated by acceleration limits, but this time the curvature has the opposite convex/concave orientation. The final spiral transition increases the radius of curvature to infinity completing the "s." A complete history of the centrifugal acceleration and lateral jerk throughout the "s" curve is shown in Figure 6-9, illustrating that both acceleration and jerk are properly controlled by this design.

Since our equations for transition spirals were developed for operation at constant speed, one approach to station lane design is to design the "s" curve to provide the required clearance between the diverging vehicle and vehicles still on the mainline. In this case the offset h should be something greater than the width of the vehicle. To maintain mainline headways without reduction in mainline speed, vehicles on the station lane must maintain cruise speed until they have left the "s" curve and have adequate lateral clearance vis-à-vis the high speed mainline vehicles. After the front of the vehicle leaves the "s" curve, an additional vehicle length must be traversed to clear the rear of the vehicle. Then the vehicle may begin decelerating.

Design of Curves and Transition Spirals for an Offline Station

The preceding discussion, which follows the approach taken by Jack Dais,[6]

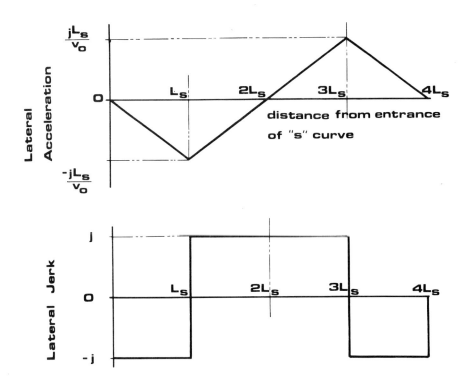

Figure 6-9. Acceleration and Jerk Levels in an "S" Turn Composed of Four Spiral Transitions

leads to a design that is readily analyzed. Each "s" curve is composed of four spiral transitions, each of length L_s. Two "s" curves are required for the station, one at the diverge section where vehicles leave the main line, and the other at the merge section where vehicles are inserted back onto the mainline. The total offline guideway required by the "s" curves is thus:

$$s_2 = 8L_s \qquad (6.38)$$

In general, comfort requirements will dictate that the "s" curve spirals be fairly gentle, in which case it will be reasonable to assume, referring to Figure 6-6, that $s \approx x$. This means that $\sin \theta \approx \theta$ and $\cos \theta \approx 1$. The total offset of the station lane from the mainline, h, is related to L_s by the equation:

$$h \approx 2L_s \sin 2\theta \qquad (6.39)$$

Converting θ^* as given in equation 6.34 into radians we obtain:

$$\theta = \theta^* \pi / 180 = L_s/2R_0 \qquad (6.40)$$

Letting $\sin 2\theta \approx 2\theta$ equation 6.39 becomes:

$$h \approx 2L_s^2/R_0 \tag{6.41}$$

Then substituting $R_0 = v_0^3/(jL_s)$ from equation 6.28 and rearranging terms we obtain:

$$L_s = v_0 \, (h/2j)^{1/3} \tag{6.42}$$

And, since s_2 equals $8L_s$:

$$s_2 = 6.35v_0(h/j)^{1/3} \tag{6.43}$$

Using a jerk limit of 2 feet/second³ and specifying a station offset of ten feet, a 30 mph system will require a total of 478 feet of guideway. At 60 mph the requirement would be twice that or 956 feet.

Total Offline Station Requirements

Total offline station requirements for "s" curves and acceleration and deceleration lanes can now be readily computed. (Of course an actual station will also require additional room for station berths and queues which can be estimated using the analytical methods of chapter 5.) The total guideway required is given by:

$$s_g = s_a + s_d + pL + s_2 \tag{6.44}$$

Here s_a and s_d refer to the distance required to accelerate and decelerate the vehicle on the offline spur, which can be obtained from the stopping distance equation including jerk as derived in chapter 2.

Assuming equal limits for acceleration and deceleration equation 6.44 becomes:

$$s_g = \frac{v_0 a}{j_1} + \frac{v_0^2}{a} + pL + 6.35v_0 \left(\frac{h}{j_2}\right)^{1/3} \tag{6.45}$$

v_0 = vehicle cruise speed—feet per second

a = vehicle acceleration and deceleration rate—feet per second²

j_1 = vehicle longitudinal jerk limit—feet per second³

j_2 = vehicle lateral jerk limit—feet per second³

p = number of vehicles in a train

L = vehicle length—feet

s_g = total offlane guideway required by "s" curves and acceleration-deceleration lanes

Table 6-2
Grades Typical of Transportation Systems

Application	Percent
Superhighways (interstate)[a]	3-5
Good Mountain Highways[b]	12
Steepest Mountain Roads[b]	32
Normal Railroad Practice[c]	
High Speed Mainline	1
Maximum Usually Encountered	2.5
Bicycle[d]	
Can Be Maintained Indefinitely by Rider	1.5
Preferred Maximum	3
Absolute Maximum	5

[a]From *Civil Engineering Handbook*, 4th edition, L.C. Urquhart, McGraw-Hill Book Company, New York, 1959, page 2-66.

[b]From "Mechanics of Vehicles," Jaroslav J. Tarorek, *Machine Design*, Penton Pub. Co., Cleveland Ohio, Reprinted from issues May 30 through Dec. 26, 1957 inclusive, page 34.

[c]From *Fundamentals of Transportation Engineering*, 2nd edition, Hennes and Ekse, Mc-Graw-Hill Book Company, New York, 1969, page 322.

[d]From "Planning Criteria for Bikeways," Vincent R. DeSimone, P.E., American Society of Civil Engineers, National Transportation Engineering Meeting, Milwaukee, Wisconsin, July 17-21, 1972, pages 15-16.

Grades

The ability of a vehicle to climb grades is also an important factor in the layout of a transit system. Although passenger comfort and safety play some role in grade design, the major limitation on grade is usually the propulsion and traction capability of the vehicles. This important subject is treated in chapter 8. Figure 8-2 shows a vehicle on a grade. θ_g is the angle of grade. The "percent grade," G, is defined as:

$$G = 100 \tan \theta_g \qquad (6.46)$$

For grades below 10 percent, $\tan \theta_g$ may be assumed equal to $\sin \theta_g$.

Typical Grades for Actual Systems

It is valuable to have an idea of the maximum grades encountered with actual transportation systems. Table 6-2 gives grades normally encountered for various systems.

Notes

1. *Traffic Engineering Handbook*, 3rd edition, edited by John Baerwold, Institute of Traffic Engineers, Washington, D.C., 1965, page 461.

2. "Noise and Vibration Characteristics of High Speed Transit Vehicles," Wilson Ihrig and Associates, Berkley, California, September 8, 1970, page 5.

3. "De Leuw, Cather and Company Long Range Transportation Plan for the Central Business District," Dallas, Texas, and Chicago, Illinois, 1965. Published in "Future Urban Transportation Systems, Descriptions, Evaluations, and Programs," PB 178265, Stanford Research Institute, Menlo Park, California, March 1968, page 89.

4. *An Introduction to Highway Transportation Engineering*, edited by Donald G. Capelle, Donald E. Cleveland, and Woodrow W. Rankin, Institute of Traffic Engineers, Arlington, Virginia, 1968, page 64.

5. *Transition Curves for Highways*, Joseph Barrett, Federal Works Agency, United States Government Printing Office, Washington, D.C., 1940, page 6.

6. Dais, Jack L., "Minichanges, Stations and Geometry in PRT," in *Personal Rapid Transit*, edited by J.E. Anderson, J.L. Dais, W.L. Garrard, and A.L. Kornhauser, Institute of Technology, University of Minnesota, Department of Audio Visual Extension, Minneapolis, Minnesota, April 1972, page 320-322; and "Planning for Personal Rapid Transit," Report by the Task Force on New Concepts in Urban Transportation, Center for Urban and Regional Affairs, University of Minnesota, Minneapolis, Minnesota, December 1972.

7

Energy and Environmental Impacts

Transit Role in Energy Consumption

In 1970, transportation accounted directly for 24 percent of the total U.S. raw energy consumption. In addition, as much as another 12 percent of the total U.S. energy consumption was attributed indirectly to transportation.[1] This indirect transportation energy is used for the production and maintenance of vehicles, guideways, facilities, fuels, etc.

The transportation portion of our energy consumption is especially important because 96 percent of it is served by petroleum based fuels—and it is just these fuels that are projected to be in continuing short supply in the years ahead.[2] At the present time, transportation is responsible for over 55 percent of U.S. petroleum consumption.[3]

Figure 7-1 places the energy situation in the United States in perspective, graphically showing not only the significance of transportation in the energy picture, but also the overwhelming dominance of petroleum as the source of transportation energy. This reliance on petroleum occurs because it has a high energy content on both a per unit weight and a per unit volume basis—and because it is easily stored, transported, and distributed.

How does energy consumption break down among the various transportation modes? Table 7-1 shows that highway traffic is by far the single largest consumer of transportation energy, accounting for 76 percent of the total. Aircraft are a distant second with a combined total for freight and passengers of 10 percent.

Slightly over half of all vehicle miles are travelled in urban areas where fuel consumption may be assumed about 25 percent above the highway average. On this basis, about 35 percent of the nation's transportation energy is consumed by automobiles in our urban areas, compared with only 0.5 percent attributed to mass transit. The difference is readily explained, since the passenger car presently accounts for 93.9 percent of the passenger miles of travel within our urban areas.[4]

Because of this overwhelming dominance of the automobile, attempts to improve the energy efficiency of urban transportation must center upon three basic approaches:

1. Reducing the fuel consumption of the automobile
2. Improving the efficiency of utilization of the automobile (load factor)
3. Diverting traffic from the automobile to mass transit

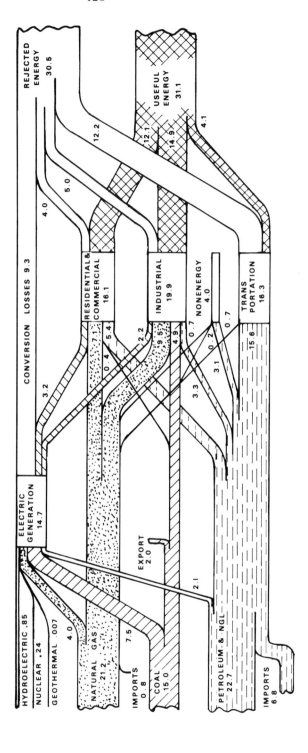

Source: "U. S. Energy Flow Charts for 1950, 1960, 1970, 1980, 1985 and 1990," A.L. Austin and S.D. Winter, Lawrence Livermore Report UCRL-51487, November 16, 1973, page 6. Reprinted with permission.

Figure 7-1. U. S. Energy Flow—1970. (All values × 10¹⁵ BTU—2.12 × 10¹⁵ BTU = 10⁶ bbl/day oil—total energy consumption = 67.5 × 10¹⁵ BTU)

Table 7-1
Energy Consumption by Various Transportation Modes in 1970

Transportation Mode	Percentage of Transportation Energy Consumed
Highway	
Passenger traffic	54
Cargo	22
Air	
Passenger traffic	9
Cargo	1
Water	
Passenger traffic	0.7
Cargo	4.2
Rail	
Passenger traffic	0.1
Cargo	3.4
Pipeline	
Cargo	5.1
Urban transit	
Passenger traffic	0.5
Total	100

Source: "Demand for Energy by the Transportation Sector and Opportunities for Energy Conservation," A.C. Malliaris and R.L. Strombotne, ASME 73-ICT-87 Intersociety Conference on Transportation, Denver, Colorado, September 23-27, 1973, Table 3, page 5. Reprinted with permission.

Malliaris and Strombotne[5] of the U.S. Department of Transportation have estimated the effect of these three policies upon our transportation energy consumption. Table 7-2 gives their results. In addition, items "b" and "d" have been added to show the effect of implementing their suggested policies only upon urban automobile traffic.

Improved fuel economy has by far the largest single impact, followed by approaches to improve the auto utilization. The encouragement of mass transit does not appear to have a very significant impact. This is because it is assumed mass transit primarily services trips to work in the downtown area (which is the case at present)—and such trips represent a very small percentage of the total urban traffic. If mass transit is to reduce energy consumption significantly, it must offer a high level of service on an areawide basis so that significant diversion of automobile traffic becomes possible.

Computation of Energy Efficiencies

In computing the energy efficiency of various transit modes, two ap-

Table 7-2
Effects of Various Actions on Petroleum Conservation

Action Taken	Percent of Total U.S. Transportation Energy Conserved
Class 1 Reduced Fuel Consumption	
(a) Convert 50 percent of entire passenger car population to small cars (22 mpg)	9
(b) Convert only 50 percent of urban passenger cars to small cars	6
(c) Introduce in 50 percent of all highway vehicles a 30 percent reduction of fuel consumption	11.4
(d) Introduce a 30 percent reduction of fuel consumption for 50 percent of urban passenger cars	5.3
Class 2 Improve Auto Utilization	
Persuade half of urban commuters to car pool	3.1
Class 3 Diversion to Mass Transit	
Shift half of commuters to and from city centers to dedicated bus service	1.9

Source: "Demand for Energy by the Transportation Sector and Opportunities for Energy Conservation," A.C. Malliaris and R.L. Strombotne, ASME 73-ICT-87 Intersociety Conference on Transportation, Denver, Colorado, September 23-27, 1973, page 7. Portions of table reprinted with permission. (Items b and d added by author).

proaches are possible: (a) the statistical approach, and (b) the driving cycle approach. Generally, the statistical approach is probably the more reliable. However, because of significant uncertainties in the accuracy of available transportation data, it is advisable to use both approaches when possible. Furthermore, when assessing the impact of a new transit technology, statistical data will be unavailable and the driving cycle approach will have to be used.

The Statistical Approach

The statistical approach is based upon the use of published data on fuel consumption, passengers carried, etc., which are available for the various transit modes. Typically, transit systems provide the following data:

1. Vehicle miles traveled
2. Total passengers carried
3. Total electric power or gallons of fuel consumed

This information is insufficient by itself to determine the energy efficiency. It will be necessary to assume or obtain one of the following additional pieces of information:

1. Load factor (passengers per vehicle, including effects of any deadheading or empty vehicles)
2. Average trip length
3. Vehicle fuel consumption per mile—miles per gallon of fuel or per killowatt-hour of electrical energy

It is important to recognize that electric energy is not nonpolluting. Such energy must be generated and, since two thirds of America's electric power is generated using coal and petroleum, the pollution is simply shifted to the power plant. Even with nuclear plants, serious problems exist concerning thermal pollution, radioactivity at the plant, and disposal of radioactive wastes. In comparing electric power with fuel powered vehicles it is important to account for the energy conversion efficiency of the power plant—plus any transmission line losses. Typical power plant efficiencies are around 40 percent and transmission losses about 10 percent. The relationship between BTUs of fuel and killowatt hours of electric power is given by:

$$E = \frac{3413E_k}{\eta_p(1 - r)} \qquad (7.1)$$

E_k = electrical energy consumed—killowatt hours

E = fuel energy required to generate E_k—BTU

η_p = power plant overall efficiency expressed as a decimal fraction

r = transmission line losses expressed as a decimal fraction

For the typical values cited:

$$E = 9480E_k \qquad (7.2)$$

Energy efficiency is best compared by reducing the fuel consumption of various modes to BTUs per passenger mile. The system with the lowest consumption on this basis has the highest energy efficiency. Computation of the energy consumption per passenger mile will generally use one of the following equations:

$$e = \frac{E}{P_0 L_0} = \frac{E}{V_m \gamma N} = \frac{E}{P_m} = \frac{H}{\gamma N M} \tag{7.3}$$

e = energy consumption—BTUs per passenger mile

E = annual system energy consumption—BTU per year

P_0 = annual number of passengers carried

L_0 = average trip length—miles

V_m = total number of vehicle miles traveled in a year

γ = vehicle average load factor including deadheading

N = vehicle design capacity

P_m = total number of passenger miles traveled per year

H = heating value of fuel—BTU per gallon

M = vehicle mileage—miles per gallon

Table 7-3 gives typical values of the heating value H for a variety of common fuels.

If the vehicle burns a fossil fuel, the annual fuel consumption may be given in gallons. Multiplication of this figure by the heating value H will give the annual fuel consumption in BTUs—E. In the case of an electrically powered transit system, the data provided will be in terms of killowatt-hours of electricity consumed. To obtain E, use the relationships given by equations 7.1 or 7.2.

The Driving Cycle Approach

In this approach, the energy consumption is calculated based upon an assumed driving cycle. It is necessary to have complete information on fuel or electrical energy conversion efficiency at all speeds and loads—including when the vehicle is stationary. Energy is required for the following loads:

1. To climb hills
2. To accelerate the vehicle
3. To overcome rolling friction
4. To overcome aerodynamic drag
5. To operate the vehicle accessories—especially the air conditioning system

The detailed approach for computing the force required for grade

Table 7-3
Higher Heating Value of Common Fuels

Fuel	H BTU/pound	Density pounds/gallon	H BTU/gallon
Gasoline	20,500	5.9	120,950
Kerosene	19,750	6.9	136,275
Diesel Oil	19,100	7.7	147,070

Source: *CRC Handbook of Tables for Applied Engineering Science*, R.E. Bolz and G.L. Tuve, Chemical Rubber Co., Cleveland, Ohio, 1970 page 304.

climbing, acceleration, rolling friction, and aerodynamic drag is covered in chapter 8. To a first approximation:

$$F_r = fW \tag{7.4}$$

$$F_i = Wa/g \tag{7.5}$$

$$F_a = 0.0012C_dAv^2 \tag{7.6}$$

$$F_g = GW/100 \tag{7.7}$$

F_r = rolling drag—pounds

f = coefficient of rolling friction

W = vehicle weight—pounds

F_i = inertial force—pounds

F_a = aerodynamic drag—pounds

F_g = force required to climb uphill—pounds

a = acceleration—feet/second²

g = gravity constant—32.2 feet/second²

A = vehicle frontal area—square feet

v = vehicle speed—feet/second

G = percent grade

The energy required by the vehicle may be approximated by the equation:

$$E_0 = \int_{x=0}^{L_t} \frac{(F_r + F_i + F_a + F_g)}{778\eta_d} dx + \frac{0.706P_aL_t}{v_s\eta_a} + m_iT_i \tag{7.8}$$

L_t = total route length—feet

η_d = energy conversion efficiency from power source to driving wheels—expressed as a decimal fraction

η_a = energy conversion efficiency from power source to accessory drive—expressed as a decimal fraction

v_s = schedule speed—feet per second

P_a = accessory power required—horsepower

m_i = energy consumption—exclusive of accessories—required with vehicle stopped and idling—BTU/second

T_i = time at idle—seconds

E_0 = total energy required for trip—BTUs

The energy consumption in BTUs per passenger mile, e, is given by:

$$e = 5280E_0/L_t\gamma N \qquad (7.9)$$

Efficiency of Energy Conversion. The energy conversion efficiency[6] includes all losses associated with delivering energy to the driving wheels. Many devices are used in the transportation field to convert energy from one form to another. For example, internal combustion engines convert the energy in gasoline to heat and mechanical energy. In this case the energy converted to heat is waste—except for the relatively small amount used for heating automobiles in colder climates. The mechanical energy output of the auto engine would be termed the useful energy since it is the desired end product of the internal combustion process. The quantity η, called the *efficiency* of a device, may be defined as:

$$\eta = \frac{\text{useful energy}}{\text{energy input}} \qquad (7.10)$$

All devices are less than 100 percent efficient. For a series of devices operated in tandem, the net efficiency will be the product of the efficiencies of each separate process. Thus:

$$\eta = \prod_{i=1}^{n} \eta_i \qquad (7.11)$$

The efficiency of an automobile engine is about 25 percent. This means that an auto engine can at best convert 25 percent of the energy content of gasoline into mechanical energy. The other 75 percent is converted into heat, most of which is wasted.

It must be emphasized that 25 percent is the *best* that an auto engine can do. Over portions of a typical driving cycle, the engine's performance will be significantly less than 25 percent. For example, when the auto is stopped

Table 7-4
Energy Conversion Losses for a Third Rail Powered Electric Vehicle

Source	Efficiency
Electrical power generation	0.40
Transmission line	0.90
Motor and drive train efficiencies	0.90

for a signal light, the engine is not supplying any mechanical energy to the automobile and so its efficiency is then zero. (For this reason, idle energy consumption is broken out as a separate term in equation 7.8.) More generally, efficiency figures close to 25 percent are obtained only when the engine is delivering a significant fraction of its rated horsepower. Otherwise the efficiency will be considerably less than 25 percent.

Another automobile device is the transmission. Transmissions provide a "lever" effect to multiply the available torque by reducing the shaft speed. Transmissions are about 95 percent efficient. From equation 7.11 the maximum possible *overall efficiency* of the engine-transmission combination is $0.25 \times .95$ or 0.24. This means that 24 percent of the energy in gasoline is available to overcome the forces resisting the vehicle's motion—the other 76 percent is converted to heat by the engine transmission combination.

As another example, consider the overall efficiency of an electrically operated urban transportation system receiving its power from a "third rail" distribution system. We have already seen that power plant efficiencies typically run about 40 percent and transmission line losses about 10 percent. In addition to these losses, we must also consider the efficiency with which electrical energy is converted to mechanical energy by the electric motors and their controllers plus any drive train losses associated with transmitting power from the motors to the driving wheels. Table 7-4 summarizes the applicable efficiencies. For the entire set of processes, equation 7.11 gives an overall efficiency of 32.4 percent.

This is somewhat better than the internal combustion engine can provide even at its best. In addition, the electric motors do not use as much energy when the vehicle is stopped, and have better part load and part speed efficiencies with properly designed solid state motor controllers. A further advantage is that electrical power generation can use nuclear or coal energy rather than scarce petroleum reserves.

As another example, let's consider the efficiency that would result for a battery powered electric automobile. Table 7-5 summarizes the conversion efficiencies. The set of processes in Table 7-5 converts fuel to mechanical energy for vehicle propulsion. The overall efficiency of the process would be, from equation 7.11, 24.3 percent. We see that the overall efficiency of

Table 7-5
Conversion Efficiencies for a Battery Powered Electric Automobile

Source	Efficiency
Electric power generation	0.40
Transmission line	0.90
Charging and discharging storage batteries	0.75
Motor and drive train efficiencies	0.90

the internal combustion engine and battery powered auto are about the same.

Computation of Energy Consumption Using the Driving Cycle Technique. To illustrate the driving cycle technique, consider a 3500 pound vehicle which operates over a two mile long route. Ten percent of the route length is spent accelerating the vehicle at a rate of 0.1 g and another ten percent is spent braking. The schedule speed for the route is 20 feet/second. Accessories require an additional five horsepower. Twenty percent of the route has an uphill grade of 3 percent, the rest of the route is level. Rolling friction may be estimated as two percent of the vehicle weight and aerodynamic drag may be estimated as 35 pounds. The vehicle carries an average of three passengers and is powered by an electrical "third rail."

Since the vehicle is electrically powered, we will assume the energy consumed while the vehicle is braking or idling is negligible, except for the accessory load. For this system the integral in equation 7.8 may be split into three constant segments, leading to:

$$E_0 = \frac{0.1L_t(F_r + F_i + F_a)}{778\eta_d} + \frac{0.2L_t(F_r + F_a + F_g)}{778\eta_d}$$
$$+ \frac{0.6L_t(F_r + F_a)}{778\eta_d} + \frac{0.706P_aL_t}{V_s\eta_a} \tag{7.12}$$

The first term gives the energy required by the acceleration portion of the cycle. The second term gives the energy required by the portion of the cycle with a three percent grade. The third term gives the energy required for straight and level cruising. The last term gives the accessory power. Simplifying:

$$E_0 = \frac{L_t}{778\eta_d}(0.9F_r + 0.9F_a + 0.1F_i + 0.2F_g) + \frac{0.706P_aL_t}{V_s\eta_a} \tag{7.13}$$

Substituting the proper values:

$$E_0 = \frac{10560}{778 \times .324}(0.9 \times .02 \times 3500 + 0.9 \times 35$$

$$+ \quad 0.1 \times 0.1 \times 3500 + 0.2 \times 0.03 \times 3500)$$

$$+ \quad \frac{0.706 \times 5 \times 10560}{20 \times 0.324} \tag{7.14}$$

We have assumed as shown earlier that the overall conversion efficiency is 32.4 percent, and we have assumed the same value of efficiency for the accessory system. Solution of equation 7.14 gives an energy consumption for the trip of 12,057 BTU. To obtain the energy consumption per passenger mile, we use equation 7.9:

$$e = 5280 \times 12057/(10560 \times 3)$$

$$= 2010 \text{ BTU/passenger mile} \tag{7.15}$$

Energy Consumption of Typical Transit Systems

It is of interest to compare the energy efficiency of different urban transit modes.[7] The efficiency depends very heavily on the load factor chosen. Table 7-6 estimates the average load factor for a variety of urban transit vehicles along with their seated capacity, design capacity, and crush load.

Figure 7-2 displays the range of energy consumption per passenger mile for these vehicles as a function of the number of passengers carried. The lower limit is based on the average load factor as given in Table 7-6. The upper limit is the maximum efficiency achieved with a crush loaded vehicle. Typical values of energy consumption at the average load factor are summarized in Figure 7-3. Notice that virtually all urban transportation modes are more efficient than the automobile. Typically the auto requires about 6400 BTU per passenger mile while the subway and bus require 2500 and 2700 BTU per passenger mile.

It is interesting to break the sources of the energy consumption into their constituent parts—namely:

1. Grade
2. Acceleration
3. Rolling resistance
4. Aerodynamic drag
5. Accessories
6. Energy conversion losses

The result, shown in Figure 7-4 for the automobile, is typical of the situation

Table 7-6
Characteristics of the Vehicles of Various Urban Passenger Ground Transportation Modes

	Conventional Modes								New Systems		
	Passenger Car	Light Truck	Motorcycle	Commercial Bus	Rapid Rail	Street Car	Trolley Bus	School Bus	Large Vehicle PRT	Small Vehicle PRT	Dual Mode
Seats	6	3	2	50	60	37	50	60**	12	4	20
Full Load* (with standees)	6	3	N/A	70	120	74	70	60	20	4	28
Crush Load	6	3	N/A	80	160	89	80	60	25	4	32
Average Load	1.5	1.3	1.1	11	24	13	9	23	6	1.2	8.4

*Standees are comfortable.
**Children.
Based on "A Comparative Analysis of the Energy Consumption for Several Urban Passenger Ground Transportation Systems," John G. Lieb, MITRE Corp., MTR6606, McLean, Virginia, February 6, 1974.

137

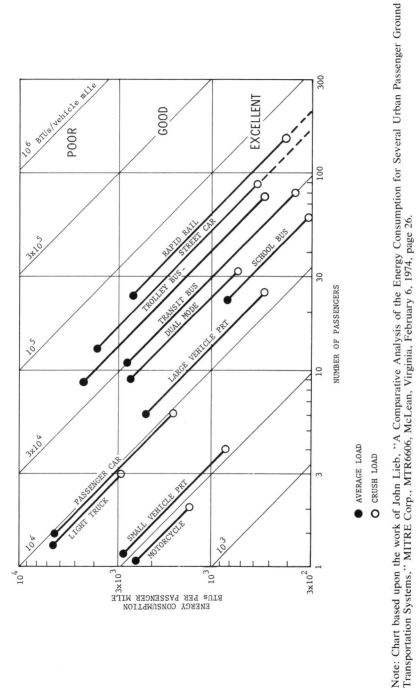

Figure 7-2. Energy Consumption of Transit Systems

Note: Chart based upon the work of John Lieb, "A Comparative Analysis of the Energy Consumption for Several Urban Passenger Ground Transportation Systems," MITRE Corp., MTR6606, McLean, Virginia, February 6, 1974, page 26.

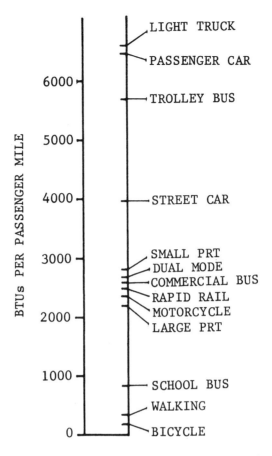

Note: Chart based upon the work of John Lieb, "A Comparative Analysis of the Energy Consumption for Several Urban Passenger Ground Transportation Systems," MITRE Corp., MTR6606, McLean Virginia, February 6, 1974, page 26.

Figure 7-3. Energy Consumption of Various Transportation Modes (based upon average load factor)

for all urban transit modes. In general 65 to 85 percent of the total energy requirement will be traceable to energy conversion losses. It is a mistake to assume from this that it does little good to reduce the other drag components. To the contrary, any savings in the road drag will be multiplied by a proportionately greater savings in energy conversion losses.

Emissions

Transportation is responsible for sixty percent of our atmospheric pol-

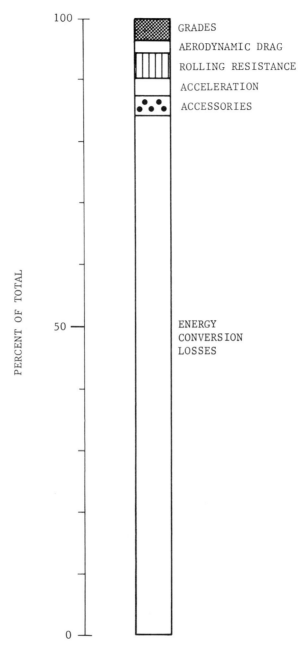

Note: Chart based upon the work of John Lieb, "A Comparative Analysis of the Energy Consumption for Several Urban Passenger Ground Transportation Systems," MITRE Corp., MTR6606, McLean, Virginia, February 6, 1974, page 26.

Figure 7-4. Energy Requirements for Automobiles

lutants.[8] These transportation related emissions consist primarily of three chemical compounds, unburned hydrocarbons, carbon monoxide, and oxides of nitrogen.[9] Transportation is responsible for 65 percent of the hydrocarbon emissions, 92 percent of the carbon monoxide emissions, and 39 percent of the nitrous oxide emissions in the United States.

Unburned hydrocarbons (UHC) are emitted from three sources: fuel evaporation, crankcase blowby, and engine exhaust. The latter contributes 55 percent of the total for an uncontrolled vehicle. UHC in the exhaust will increase with a decrease in air/fuel ratio, such as during warm-up, idle, and deceleration. The health significance of UHC is not well understood. Some carcinogenic effect is believed possible but has yet to be proved. Some UHC react in sunlight with oxides of nitrogen to produce smog, eye irritation, and vegetation damage.

Carbon monoxide (CO) is a result of incomplete combustion and is therefore emitted in greater quantities when the air/fuel ratio is less (i.e., during warm-up, idle, and deceleration). The health aspects of CO are relatively well known. By replacing oxygen in the bloodstream, CO cumulatively reduces the ability of the blood to carry oxygen to the body tissues.

Oxides of nitrogen (NO_x) result from the combining of nitrogen (carried along by the air) with oxygen not consumed in the combustion process. The extent to which available nitrogen and oxygen combine depends strongly on the temperature of the gases, the time of contact, and, to a lesser degree, the pressure level. The air/fuel ratio determines the quantity of excess oxygen and the reaction temperature, two of the most important factors in NO_x production. For the internal combustion (IC) engine, NO_x emissions are greatest near the stoichiometric air/fuel ratio where present-day IC engines are designed to operate. NO_2 is toxic to man and animals, can cause acute damage to plants at concentrations as low as 1 ppm, and causes atmospheric discoloration by absorbing light in both ultraviolet and visible spectrums.

Reporting Basis

Emissions for automobiles are usually reported on a grams per mile basis. To assure repeatable results, the driving cycle must be rigidly specified. For trucks and buses the payload must be taken into account as well as the distance traveled. California therefore specifies emissions for these vehicles in terms of grams per horsepower hour of energy delivered by the engine. Again duty cycle must be specified to assure repeatable results. Table 7-7 lists emission levels for some typical vehicle-engine combina-

Table 7-7
Typical Emission Levels

Engine/Vehicle System	Emission grams/engine hp-hr			Emission grams/mile		
	CO	UHC	NO_2	CO	UHC	NO_2
Steam Bus[a]	4	0.9	1.8	11.0	2.5	5.0[f]
Diesel Bus[a]	4.3	1.4	10.4	11.8	3.9	28.6[f]
Regenerative Gas Turbine Bus[b]	5.9	0.5	3.7	16.3	1.5	10.3[f]
Nonregenerative Gas Turbine Bus[b]	11.9	1.1	7.5	32.7	2.9	20.6[f]
Electric Bus[c]	0.0	0.07 (+1.2 sulfur)	2.3	0.0	0.2 (+3.3 sulfur)	6.3
Unmodified Car[c]				90	15	4-6
1973 Standards[d]				28	3.1	3.0
1976 Standards[d]				3.4	0.41	3.0
1977 Standards[d]				3.4	0.41	0.4
Car with Gas Turbine Engine[e]				1.37	0.15	4.13
California Diesel Standards[a]						
1973	40	16 (HC and NO_2)				
1975	25	5 (HC and NO_2)				

[a]"California Steam Bus Project Final Report," Assembly Office of Research, California Legislature, Sacramento, January 1973.

[b]"A Survey of Propulsion Systems for Low Emission Urban Vehicles," W. Fraize and R. Lay, MITRE Corp., M70-45, McLean, Virginia, September 1970.

[c]*CRC Handbook of Tables for Applied Engineering Sciences*, R.E. Bolz and G.L. Tuve, Chemical Rubber Co., 1970, Cleveland Ohio, page 545. Assumes a heating value of 147,070 BTUs per gallon, power plant efficiency 40 percent, transmission line losses 10 percent, and an oil fueled power plant with fuel with 0.35 percent sulfur.

[d]"Factors Affecting Vehicle Fuel Economy," Clayton LaPointe, SAE730791, presented at SAE National Off-Highway Vehicle Meeting, Milwaukee, Wisconsin, 1971.

[e]"A Low Emission Gas Turbine Passenger Car." T.F. Nagey, Mykolenko et al. (General Motors) *Mechanical Engineering*, New York, N. Y. January 1974, pages 14-20.

[f]From "California Steam Bus Project Final Report," bus requires 2.34 hp hr per mile at rear wheels. Assuming 85 percent drive line efficiency there are 2.75 engine hp hr per mile.

tions. Bus data has been reduced also to a grams per mile basis. In comparing these with the automobile their greater passenger carrying capacity must be remembered. Steam bus data is based on tests with prototype buses developed under the California Steam Bus programs. The electric power data assumes an oil fueled power plant. The use of coal will reduce oxides of nitrogen to about a fifth of the value cited but will increase the sulfur levels and add significant particulate emissions.

Table 7-8

Chronological Summary of 49-State Emission Standards and Corresponding Fuel Economy Losses[a]

	49-State Standards				Fuel Economy Change[b] percent	
Year	UHC, grams/mile	CO, grams/mile	NO$_x$, grams/mile	Evaporation, grams/test	By Regression Analysis	By Efficiency Analysis
1967[c]	(15)	(90)	(4-6)	(40)	0	0
1968	6.3	52	—	—	0	−2
1969	6.3	52	—	—	+2.2	+1.3
1970	4.1	34	—	—	−1.3	−1.6
1971	4.1	34	—	6	−4.5[d]	−4.9[d]
1972	3.0	28	—	2	−7.6	−7.7
1973	3.0	28	3.1	2	−13.6	−13.2

[a]All emission levels are in terms of 1975 CVS-CH procedure.

[b]Fuel economy losses due to emission controls only—city suburban cycle (8-car-line average)—cumulative losses referred to 1967 base line.

[c]1967 emission levels shown are for uncontrolled vehicles. These values have recently been criticized as being too high.

[d]1971 compression ratios were reduced in most engines, so they could use 91-octane low-lead or no-lead fuel, thus lowering fuel economy.

Source: "Factors Affecting Vehicle Fuel Economy," Clayton LaPointe, SAE 730971, Society of Automotive Engineers National Off-Highway Vehicle Meeting, Milwaukee, Wisconsin, 1974. Reprinted with permission.

Emission Standards and Their Impact on Energy

Table 7-8 shows the Federal emission standards for automobiles since 1967 along with the change in fuel economy. It shows that present emission control devices have adversely affected fuel economy. For the future, the Environmental Protection Agency has set the 1975 49-state interim UHC and CO standards at 1.5 and 15 grams/mile respectively. In 1976, permissible levels of UHC, CO, and NO$_x$ are scheduled to be 0.41, 3.4 and 3.0 grams/mile. The relationship between environmental and energy factors will be the subject of serious debate in the years ahead.

Notes

1. "Demand for Energy by the Transportation Sector and Opportunities for Energy Conservation," A.C. Malliaris and R.L. Strombotne,

ASME 73-ICT-87, Intersociety Conference on Transportation, Denver, Colorado, September 23-27, 1973.

2. Ibid.

3. "Energy Requirements for Passenger Ground Transportation Systems," Goss McGowan, 73-ICT-24, Intersociety Conference on Transportation, Denver, Colorado, September 23-27, 1973.

4. "1972 National Transportation Report" U.S. Department of Transportation, Washington, D.C., July 1972, page 189.

5. See note 1.

6. This section is based upon lecture notes from a course in transportation taught by Jack Dais of the University of Minnesota.

7. This section is based upon "A Comparative Analysis of the Energy Consumption for Passenger Ground Transportation Systems," by John G. Lieb, MITRE Corporation, MTR6606, McLean, Virginia, February 6, 1974.

8. *CRC Handbook of Tables for Applied Engineering Science*, R.E. Bolz and G.L. Tuve, Chemical Rubber Company, Cleveland, Ohio, 1970, page 544.

9. "A Survey of Propulsion Systems for Low Emission Urban Vehicles," W. Fraize and R. Lay, MITRE Corporation, M70-45, McLean, Virginia, September 1970. In addition to specific data cited, much of the emissions section is based upon this report by Fraize and Lay.

8 Propulsion System Requirements

The primary purpose of any transportation system is to move people or goods. This chapter discusses the requirements for the propulsion system, which provides the force necessary to move the vehicle. According to Newton's first law of physics, if a balanced force system acts on a body in motion it will remain in motion in a straight line and without acceleration. One might think this means that once a vehicle is accelerated up to speed it will continue moving indefinitely until the brakes are applied. Of course, as we know from personal experience, this is not the case. The key is in the words "balanced force system."

A moving vehicle has two sources of "drag forces" tending to slow it down. First it must overcome the air resistance caused by pressure differentials and skin friction as the vehicle moves relative to the air. For high speed vehicles. some investigators have proposed operation in tubes that have been partially evacuated of air, as one means of reducing the air resistance. The second source of drag is the frictional losses associated with the support and guidance system. To maintain a constant speed on a level guideway, propulsive thrust must be provided to overcome both air resistance and frictional drag forces.

In addition to overcoming these drag forces, a vehicle propulsion system must provide adequate thrust to climb hills and to accelerate the vehicle up to speed. Figure 8-1 shows the forces acting on a vehicle that must be overcome by the propulsion system. Both acceleration (or inertial) forces and the gravity component on a hill are body forces that may be assumed to act through the center of gravity of the vehicle. The aerodynamic drag force, on the other hand, is a surface force that acts at the center of pressure of the vehicle frontal area. Location of the friction and propulsive force vectors will depend upon the particular vehicle configuration.

Figure 8-1 shows the propulsive thrust vector at the driving point—in this case the interface of the rear wheels with the guideway. The power plant must supply extra power to compensate for losses in the drive train between the power plant and this driving point. In addition, engine power must be adequate to operate the vehicle accessory loads. These include air brakes, power steering, automatic doors, and air conditioning. To summarize then, propulsive power is required for six purposes:

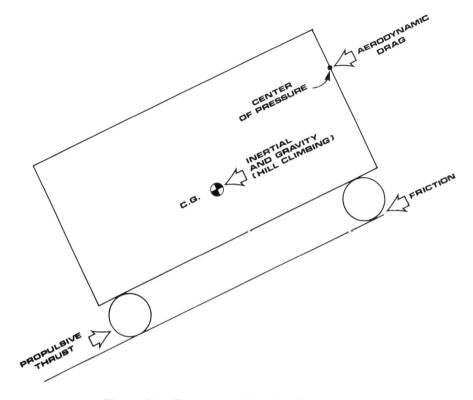

Figure 8-1. Forces on a Moving Vehicle

1. To overcome aerodynamic drag
2. To overcome frictional losses associated with the support and guidance system
3. To climb hills
4. To accelerate the vehicle
5. To overcome drive train losses
6. To power the vehicle accessories

Inertial Forces

Inertial forces must be overcome when the vehicle is accelerated. The force required to accelerate the vehicle includes both that required to accelerate the vehicle mass linearly and that required to "spin up" any rotating parts in the vehicle system. Such rotating parts might include wheels, flywheels, and motor armatures.

It is common to define an equivalent mass m_e which provides a translational inertia equivalent to the combined translational and rotational inertia of the actual vehicle system. Based on the law of conservation of energy, the equivalent mass is given by:[1]

$$\frac{m_e v^2}{2} = \frac{mv^2}{2} + \sum_{i=1}^{n} \frac{I_i \omega_i^2}{2} \qquad (8.1)$$

m_e = vehicle equivalent mass—slugs[a]

v = vehicle speed—feet per second

ω_i = rotational speed of the ith rotating mass—radians per second

I_i = moment of inertia of the ith rotating mass—foot-pound-second^2

n = number of rotating masses

m = actual vehicle mass—slugs

For rubber tired or steel wheeled vehicles, the rotational speed of the various parts may be related to the rotational speed of the driving wheels by the reduction ratio. In other words:

$$\xi_i = \omega_i / \omega_d \qquad (8.2)$$

ξ_i = reduction ratio between the rotating part and the driving wheels

ω_d = angular rotation of the driving wheels—radians per second

If wheel slip is assumed negligible between the driving wheels and the guideway, then:

$$\omega_d = v/r \qquad (8.3)$$

v = vehicle speed—feet per second

r = driving wheel radius at point of guideway contact—feet

From combination of equations 8.2 and 8.3:

$$\omega_i = v\xi_i / r \qquad (8.4)$$

Substitution of equation 8.4 into equation 8.1 gives a relationship for the equivalent mass:

$$m_e = m + \sum_{i=1}^{n} \frac{I_i \xi_i^2}{r^2} \qquad (8.5)$$

[a] For these units, the slug equals pounds mass divided by 32.2.

Notice that m_e is not dependent upon the vehicle speed but only upon the reduction ratios and other speed invariant parameters.

As an example, consider the equivalent mass of a two ton vehicle driven by an electric motor with a 500 pound armature. The electric motor drives three foot diameter wheels through a ten to one speed reducer. The armature is solid copper with an outer diameter of one foot. We assume the rotational inertia of all components besides the armature is negligible.

For a solid disc the moment of inertia is given by I equals $mr^2/2$ equals 1.94 foot pound second^2. Therefore:

$$m_e = \frac{4000}{32.2} + \frac{1.94 \times 10 \times 10}{1.5 \times 1.5} = 210 \text{ slugs}$$

Thus the equivalent mass is 210 slugs or 6762 pounds, an increase of 69 percent. Notice the tremendous effect of the reduction ratio. For a 3 to 1 reduction ratio the increase would have been only 6 percent! It is common to define a mass factor γ as:

$$\gamma = m_e/m \tag{8.6}$$

For the example above γ would be 1.69 for the ten to one reduction and 1.06 for the three to one reduction. Typical values of the mass factor as given by Taborek for passenger cars and by Baumeister and Marks's *Handbook* for trains are summarized in Table 8-1.

Notice that for direct drive, values of γ between 1.05 and 1.10 would be typical, and are often used without bothering with a calculation. However, with large gear reductions, mass factors can become quite significant and a calculation using equation 8.5 is recommended.

Once the mass factor has been computed, the force required to accelerate the vehicle may be obtained readily from Newton's Law:

$$F_i = m_e a = \gamma \, ma = \gamma \, (GVW)a/32.2 \tag{8.7}$$

F_i = inertial force—pounds

a = vehicle acceleration—feet per second^2

GVW = gross vehicle weight—pounds

Grade Climbing Force

Force is also required to push a vehicle uphill against the force of gravity. Figure 8-2 shows the situation. For a slope inclined at an angle θ_g with the horizontal:

$$F_g = (GVW) \sin \theta_g \tag{8.8}$$

Table 8-1
Mass Factors for Typical Vehicles

Vehicle	Mass Factor—γ
Train[a]	1.06-1.12
Passenger car[b]	
High Gear	1.09-1.11
Second Gear	1.14-1.20
First Gear	1.30-1.50
Truck—low gear[b]	2.5

[a]From *Standard Handbook for Mechanical Engineers*, T. Baumeister and L.S. Marks, 7th edition, McGraw-Hill Book Company, New York, 1967.

[b]From "Mechanics of Vehicles," Jaroslav J. Taborek, *Machine Design*, Penton Pub. Co., Cleveland, Ohio, Reprinted from issues of May 30 through December 26, 1957 inclusive.

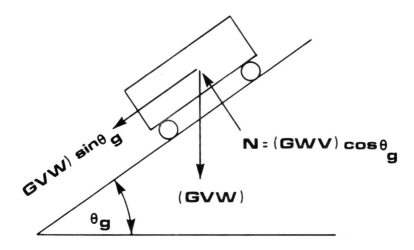

Figure 8-2. Gravity Force on a Vehicle Climbing a Hill

F_g = grade force—pounds

The percent grade is commonly defined as:

$$G = 100 \tan \theta_g \qquad (8.9)$$

For grades below 10 percent as are usually encountered in most transportation applications, $\tan \theta_g$ is approximately equal to $\sin \theta_g$ so that:

$$F_g \approx (GVW)G/100 \qquad (8.10)$$

Aerodynamic Drag

The aerodynamic drag resistance to motion of a train, automobile, bus, or other transportation vehicle is composed of profile drag and skin friction. Profile drag is caused by the pressure distribution created by the relative velocity between the vehicle and the airstream. Skin friction is caused by viscosity effects in the fluid boundary layer. The net effect of drag on a vehicle may be estimated using the usual drag equation:

$$F_a = (1/2) \ C_d \rho_s A v_r^2 \tag{8.11}$$

F_a = aerodynamic drag force—pounds

C_d = drag coefficient

ρ_s = density of air—slugs per cubic foot (density in pounds mass per cubic foot divided by 32.2)

A = vehicle projected frontal area—square feet

v_r = speed of vehicle relative to air—feet per second

At atmospheric temperature and pressure, the density of air may be assumed to be 0.0024 slugs per cubic foot (0.077 pounds per cubic foot).[2] Thus equation 8.11 may be written:

$$F_a = 0.0012 C_d A v_r^2 \tag{8.12}$$

Table 8-2 gives typical values of drag coefficient C_d for use in equation 8.12. Notice that the lead car in a train has a higher drag than the following vehicles since they travel in the wake of the lead car. This principal is sometimes made use of by racing car drivers who tailgate one another to get a "free ride."

Effect of Headwind

The velocity used in equation 8.12 should be the velocity of the vehicle relative to the air. If the vehicle is operating in a headwind v_w at a vehicle ground speed v then equation 8.12 may be written:

$$F_a = 0.0012 C_d A (v + v_w)^2 \tag{8.13}$$

It is not uncommon to size vehicle propulsion systems assuming a headwind of fifteen miles per hour (v_w equals 22 feet/second). This, of course, assumes that some performance degradation is acceptable in very high winds. For certain types of automated transit systems where the speeds of all vehicles are closely synchronized, it is probably necessary to design for higher headwinds of at least 30 to 40 miles per hour, to prevent wind gusts from breaking the synchronism and shutting down the system.

Table 8-2
Aerodynamic Drag Coefficients for Urban Vehicles

Vehicle Configuration	Coefficient C_d
First Car in a Train[a]	0.47-0.50
Other Cars in a Train[a,b]	0.15-0.18
Bus[c]	0.5
Conventional Automobile (sedan)[b]	0.52
Moderately Streamlined Automobile[b]	0.34
Well Streamlined Automobile[b]	0.23
Open Convertible Automobile[c]	0.9
Passenger Car[d]	0.46
Motorcycle and Rider ($A = 6$ ft²)[c]	0.9
Truck[d]	0.77

[a]From "Performance of Land Transportation Vehicles," R.H. Haase, W.H.T. Holden, AD428668, The Rand Corp., Santa Monica, Cal., January, 1964.
[b]From *Standard Handbook for Mechanical Engineers*, 7th edition, T. Baumeister and L.S. Marks, McGraw-Hill Book Co., New York, 1967.
[c]From *CRC Handbook of Tables for Applied Engineering Science*, R.E. Bolz and G.L. Tuve, Chemical Rubber Corp., Cleveland, Ohio, 1970, page 434.
[d]From *Civil Engineering Handbook*, 4th edition, L.C. Urquhart. McGraw-Hill Book Co., New York, 1959.

It is worth remarking that a sixty mile per hour relative air speed causes a drag force of roughly ten pounds per square foot assuming a drag coefficient of unity.[b]

For operation in evacuated tubes, the density used in equation 8.11 should be that in the unperturbed air in the tube. Assuming the tube is at ambient temperature, the perfect gas law states that the pressure ratio is equal to the density ratio. Thus if we operate at one half atmosphere (7.35 psia) the appropriate density would be 0.0012 slugs per cubic foot. Of course operation in a tube causes a "piston effect," so that drag coefficients valid for operation in free air can not necessarily be used.

Support and Guidance Losses—Steel Wheel on Rail

At lower speeds a preponderant source of drag is caused by energy expended in supporting and guiding the vehicle. A ground transportation vehicle depends upon forces exerted by the guideway upon the vehicle, both to constrain it to follow the path of the essentially one dimensional

[b]This is a rough approximation. From equation 8.12 the exact value would be 9.29 pounds per square foot.

guideway and to support the weight of the loaded vehicle. The precise form of these forces depends upon the type of vehicle suspension.

Railroad trains and subway cars use a flanged steel wheel running on a steel rail (see Figure 8-3). Guidance is provided by lateral forces acting between the steel rails and either the flange or the wheel running surface. The vehicle weight is reacted by the normal forces between the steel wheel and the rail. Both the lateral guiding or tracking forces and the forces supporting the vehicle weight generate frictional forces resisting vehicle motion if the vehicle is moving along the track. When the vehicle is going around a curve, the lateral guiding forces become larger because of centrifugal acceleration, causing a corresponding increase in the frictional drag.

The frictional forces generated when the vehicle is moving on straight track are commonly referred to as "rolling friction." Rolling friction is primarily dependent upon the total weight of the vehicle and its payload. We call this the "gross vehicle weight" (GVW). Steel wheel on rail systems typically have a rolling drag of about four pounds per ton. We may define the rolling friction coefficient f as:

$$f = F_r/N \qquad (8.14)$$

F_r = total rolling friction drag—pounds

N = normal force between wheels and track—pounds

From Figure 8-2, for a vehicle on a grade at an angle θ_g with the horizontal:

$$f = F_r/(GVW) \cos \theta_g \qquad (8.15)$$

In most practical situations, $\cos \theta_g$ may be assumed approximately equal to one. For typical rail systems with a rolling friction of four pounds per ton, the rolling friction coefficient f would be 0.002.

Steel wheel on rail systems have probably the lowest rolling friction per ton of payload of any support concept. This efficiency is very important in hauling heavy freight loads and will increase in significance as energy supplies become tighter and more expensive. In urban transportation, where payloads are lighter, the energy efficiency of the support system is a less significant factor.

Starting Resistance

The force required to produce an oil film on a journal is considerable and, if all wheels must be started simultaneously, 35 to 40 pounds per ton will be required to start the train moving from rest.[3] This is equivalent to a rolling friction coefficient of 0.0175 to 0.02. Slack in the couplings between cars

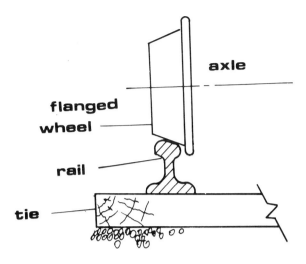

Figure 8-3. Railroad Guidance and Support

usually permits a more gradual start, which permits a passenger train to start with a force of 25 to 30 pounds per ton—or a rolling friction coefficient of 0.0125 to 0.015.[4]

Curve Resistance

As has been mentioned previously, taking a corner increases the frictional losses associated with the guidance system. For trains, Hennes suggests an increase in drag of 0.8 pound/ton per degree curvature.[5] This is equivalent to an increase in the rolling friction coefficient of 0.0004. Thus for a typical rail vehicle with a rolling friction coefficient of 0.002, taking a one degree curve will increase the rolling friction coefficient to 0.0024. The turning radius of a one degree curve may be obtained from equation 6.32 of chapter 6.

$$R_0 = 18000/\pi D_c \qquad (8.16)$$

D_c = degree of curvature—degrees per hundred feet

R_0 = radius of curvature—feet

Thus a one degree curve has a radius of 5730 feet.

Typical train curvatures are 1 to 2 degrees on flat terrain, 10 degrees in mountainous terrain and 40 degrees in yards.[6] This represents curve radii from 5730 feet down to 143 feet. Some older subway lines, including the New York City Transit Authority, the Chicago Transit Authority, the Port Authority Trans Hudson, the Southeastern Pennsylvania Transit Authority, and the Metropolitan Boston Transit Authority, have curve radii as small as 90 to 100 feet (about a 60 degree curve).[7] This results in a piercing wheel screech as the wheels drag through the tight turn. The problem is caused by at least two separate factors. One is the greater distance that the wheels on the outside of the turn must travel compared with the wheels on the inside of the turn. Since both wheels are rigidly connected by a solid axle, wheel slip at the wheel rail interface is inevitable. However, tests with differential units at the Bay Area Rapid Transit District's Diablo test track have indicated that elimination of this factor is by itself insufficient to eliminate screech.[8] Centrifugal force causes the wheel flange to rub against the side of the rail on turns, producing a second source of metal on metal sliding.

The Davis Formula

It is common in the railroad industry to lump together the combined effects of rolling friction and aerodynamic drag into a single term called the "inherent resistance." This represents the total force required to move a train at constant speed on a straight and level track. It does *not* include the friction caused by curves discussed in the previous section.

Inherent resistance is usually computed using the Davis formula:[9]

$$F_{(a+r)} = 1.3 + 29/w + ku + KAu^2/wn \qquad (8.17)$$

$F_{(a+r)}$ = inherent resistance—pounds/ton of car weight

w = average load per axle—tons

u = train speed—miles per hour

n = number of axles

A = cross section area—feet^2

k and K are coefficients applicable to different types of equipment.

Table 8-3 lists values of k, K, and A that are reasonable for current transit equipment.

Support and Guidance Losses—Rubber Tires

A rubber tired automobile or bus also has frictional drag forces. In this

Table 8-3
Values for Use in the Davis Formula

Equipment	k	K	A
Lead car or locomotive	0.03	0.0016	120
Trailing cars	0.03	0.00034	120

case, lateral guidance of the vehicle is provided by frictional forces generated between the tire and the road. When the steering wheel is turned, the tires on the front wheels are no longer rotating in the direction of the vehicle's motion. In other words, the tires would like to make the vehicle move in a different direction from that in which it is actually moving. The difference in these two directions is called the tire "slip angle." The tire is dragged sidewise by this discrepancy between its natural direction of motion and the path of the vehicle; and this tire scrubbing generates a lateral friction force that tends to align the vehicle path with the direction of motion dictated by the steering input. The tire scrubbing required for lateral guidance of a rubber tired vehicle also generates drag forces opposing the motion of the vehicle that must be overcome by propulsive thrust. Obviously this lateral guidance drag is greatest on curves.

The rubber tire, even when properly aligned with the direction of vehicle motion, must also support the weight of the moving vehicle. This results in a rolling friction force. Rolling friction is caused by several phenomena.[10] First, pure rolling does not occur. A small amount of tire sliding at the tire-roadway interface is necessary in order to transmit the required thrust. This is called "tire slip." The second cause of tire rolling friction is the continual flexing of the tire as different portions of the rotating casing move into and out of the region of contact with the roadway (the tire "footprint area"). Friction caused by inelasticity in this flexing process is known as "tire hysteresis." Because the amount of flexing is speed dependent, tire hysteresis tends to increase with vehicle speed.

Especially important with soft road surfaces is the energy expended in compressing the road surface as the vehicle passes over it. For this reason frictional losses are greatest on soft surfaces such as earth or sand, and lowest on a hard surface such as concrete.

A final minor source of frictional losses for rubber tired vehicles is caused by the circulation of air within the rotating tire, and the fan effect of the rotating wheel on the outside air.

For a vehicle traveling in a straight line, the rolling friction coefficient as defined by equation 8.14 may be estimated by the equation:[11]

$$f = (a + bv)S \tag{8.18}$$

$v =$ vehicle speed—feet per second

$S =$ road surface factor

$a, b =$ constants

Table 8-4 suggests values for S based on S equals one for concrete in good condition. Taborek[12] suggests values for a of 0.01 and for b of 6.8×10^{-5} for equation 8.18.

Smith recommends values for a of 0.0068 and for b of 5×10^{-5} for trucks, and that a equal 0.0116 and b equal 1.6×10^{-4} for pickup trucks.[13] In an earlier work, Hay[14] suggests an equation which for a two ton automobile would be equivalent to using values for a of 0.0064 and b of 2.3×10^{-4} in equation 8.18. Smith's studies indicate that rolling resistance is nearly independent of load distribution and the number of tires carrying a given load, and also tend to discount the effect of tire and axle alignment. For typical hard surfaced roads at speeds of interest, f will usually be between 0.01 and 0.02. (Rolling drag for an automobile is thus about 1 to 2 percent of the vehicle weight.)

Drag from Side Loads

Because of the tire drag required to react side loads, significant frictional forces are generated. Figure 8-4 shows a tire reacting a lateral side load L. This load will be required to react centrifugal forces on turns or wind loads acting on the side of the vehicle. If the tire slip angle is α, the tire scrubbing force[c] will produce a longitudinal drag F_c given by:

$$F_c = F_\alpha \sin \alpha \qquad (8.19)$$

$F_\alpha =$ tire scrubbing force—pounds

The magnitude of the tire scrubbing force is proportional to the slip angle. The relationship is usually expressed by the "tire cornering coefficient" given in pounds per pound load per degree slip. That is:

$$F_\alpha = nc\alpha(GVW/n) = (GVW)c\alpha \qquad (8.20)$$

$F_\alpha =$ total cornering force—pounds

$n =$ total number of tires on vehicle

$\alpha =$ slip angle—degrees

$c =$ tire cornering coefficient—pounds per pound load per degree

[c] When the tire scrubbing force is entirely reacting centrifugal force in a turn it is called the "cornering force."

Table 8-4
Road Surface Factors

Material	S
Concrete[a]	
Good Condition	1.0
Fair Condition	1.5
Poor Condition	2.0
Macadam[a]	
Good Condition	1.5
Fair Condition	2.25
Poor Condition	3.5
Earth Roads[a]	
Good Condition	3.5
Fair Condition	4.5
Poor Condition	7.5
Hard Sand[b]	30.0
Rough Gravel[c]	2.5
Muddy Earth Roads[c]	5.0

[a]From *An Introduction to Transportation Engineering,* William W. Hay, John Wiley and Sons, New York, 1967.
[b]From "Mechanics of Vehicles," Jaroslav J. Taborek, *Machine Design*, Penton Pub. Co., Cleveland, Ohio, reprinted from issues of May 30 through December 26, 1957 inclusive.
[c]From *Civil Engineering Handbook*, 4th edition, L.C. Urquhart, McGraw-Hill Book Co., New York, 1959.

Since $F_\alpha \cos \alpha$ must be equal to the total lateral side load L:

$$\alpha \cos \alpha = L/(GVW)c \qquad (8.21)$$

Using small angle approximations for $\cos \alpha$ and $\sin \alpha$, and combining equations 8.19, 8.20 and 8.21 we obtain:[15]

$$F_c = \pi L^2/180(GVW)c \qquad (8.22)$$

If the lateral force is composed entirely of centrifugal force:

$$F_c = \frac{\pi}{180c(GVW)} \left[\frac{(GVW)v^2}{32.2 \, R} \right]^2 = 16.8 \times 10^{-6} \frac{(GVW)v^4}{R^2 c} \qquad (8.23)$$

Typical values of c range from 0.1 to 0.2 pounds per pound load per degree. The drag caused by a 4000 pound automobile taking a 400 foot radius curve at a speed of 40 mph, with c equaling 0.2 pounds per pound load per degree, would be 25 pounds. This represents an increase in rolling coefficient of 0.0062. If the vehicle is traveling on concrete at 40 mph, the rolling coefficient (using Taborek's values) would be 0.014. Cornering increases the rolling drag by 44 percent. This represents a significant increase in the drag.

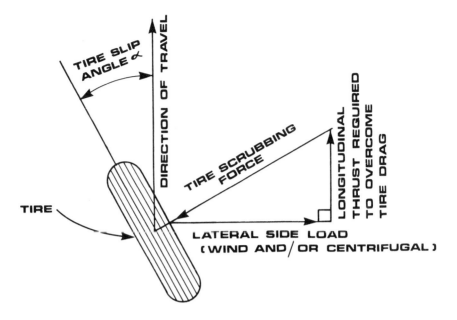

Figure 8-4. Forces Acting on a Tire Subject to a Sideload

Side winds will usually have less effect than centrifugal loads. The side wind may be computed from the formula:

$$L_w = 0.0012 \; C_d \; A v_w^2 \qquad (8.24)$$

v_w = crosswind speed—feet/second

A = area of the side of the vehicle—square feet

C_d = drag coefficient of vehicle side profile

For an automobile with a drag coefficient of unity and a side area of eighty square feet, the wind speed would have to be 72 miles per hour to produce the same 25 pound tire scrubbing drag. In general, for wind speeds below 30 mph, the effect on tire friction can be assumed negligible.[16]

Support and Guidance—Air Cushion Vehicles

One of the newer vehicle guidance and support concepts uses air cushions to levitate the vehicle. Air cushions support the vehicle by means of the pressure forces generated by a quantity of air trapped between the air cushion and the guideway. The required clearance between the air cushion and the guideway, caused by roughness of the guideway surface and construction tolerances, permits a continual leaking of the air out of the air cushion "plenum" chamber.

The cushion pressure multiplied by the total plenum chamber area must be large enough to support the total vehicle load. Thus the required pressure may be computed as:[17]

$$\Delta P = K(GVW)/144nA \qquad (8.25)$$

$K =$ dynamic load factor

$n =$ number of air cushions

$A =$ area of one cushion plenum chamber—square feet

$GVW =$ gross vehicle weight—pounds

$\Delta P =$ cushion pressure—pounds per square inch gauge

Thus a 10,000 pound vehicle with a dynamic load factor of 1.2 and eight air cushion pads each with 5 square feet of plenum chamber area would require a cushion pressure of 2.08 pounds per square inch gauge.

The volume flow rate of air required to maintain this pressure in the plenum chamber is primarily a function of the cushion perimeter and the clearance required between the cushion and the guideway. From the Bernoulli Equation:

$$\Delta P'/\rho = V^2/2g \qquad (8.26)$$

$V =$ velocity of fluid leaking through plenum chamber—feet/second

$\rho =$ density of air—pounds mass/feet^3

$\Delta P' =$ plenum pressure differential over atmospheric—pounds/feet^2

Using $\rho = 0.077$ pounds mass/feet^3 and converting $\Delta P'$ into pounds per square inch gauge we obtain:

$$V = 347 \sqrt{\Delta P} \qquad (8.27)$$

The mass flow rate from the continuity equation is:

$$m = C_c nLt\rho V/12 \qquad (8.28)$$

$L =$ perimeter of one cushion—feet

$n =$ number of cushions

$t =$ clearance—inches

$C_c =$ coefficient of flow contraction $= 0.611$

$m =$ mass flow rate—pounds per hour

Combining with equation 8.27:[18]

$$m = 1.36nLt\sqrt{\Delta P} \qquad (8.29)$$

The power required to maintain this flow rate, assuming a combined duct loss and fan efficiency η, will be:[19]

$$\text{Power} = m\Delta P'/\eta\rho \quad \text{(foot-pound/second)} \qquad (8.30)$$

Assuming an 80 percent fan efficiency and duct loss and substituting for m from equation 8.29:[d]

$$HP = 5.77nLt\Delta P^{1.5} \qquad (8.31)$$

$HP =$ compressor power—horsepower

$\Delta P =$ cushion pressure—pounds per square inch gauge

Peripheral Jet Air Cushions

The previous analysis is valid for a plenum chamber type air cushion in which the supporting air is contained in a large cushion chamber, where its velocity is very low compared to the velocity of the air leaking under the edges of the cushion. In the peripheral jet air cushion, jets of air are directed out of nozzles located on the periphery of the cushion. These jets supply lift due to momentum reaction, and also serve to confine air within the cushion, producing a lift that is many times the jet reaction. The peripheral jet design is somewhat more efficient than the simple plenum chamber. Nevertheless, most air cushion vehicles proposed for low speed urban application (below 60 mph), including the Transportation Technology Incorporated and Uniflo designs, have found it desirable to use concepts based upon the plenum type of cushion.

Notes

1. "Mechanics of Vehicles," Jaroslav J. Taborek, *Machine Design*, Penton Publishing Company, Cleveland, Ohio, reprinted from issues of May 30 through December 26, 1957 inclusive.
2. *Standard Handbook for Mechanical Engineers*, T. Baumeister and L.S. Marks, 7th edition, McGraw-Hill Book Company, New York, 1967.
3. Ibid.
4. Ibid.

---

[d]The analysis assumes incompressible flow. This assumption is reasonable provided that the cushion pressure differential ΔP is less than 0.07 times the ambient pressure in psig.

5. *Fundamentals of Transportation Engineering*, Hennes and Eske, 2nd edition, McGraw-Hill Book Company, New York, 1969.

6. Ibid.

7. "Research Requirements Survey of the Rapid Rail Industry," T.J. McGean, PB 204438, MITRE Corporation, McLean, Virginia, June 17, 1971.

8. "TR5-Transit Vehicle Truck Concepts," San Francisco Bay Area Rapid Transit District Demonstration Project, Parsons, Brinckerhoff, Tudor, Bechtel, San Francisco, January 1, 1970.

9. *Civil Engineering Handbook*, 4th edition, L.C. Urquhart, McGraw-Hill Book Company, New York, 1959.

10. See note 1.

11. See note 1.

12. See note 1.

13. "Commercial Vehicle Performance and Fuel Economy," Gary L. Smith, SAE 700194, Society of Automotive Engineers, Warrendale, Pennsylvania, January 1970.

14. *An Introduction to Transportation Engineering*, William W. Hay, John Wiley and Sons, New York, 1967.

15. See note 13.

16. See note 13.

17. *Standard Handbook of Engineering Calculations*, T.G. Hicks, McGraw-Hill Book Company, New York, 1972, pages 8-6 to 8-8.

18. Ibid.

19. Ibid.

9 Propulsion Systems

In chapter 8, methods were presented for estimating the propulsion power and thrust required for any specified mission profile. Having determined these propulsion requirements, it is next necessary to select a propulsion system suitable for the mission. Urban transit vehicle propulsion systems are generally of two basic types—electric motors and liquid fueled engines.

Electric Motors

Let us first consider the electric motor. Because it is quiet and does not require a petroleum based fuel, the electric motor is a strong candidate for future transit systems. It has the further advantage that the motor itself is pollution free. Although pollution *is* produced at the generating station, this large fixed power source may be easier to clean up than the hundreds of moving power plants in a liquid fueled transit system. Trolley and subway cars have traditionally used direct current series wound motors, because their torque-speed characteristic is well matched to the mission requirement. However, recent progress in solid state motor control technology has made both the separately excited direct current motor and the alternating current induction motor into contenders for urban transit propulsion. In addition, linear induction motors are also being touted— especially for vehicles with air cushion or magnetically levitated suspension systems.

Some Electromagnetic Theory

In order to understand the characteristics of these various types of motors, a minimal understanding of certain basic principles of electromagnetism is required. An electric motor is basically a device that produces thrust from the interaction of an electric current with a magnetic field. In 1831, Faraday discovered that a closed conductor moving in a magnetic field has a voltage induced in it proportional to the time rate of change of flux:[1]

$$E = -N \, d\Phi/dt \qquad (9.1)$$

$E = $ induced voltage—volts

N = number of turns

Φ = flux—webers

This principle, of inducing a voltage by moving a closed conductor through a magnetic field, is the principle of the electric generator. Conversely, a voltage applied to a closed conductor in the presence of a magnetic field, can be made to cause the conductor to rotate. This is the principal of the electric motor. The induced voltage in the case of a generator is called the "back EMF" of the motor, and represents the voltage drop required to sustain rotation of the conductor in the magnetic field. The output power of the electric motor is given by the product of the current in the rotating coil and the back EMF:

$$P_{out} = EI_a \tag{9.2}$$

P_{out} = output power of motor—watts

E = back EMF—volts

I_a = current in rotating coil—amperes

The torque output of a rotating machine is related to the power by the familiar relationship:

$$T' = 60\,P_{out}/2\pi n \tag{9.3}$$

T' = output torque—newton meters

n = motor speed—revolutions per minute

Converting the torque from newton meters to the more familiar foot pounds and substituting for P_{out} we obtain:[2]

$$T = 7.04EI_a/n \tag{9.4}$$

T = torque—foot pounds

To determine the back EMF for use in equation 9.4, we use Faraday's equation, which means we must know the time rate of change of the magnetic flux. To grasp the concept of magnetic flux it is useful to draw an analogy between an electric and magnetic circuit. Figure 9-1(left) shows an electric circuit. The circuit is connected by a high conductivity metal such as copper, and its opposition to the flow of a current is termed the resistance. To overcome the resistance, the flow of current requires a driving "voltage." The relationship is given by Ohms law: voltage equals current times resistance. The analogous magnetic circuit is shown in Figure 9-1(right). The circuit here is made of a high permeability metal such as iron. A high permeability metal is one that acts as a low loss conduit for lines of magnetic flux. The flux in the magnetic circuit is analogous to the

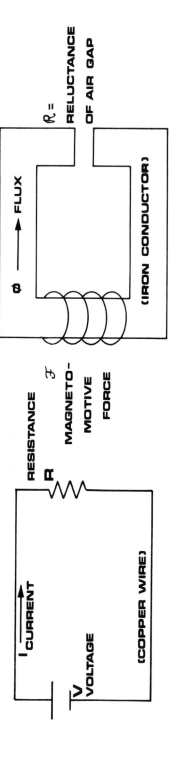

Figure 9-1. Electric Circuit and Equivalent Magnetic Circuit Elements

current in the electric circuit—and the opposition of circuit elements to the flow of flux is called the "reluctance." To overcome the reluctance a flow of flux requires a driving "magnetomotive force." Thus the equivalent magnetic circuit equation is:[3]

$$\mathscr{F} = \mathscr{R}\Phi \qquad (9.5)$$

$\mathscr{F}$ = magnetomotive force—ampere turns

$\mathscr{R}$ = reluctance—ampere turns per weber

Φ = flux—webers

From equation 9.5 we can relate the flux to the magnetomotive force, but we are still no closer to our goal, for how do we determine the magnetomotive force? The answer is that the magnetomotive force generated by an electric current is proportional to the product of the current and the number of turns of wire:[4]

$$\mathscr{F} = N_f I_f \qquad (9.6)$$

N_f = number of turns of wire on the field coil

I_f = field current—amperes

Equation 9.6 may be thought of as the complement to Faraday's Law. While Faraday's Law relates the induced electric voltage to the magnetic flux, equation 9.6 relates the induced "magnetic voltage" (i.e., magnetomotive force) to the electric current. The two equations together provide the interrelationship between the electric and magnetic circuits.

A motor is constructed of two parts. First there must be either permanent magnets or electromagnets to create the magnetic field flux. If the magnets are electromagnetic the magnetomotive force will be given by equation 9.6 with I_f the current in the magnet coil, and N_f the number of turns of wire. If the magnets are permanent magnets, their magnetomotive force will be obtained from a magnetization curve supplied by the manufacturer. The field coils of a motor are usually stationary and are referred to as the "stator."

The second part of an electric motor is the moving conductor. Its back EMF is given by Faraday's equation. This part of the motor is referred to as the rotor or armature.

To minimize losses in the magnetic circuit, the coils of both the stator and the rotor are wound on a high permeability material such as iron.

Some Limitations of This Theory

The aforementioned electric motor theory is highly simplified. The primary limitations are two:

1. The relationship between magnetomotive force and flux is assumed linear.
2. The magnetic and electric fields are assumed uniform.

The first assumption is inherent in equation 9.5, which relates magnetomotive force and flux by the constant reluctance. In fact, magnetic circuits are far less linear than electric circuits, evidencing a phenomena known as "saturation." Once the flux per unit area reaches a certain value, the magnetic circuit saturates, and additional increase in magnetomotive force causes no change in flux. Under saturated conditions, the flux is constant. Our approach is valid only under unsaturated conditions where the linear relationship implied by equation 9.5 is valid.

The second assumption can be best clarified by defining the concepts of magnetic field intensity and flux density:[5]

$$\mathcal{F} = \oint H\,ds \tag{9.7}$$

$$\Phi = \int B\,dA \tag{9.8}$$

$H =$ magnetic field intensity—ampere turns per meter

$s =$ unit conductor length—meters

$B =$ flux density—webers per meter^2

$A =$ area normal to flux lines—meters^2

For a uniform field the quantities H and B are constant and equations 9.7 and 9.8 become:

$$\mathcal{F} = Hs \tag{9.9}$$

$$\Phi = BA \tag{9.10}$$

It is implicit in magnetic circuit theory that equations 9.9 and 9.10 are adequate approximations. Permanent magnet characteristics will be given in terms of a magnetization curve giving B versus H. The proper values for use in the magnetic circuit are obtained from equations 9.9 and 9.10.

Direct Current Motors

A direct current (DC) motor consists of an armature rotating through a magnetic field generated by field coils on the stator. Current is transmitted to the armature through carbon brushes which contact a "commutator" composed of copper segments that rotates with the armature. Interaction of the electric and magnetic fields produces a torque which drives the motor.

Figure 9-2 shows a conceptual schematic of a direct current motor. It consists of a single conductor rotating in a magnetic field caused by a single pair of poles, one north and one south, between which flow a flux Φ. When the single conductor rotates one quarter revolution in this field it moves from a position where there are zero flux linkages to one where it is cutting the maximum flux. (A to B). If the conductor is rotating at f cycles per second, the flux thus changes from zero to Φ in a time $1/4f$. Therefore:[6]

$$\frac{d\Phi}{dt} \approx 4f\Phi \qquad (9.11)$$

For an armature coil consisting of N turns the back EMF from the Faraday equation becomes:

$$E = 4f\Phi N \qquad (9.12)$$

In an actual direct current motor, the armature will consist of a number of separate coils, each consisting of N turns. This is done to reduce the total current carried by each turn and to reduce the fluctuation in the back EMF—and hence the torque. The armature is generally specified in terms of the number of "conductors" it contains where a conductor represents half of a full turn of wire. If z is the number of conductors, then:[7]

$$N = z/2a \qquad (9.13)$$

N = number of turns

a = number of separate coils on armature wound in parallel

In addition, an actual DC motor may have more than a single pair of poles, in order to reduce the torque fluctuation. If the motor has p poles, the rate of change of flux with time will be $p/2$ times faster. Thus the back EMF must be multiplied by the number of pairs of poles. The total average back EMF for a DC motor is therefore given by:[8]

$$E = f\Phi zp/a = n\Phi zp/60a = k_1 n\Phi \qquad (9.14)$$

f = armature rotation speed—revolutions per second

n = armature rotation speed—revolutions per minute

z = total number of conductors in armature

p = number of poles

a = number of parallel armature paths

Φ = flux—webers

k_1 = a constant for a particular motor

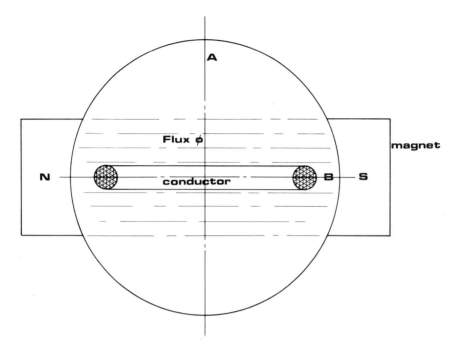

Figure 9-2. Simple Bipolar Direct Current Motor

Since for a particular motor, z, p and a are constants, the variation in the back EMF for that motor is simply proportional to the product of the speed and the flux. Thus speed can be increased either by increasing the back EMF or by decreasing the flux.

With the back EMF known, the output power can be obtained by substitution in equation 9.2:

$$P_{\text{out}} = n\Phi z p I_a / 60a \quad \text{(watts)} \tag{9.15}$$

And the torque may be obtained from equation 9.4:[9]

$$T = 0.1175 z p I_a \Phi / a \quad \text{(foot-pounds)} \tag{9.16}$$

Since z, p, and a are fixed for a given motor the torque is proportional to the product of the armature current and the flux:[10]

$$T = k_2 I_a \Phi \tag{9.17}$$

k_2 = a constant for a particular motor

The flux may be computed from equations 9.5 and 9.6 to be given by:

$$\Phi = N_f I_f / \mathcal{R} = k_3 I_f \tag{9.18}$$

k_3 = a constant for a particular motor

In other words, for a particular motor the flux tends to be proportional to the field current. This means that the torque for a DC motor is proportional to the product of the field current and the armature current.

The circuit representation of a DC motor is shown in Figure 9-3. There are three basic types of DC motors depending on the method of exciting the field winding.

1. Shunt wound—the field is wired in parallel with the motor armature.

2. Series wound—the field is wired in series with the motor armature.

3. Separately excited—the field is excited by a separate voltage supply.

In addition there is the compound wound motor with some field windings in series and some in parallel. Its performance characteristics are in between the shunt and series types.

Shunt Wound Motor. Consider first the shunt wound motor. Solution of the circuit equation provides the relationship for the back EMF:

$$E = V - I_a r_a \tag{9.19}$$

V = supply voltage—volts

I_a = armature current—amperes

r_a = armature resistance—ohms

By making use of the expression for back EMF given by equation 9.14 we obtain the so-called "speed equation" for a DC shunt motor:[11]

$$n = \frac{V - I_a r_a}{k_1 \Phi} \tag{9.20}$$

Substituting for I_a in terms of torque from equation 9.17:

$$n = \frac{V}{k_1 \Phi} - \frac{T r_a}{k_1 k_2 \Phi^2} \tag{9.21}$$

From equation 9.18, the flux is equal to $k_3 I_f$:

$$n = \frac{V}{k_1 k_3 I_f} - \frac{T r_a}{k_1 k_2 (k_3 I_f)^2} \tag{9.22}$$

From the circuit equations, I_f equals V/r_f:

$$n = \frac{r_f}{k_1 k_3} - \frac{T r_f^2 r_a}{k_1 k_2 k_3^2 V^2} \tag{9.23}$$

Equation 9.23 gives the torque speed relationship for a DC shunt motor. In general the first term is considerably larger than the second, so that the

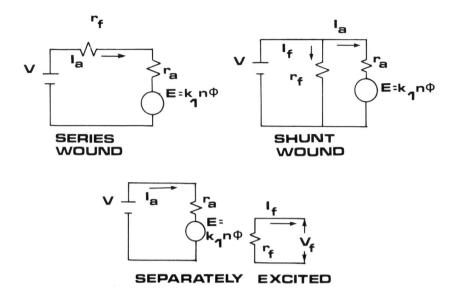

Figure 9-3. Basic Types of DC Motor Circuits

speed tends to be nearly constant regardless of torque, with a slight tendency to drop as the torque is increased.

DC Shunt Motor Control. From equation 9.23 it is clear that for a given motor (k_1, k_2, and k_3 fixed), the only ways to change the torque-speed characteristics are to change the supply voltage V or add additional resistance to the armature or field branches of the circuit. Speed is increased by adding additional resistance to the field branch, thereby increasing r_f. This increases the dominant first term in equation 9.23 thus increasing the speed for a fixed value of torque. In this manner speed may be increased to about three times the base speed. To reduce the speed below the base speed additional resistance may be inserted in the armature circuit. By increasing the second term in equation 9.23 this will *decrease* the speed for a given load. Since the second term of equation 9.23 includes the torque, armature speed control will increase the negative slope of the torque-speed curve. Speed control down to about 10 percent of the base speed is possible by the addition of resistance to the armature circuit.

Maximum Torque Limitations. The maximum torque of the motor is essentially limited by the heat rise caused by I^2R losses in the armature. This sets an upper limit to the armature current. For field control of speed, the armature voltage drop is small compared to the line voltage, so from equation 9.20 the speed is approximately $V/k_1\Phi$. The torque from equation 9.17 is proportional to the flux times the armature current. For a given limiting value of armature current the maximum torque is thus proportional to the flux. This implies that the product of maximum torque times speed is constant for field control of a shunt DC motor. Field control thus produces a constant maximum horsepower output throughout the control range.

If armature resistance is increased to decrease the speed, the current and hence the flux in the field will remain unchanged. In this case the torque from equation 9.17 will be proportional to the armature current. For a given limiting value of armature current the *torque* will be a constant. Armature speed control thus produces a constant maximum torque output throughout the control range.

Figure 9-4 summarizes the characteristics of the DC shunt wound motor. The base speed-torque characteristic is shown as a heavy line. Notice that base speed is nearly independent of load, dropping only slightly as load is increased. Increasing the field resistance increases the speed, moving the torque speed curve to the right. The maximum torque decreases as the speed is increased to maintain a constant horsepower output. Thus the maximum torque curve appears as the dotted line in Figure 9-4.

To decrease speed below the baseline, armature circuit resistance is increased. This causes an increasing drop of speed with load. Maximum torque in this range tends to be constant.

A maximum torque speed curve as shown by the dotted line may be achieved using a combination of armature and field resistance variation. Torque is constant up to the motor base speed. Above that speed motor output horsepower is constant. Each solid line on Figure 9-4 represents the torque-speed curve for a given setting of armature and field resistance. The more nearly vertical these curves are, the more closely will the motor maintain a given speed setting regardless of grades, winds, or other variations in load. This ability to maintain a set speed is called "speed regulation" and is considered a major attribute of the shunt wound motor. On the other hand, it means that to accelerate a vehicle from rest, using a shunt motor, it is necessary to vary the armature and field resistance values continuously. This requires a feedback control system. If maximum thrust is desired, the feedback control would be adjusted to provide a specified limiting value of armature current until the desired operating speed is achieved. Once at that speed the motor will tend to be self-regulating.

Series Motor. The series wound DC motor has traditionally been the most widely used for transportation vehicle applications. Referring to Figure 9-3, solution of the circuit equations gives for the back EMF:

$$E = V - I_a(r_f + r_a) \tag{9.24}$$

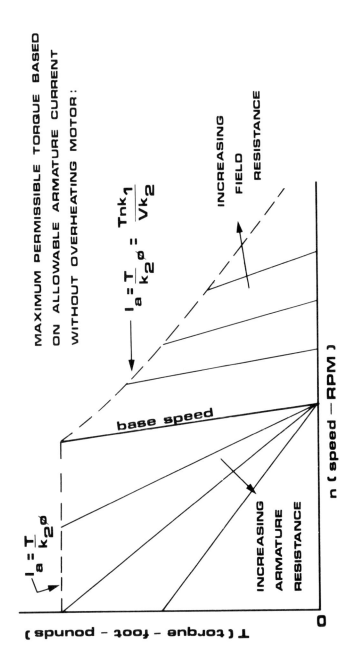

Figure 9-4. Torque versus Speed Curves for a Shunt Wound Direct Current Motor

Substituting for the back EMF from equation 9.14 we obtain the speed equation for the series wound motor:[12]

$$n = \frac{V - I_a (r_f + r_a)}{k_1 \Phi} \qquad (9.25)$$

Flux is proportional to field current, but for the series wound motor the field current and armature current are the same. Thus equation 9.18 becomes Φ equals $k_3 I_a$ and:[13]

$$T = k_2 k_3 I_a^2 \qquad (9.26)$$

Substituting for Φ and I_a and rearranging terms we obtain the torque-speed relationship for a series wound motor:

$$T = \frac{k_2 k_3 V^2}{(k_1 k_3 n + r_f + r_a)^2} \qquad (9.27)$$

The torque for a series wound motor is a maximum at zero speed and decreases to zero at infinite speed. The high torque available under starting conditions has made the series wound motor a frequent choice for transportation applications. Notice that the speed can be changed either by varying the supply voltage or by inserting additional resistance. In this way a family of torque speed curves as shown in Figure 9-5 can be generated. Both techniques are used in transit vehicles.

Conventional Cam Control of a Series Motor. Figure 9-6 shows a conventional control circuit for a transportation vehicle.[14] It is typical of the technique that has been used on subway cars in the United States for over 70 years. The power supply is 600-700 volts DC. In general one motor is provided for each car axle and there are four axles on each vehicle. During acceleration at low speed all motors are connected in series. As the speed increases, the resistors are shunted out in steps to maintain constant acceleration. When the resistance has been completely shunted out the motors are reconnected two in series and two in parallel and the resistors are reconnected in series with the motors. With the motors connected two in series and two in parallel the voltage across each motor is doubled. This compensates for the reduced torque available from the series wound motor at higher speeds. As speed is further increased the resistors are once again shunted out sequentially until the motors are directly connected to the line voltage. Above this speed, the torque-speed relationship is governed by the performance characteristic of the motor, with torque decreasing as speed is increased.

The combination of voltage and resistor speed control limits the armature current to the maximum permitted by thermal limitations, providing an approximately constant torque output. This limit is indicated by the

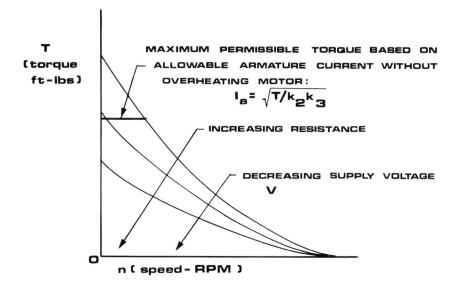

Figure 9-5. Torque-Speed Curves for a Series Wound Direct Current Motor

heavy black line in Figure 9-5. When the motor is directly connected to the supply voltage, motor torque is inversely proportional to the speed squared and drops off rapidly. The controlled motor thus has a torque-speed characteristic as shown by Figure 9-5.

"Chopper" Speed Control. The problem with cam control is that the full armature current must flow through the additional resistance, leading to considerable energy dissipated in heat. The modern trend is towards control of the supply voltage using solid state devices to avoid the high resistive losses.

The most common electronic technique for controlling the DC voltage supply to a series motor is known as "chopper control." The chopper is essentially a fast switch inserted between the DC power supply and the motor. The basic principal of chopper operation, which is pulse width modulation (PWM), is illustrated in Figure 9-7.[15] For simplicity the chopper is shown as a switch that opens and closes a given number of times per second (chopper frequency). The amount of time during each cycle that the switch remains open is varied to control the effective voltage and current levels. The effective voltage and current are equal to the maximum values passed when the switch is closed multiplied by the percentage of the total cycle time that the switch is closed. Thus by having the switch closed a third of the time, the current and voltage can be reduced to a third of their

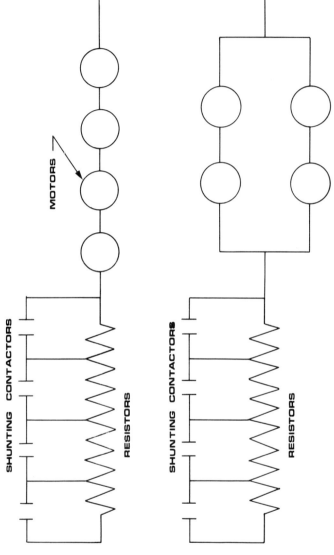

Figure 9-6. Conventional "Cam" Control for a Series DC Motor

nominal values. Since the chopper is a switch, it has the property of having high resistance when the current flow is low (circuit open), and low resistance when the current flow is high (circuit closed). Thus the I^2R heat loss dissipated in the chopper is low, since either the current is negligible (circuit open), or the resistance is very low (circuit closed). By comparison, if the series wound motor is controlled by inserting additional resistors, the high motor armature current must flow through the resistor, resulting in considerable heat dissipation. In addition to reduced heat dissipation, the chopper has the advantage of providing continuous stepless control of voltage.

The chopper has been made possible by the development of the thyristor, more frequently called the SCR (Silicon-Controlled Rectifier). The SCR is a transistor semiconductor device. Like a diode, it will only pass current in one direction. In addition, the SCR has a gate electrode that is used to initiate the flow of current. An electrical pulse, applied to the gate electrode, effectively "opens the valve" to start current flowing. Unfortunately the gate electrode can not stop the current flow once it has been initiated. For this purpose a capacitor is discharged to momentarily drop the current below a threshold value. Once the current drops below this value the SCR "valve" is shut again and no current will flow until another electrical pulse is applied to the gate. The capacitor is coupled with an inductor into an oscillator circuit that determines the triggering frequency. The duration of the current flow during each cycle is regulated by adjusting the phase angle between the trigger pulse and the capacitor discharge.

Externally Excited Motor. The externally excited motor has a separate voltage supply for the field and armature circuits. Solution of its circuit equation will lead to the same torque-speed relationship as was found in equation 9.22 for the shunt wound motor. The field current however, is now given by V_f/r_f, where V_f is the separately excited field supply voltage, instead of by V/r_f. This leads to:

$$n = \frac{Vr_f}{k_1 k_3 V_f} - \frac{Tr_f^2}{k_1 k_2 k_3^2 V_f^2} \tag{9.28}$$

Control of speed is obtained by increasing or decreasing the field voltage and the armature voltage. Notice that speed is increased by decreasing the field voltage, since the first term in equation 9.28 is much larger than the second. On the other hand speed is *decreased* by decreasing the armature voltage. Motor performance is similar to the shunt DC motor. Reduction in armature voltage is used to decrease the speed below baseline; speeds above baseline are obtained by decreasing the field voltage ("field weakening").

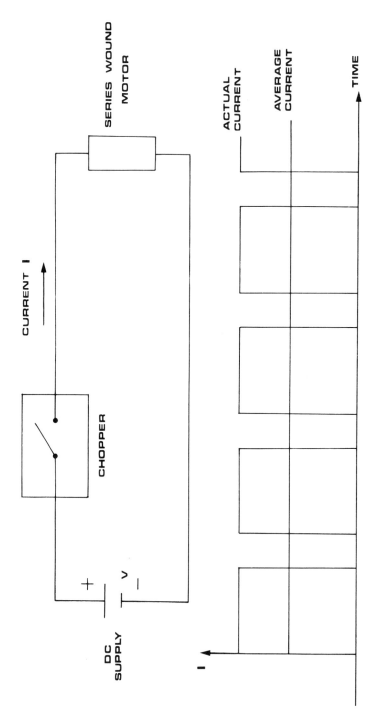

Figure 9-7. Principle of DC Chopper Control

Thyristor (or SCR) controllers are usually used to regulate armature and field voltage. Usually separately excited motors are run off rectified three phase AC current. The sixty hertz source can be used to regulate the pulse frequency, simplifying the triggering circuit over that required for the DC "chopper" system.

Output Limitations on DC Motors. The output of a DC motor can be limited in either of two ways:

1. The temperature of the motor can exceed the permissible limit.
2. The current can exceed that which can be handled by the commutator without excessive sparking, flashing, or heating at the brush contacts.

It is usual for the limitation to be temperature. The heating of a DC motor is caused by several factors:

1. I^2R losses in the armature
2. I^2R losses in the field
3. Friction losses
4. Windage losses
5. Core losses (from magnetic hysterisis and eddy currents in the iron core)

It is the I^2R losses that are most dependent upon the load, since the current must increase to produce added torque. For a series motor both field and armature I^2R losses are significant, while for a shunt or externally excited motor the field losses will be minor. Friction, windage, and core losses tend to be relatively independent of the load.

The temperature limitation will usually be set by the quality of the insulation used in the motor and will in turn impose a maximum current limitation on the motor. For short periods of time it is safe to exceed this current limitation. The motor is designed to a specified temperature rise for continued operation at the rated current. To determine the temperature rise for a variable duty cycle as is used in a transit application with much starting and stopping, it is necessary to compute the I^2R losses for the various operating load conditions.

The power loss at each operating load is multiplied by the portion of the duty cycle over which the particular load occurs. The summation of all these energy terms when divided by the total duration of the duty cycle gives the average power loss. The ratio of this value to the power loss at rated current is multiplied by the rated temperature rise to estimate the temperature rise of the motor when operated on that duty cycle. So long as the average power loss does not exceed the power loss for continuous duty operation at rated current, it is permissible for portions of the duty cycle to exceed the rated current. This enables DC motors to deliver considerable torque for brief periods of time. Under short term conditions with the motor operating above rated current, it is quite likely that ultimate current capacity will be limited by flashing at the commutator.

Induction Motors

The principle of the induction motor may be illustrated by suspending a magnet on a string over a copper or aluminum turntable. If the magnet is allowed to spin, the turntable will also rotate. This effect is caused by eddy currents induced in the turntable by the relative motion between a conductor (the turntable) and a magnetic field. Notice that the disc must always rotate at a speed less than the magnet—otherwise there will be no relative motion between the conductor and the magnetic field and consequently no eddy currents will be produced in the disc.[16]

In an induction motor, the rotation of the magnetic field is achieved by application of an alternating current to the field windings or stator. This causes a magnetic field to rotate about the stator at a speed equal to the line frequency divided by the number of pole pairs in the stator.[17]

$$n_f = \frac{120f_0}{p} \tag{9.29}$$

f_0 = alternating current line frequency—hertz

p = number of poles in field winding

n_f = magnetic field rotational speed—revolutions per minute

According to Faraday's Law a voltage is induced in any conductor in a moving magnetic field proportional to the rate at which the magnetic flux is changing. Since the magnetic field is rotating at a frequency of $2f_0/p$, a voltage is induced in the stator or field winding given by:

$$E_s = \frac{-4\pi f_0}{p} N\Phi \cos\frac{(4\pi f_0 t)}{p} \tag{9.30}$$

In phasor notation:

$$\mathbf{E}_s = \frac{-4\pi f_0 N\Phi \mathbf{j}}{p} \tag{9.31}$$

Assume the armature rotor is turning at a speed of n revolutions per minute. In that case the *relative* speed at which the magnetic field from the stator rotates with respect to the armature is given by:

$$n_m = n_f - n \tag{9.32}$$

n_m = relative speed of magnetic field rotation with respect to armature—revolutions per minute

We define the "slip" s as:[18]

$$s = \frac{n_f - n}{n_f} \tag{9.33}$$

Thus the speed at which the magnetic field rotates *relative* to the rotor is equal to its actual rotation multiplied by the slip, or $2sf_0/p$ hertz. Accordingly a magnetic flux is induced in the *rotor* by Faraday's Law equal to:

$$\mathbf{E}_r = \frac{-4\pi s f_0 \Phi N \mathbf{j}}{p} \tag{9.34}$$

Notice that the voltage induced in the secondary or rotor is only s times the voltage induced in the primary windings:

$$\mathbf{E}_r = s\mathbf{E}_s \tag{9.35}$$

Now the rotor of an induction motor consists of short-circuited conductors, so the current in the rotor will be simply the induced voltage divided by the impedance of the secondary. (Since this is an AC circuit we must use impedance rather than resistance.)

$$\mathbf{I}_r = \mathbf{E}_r/\mathbf{Z}_r \tag{9.36}$$

$\mathbf{I}_r$ = rotor current

$\mathbf{Z}_r$ = rotor impedance

The impedance of the secondary (or rotor) is composed of its resistance plus the leakage reactance caused by flux not inductively coupled with the primary field winding:

$$\mathbf{Z}_r = r_r + \mathbf{j}4\pi s f_0 L/p \tag{9.37}$$

r_r = secondary resistance—ohms

L = secondary inductance—henries

(Since the voltage induced in the rotor is at $2s/p$ times the line frequency, $2sf_0/p$ is the correct frequency for the leakage reactance term.) Combining equations 9.36 and 9.37 we obtain:

$$\mathbf{E}_r = \mathbf{I}_r (r_r + \mathbf{j}4\pi s f_0 L/p) \tag{9.38}$$

Recalling that the induced voltage in the stator is $\mathbf{E}_r$ divided by s we may rewrite equation 9.38 as:

$$\mathbf{E}_s = \mathbf{I}_r(r_r/s + \mathbf{j}4\pi f_0 L/p) \tag{9.39}$$

It is common to assume that $\mathbf{E}_s$ is approximately equal to the line voltage $\mathbf{V}$ and to add the primary resistance and leakage reactance to the secondary values. In that case equation 9.39 becomes:

$$\mathbf{V} = \mathbf{I}_r(r_r/s + r_f + \mathbf{j}X) \tag{9.40}$$

X = combined primary and secondary leakage reactance

r_f = primary or field resistance—ohms

V = line voltage—volts

Now the total power consumed by the rotor for a three phase induction motor is given by:

$$P_r = 3I_r^2 r_r/s \tag{9.41}$$

The power consumed by rotor copper losses in all three phases will be:

$$P = 3I_r^2 r_r \tag{9.42}$$

The difference between the total power consumed by the rotor and the rotor copper losses represents the mechanical work done by the motor.[19]

$$P_{\text{out}} = \frac{3I_r^2 r_r(1-s)}{s} \quad \text{(watts)} \tag{9.43}$$

The torque will be equal to the power divided by the armature speed in radians per second. Since the armature speed is $(1-s)2f_0/p$ hertz:[20]

$$T' = 3I_r^2 r_r p/4\pi s f_0 \quad \text{(newton meters)} \tag{9.44}$$

From equation 9.40 we obtain the magnitude of I_r:

$$I_r = \frac{V}{\sqrt{(r_r/s + r_f)^2 + x^2}} \tag{9.45}$$

Substituting 9.45 in 9.44 and converting to foot pounds we obtain:[21]

$$T = \frac{0.175V^2 r_r p s}{f_0\{(r_r + sr_f)^2 + s^2 X^2\}} \quad \text{(foot pounds)} \tag{9.46}$$

Equation 9.46 gives the expression for the torque of an induction motor as a function of the slip. Solution of equation 9.46 gives torque versus speed curves as shown in Figure 9-8. Maximum torque can be found by differentiating T with respect to s and setting the result equal to zero. The slip for maximum torque is found to be:

$$s_{\max} = \frac{r_r}{\sqrt{r_f^2 + X^2}} \tag{9.47}$$

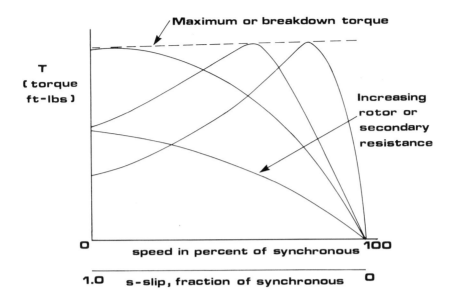

Figure 9-8. Torque-Speed Characteristics for an AC Induction Motor

Since unity slip occurs at zero speed, the maximum torque will occur at starting if $r_r \geq (r_f^2 + X^2)^{1/2}$. With lower values of r_r, the peak torque is moved towards increasingly higher speeds as shown in Figure 9-8. Thus, it is possible to increase the starting torque of an induction motor by increasing the rotor (or secondary) resistance. The penalty is of course the increased I^2R losses incurred.

Induction Motor Control. Two techniques for induction motor speed control have been used in transportation systems.

1. Pole changing
2. Variable frequency and voltage control

For pole changing the secondary resistance is selected to give a reasonable starting torque. Operating speed is varied by removing segments of the field winding, thereby changing the number of poles. This change in the number of poles affects both the synchronous (zero slip) speed and the maximum available torque.

Variable voltage and frequency control involves the use of solid state devices to change at will the voltage and frequency of the source. The change in frequency will change the synchronous speed and the change in voltage will change the torque. Together any arbitrary speed-torque relationship desired can be synthesized in this manner. Typically three phase sixty cycle AC current is rectified to DC and then reconstituted as variable frequency AC by an "inverter." The inverter uses a variety of circuits in which silicon controlled rectifiers operate as switches and synthesize the motor voltage waveform from segments of the DC voltage. The triggering rate determines the frequency of the output. The voltage level is either controlled in the rectifier preceding the inverter, or it may be controlled within the inverter by pulse width modulation. Filtering of the harmonics inevitably generated by synthesizing alternating current in this fashion is of course essential.

At the present time, inverter cost per kilowatt is about twice that of controlled rectifiers, and a complete power converter for an AC drive approaches three times the cost of a DC drive.

The Linear Induction Motor

The linear induction motor (LIM) was first patented in 1890, but it has not been until the present era that it has received serious consideration as a source of transportation propulsion. The linear induction motor may be imagined to be generated from a rotary induction motor by unwrapping the armature and the stator into flat sheets. Since the angular rotation is now zero, it is necessary for either the primary or the secondary to extend to infinity. Thus either the primary or secondary is incorporated as part of the guideway—the other element being placed in the vehicle. The result is that the linear motor thrust is developed by means of electromagnetic forces between the vehicle and the guideway so that rubber tires, steel wheels, or other friction devices are not required to push against the guideway surface to provide thrust. This makes the LIM a prime candidate for air cushion or magnetically levitated vehicles—where it is not possible to transmit thrust by vehicle-guideway rolling contact. The primary may be placed either in the vehicle or in the guideway, although most systems built to date have placed the primary on the vehicle. This is because the primary of an induction motor consists of expensive copper wound coils, while the secondary can be made simply of a laminated sheet of aluminum and steel. Therefore it is often economic to make the "infinite" portion of the LIM the relatively simple and inexpensive secondary. Unfortunately this requires brushes to be introduced into the LIM concept in order to supply power to the now moving field winding (or secondary). It is as though we had turned an ordinary rotary induction motor inside out and were supplying power to the rotating field via brushes. The rotating field would then induce a field in the stationary armature! At low urban speeds the use of sliding power pickup brushes is not a technical problem—but at the high speeds approaching 300 mph talked about for intercity high speed transit it can become a serious problem indeed.

The interaction between the primary and secondary has important effects on vehicle design. Not only is the desired thrust generated, but unintended forces pushing the vehicle towards or away from the guideway are also created. The result can be to change significantly the suspension characteristics of the vehicle.

One way to counteract these undesirable forces is to use a double-sided LIM. In this case the primary coils on the vehicle are mounted as the two sides of a sandwich with the secondary serving as the "filling." In this configuration it is necessary to mount the secondary rail vertically, which cuts the vehicle in half and reduces the designer's flexibility in locating passengers and equipment. A sketch of a double sided LIM configuration is shown in Figure 9-9.

Another problem inherent in the LIM concept is that of maintaining a small air gap between the primary and the secondary. A large air gap will naturally increase the gap reluctance and also increase the leakage flux, both of which are deleterious to performance. Unfortunately a small air gap implies a rigid suspension, meaning that an additional secondary suspension will probably be required to obtain passenger comfort. Furthermore, the heavy primary coils must not be cushioned by the secondary suspension if a close air gap is to be maintained. This means a high unsprung mass, which further complicates the ride dynamics.

The primary on the vehicle may be thought of as a segment of a rotary machine that has been cut at one point and "unwrapped." There is thus a discontinuity at each end of the primary segment. These "end effects" represent a source of error if simple rotary motor theory is extended to the LIM. At low speeds these edge effects are small and the extension of the induction motor theory is justified.

To determine the thrust and speed characteristics of a LIM, assume it is generated from a p pole machine with radius r. Then if the spacing between the magnetic poles (the magnetic pole pitch) is denoted by ℓ:

$$r = p\ell/2\pi \tag{9.48}$$

Now thrust is simply the torque of the motor divided by the torque arm r. Thus:

$$T_h = \frac{T}{r} = \frac{1.1 V^2 r_r s}{f_0 \ell \{(r_r + s r_f)^2 + s^2 X^2\}} \tag{9.49}$$

T_h = LIM motor thrust—pounds

V = supply voltage—volts

r_r = secondary resistance — ohms

s = slip

f_0 = line frequency — hertz

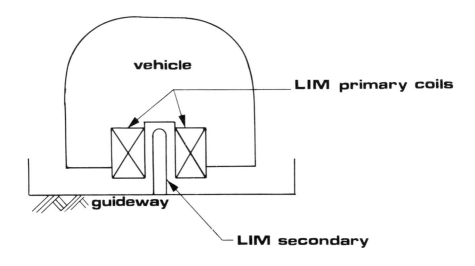

Figure 9-9. Front View of a Vehicle with a Double Sided LIM Motor

r_r = primary resistance — ohms

X = combined leakage reactance

Similarly the speed may be found by multiplying the rotary speed by the radius r. In other words:

$$v = \frac{2\pi rn}{60} = 2(1 - s)f_0\,\ell \qquad (9.50)$$

v = speed—feet per second

s = slip

f_0 = supply frequency—hertz

ℓ = pole pitch—feet

Since the difference between the equations for linear speed and thrust of a LIM and rotary speed and torque of a rotary induction motor is only a multiplying constant, the form of the thrust speed curve of the LIM is similar to Figure 9-8 shown for a rotary machine. Thus an increased secondary resistance (r_r) can be used to increase the starting torque. For this reason some LIM secondary rails are made of a higher resistance material—to get an improved thrust speed curve and permit operation without variable frequency control. Speed control techniques are similar to those discussed for rotary induction motors.

Table 9-1
Weights and Costs of Motors and Controllers

	Motors and Controls Costs (dollars/horsepower)	Weights (pounds/horsepower)
AC Motors	2	1-3
DC Motors	4	3
DC Switchgear	1	—
DC Chopper	2	0.3-0.8
Inverter (AC)	5	1.5-3.0

Source: "Electric Propulsion for Transit Vehicles," R.U. Ayres, R. McKenna, and M.L. Walker, International Research and Technology Corp., Arlington, Virginia, May 1970, Table 2. Reprinted with permission.

Costs and Weight of Electric Motors and Controllers

Table 9-1 lists estimated weights and costs for AC and DC motors and controllers. While the AC motor is both cheaper and lighter, this advantage is offset by the added weight and cost of the AC motor controller.

Heat Engines

Heat engines used or under consideration for mass transit systems are of three basic types:

1. Internal combustion engines (IC)
2. Gas turbine engines
3. External combustion engines (e.g., steam)

Internal Combustion Engines

The two basic types of internal combustion (IC) engines are the Otto cycle and the Diesel cycle. IC engines utilize an intermittent combustion process instead of the continuous combustion employed by other engines. Physically the engine consists of rows of reciprocating pistons into which a fuel-air mixture is periodically introduced. Combustion and expansion of the fuel-air mixture pushes against the pistons thereby providing the engine torque. The intermittent combustion process contributes to a generally "dirtier" exhaust than is obtained from continuous combustion.

Otto Cycle Engines. The Otto cycle engine is none other than the familiar gasoline burning reciprocating engine found in almost every automobile made today. It is distinguished from the Diesel engine by its carburetor and spark plugs. The spark plugs are used to ignite the gasoline-air mixture at the proper point in the piston's stroke. The carburetor is used to vaporize the gasoline and mix it with air. It also controls the amount and the proportions of the air-fuel mixture to be introduced into the engine. A major advantage of the Otto cycle engine is its very high state of development, which yields cost and power-to-weight ratios difficult to match. Energy efficiency of the gasoline engine is only moderate when compared with the Diesel engine.

Figure 9-10 shows the torque-speed characteristic of the Otto cycle engine. Unlike the series motor, its torque actually decreases with decreasing speed. For this reason it is necessary to couple the auto engine with a transmission in order to multiply the torque available at low speeds. A transmission is a device using gears or fluid pumps that utilizes leverage principals to trade off speed for torque. By reducing the shaft speed and multiplying the torque proportionately, the transmission provides higher torque at low engine speeds. As vehicle speed increases, it is necessary to downshift to stay within the RPM limitations of the motor. Figure 9-11 shows how the automobile transmission is used to generate a torque-speed curve that rises at low speeds.

Diesel Engines. Unlike the gasoline engine, the diesel engine does not use spark plugs to ignite the air-fuel mixture. Nor does it premix the air and fuel. Instead the fuel is injected directly into the combustion chamber. The piston compresses the air in the combustion chamber to a pressure where it will self-ignite. This requires higher pressures than are required by the gasoline engine. The higher pressures induce larger stresses, which make the Diesel engine heavier, and which also make the engine noisier. On the other hand the higher pressures and temperatures used in the Diesel engine contribute to higher operating efficiency and better fuel economy. Like the gasoline engine the Diesel has a torque-speed curve that decreases at low engine speeds and thus requires a transmission for efficient operation.

For transit use the Diesel has several serious disadvantages. First, it is noisy, especially when accelerating under load. Second, its exhaust can be very smelly. Third, the Diesel has a tendency to smoke when it is out of tune that is extremely obnoxious in a restricted urban area. Unfortunately, the Diesel achieves maximum economy at a fuel-air mixture very near that at which smoking occurs, so the operator is often running the engine very near its smoking air-fuel ratio.

Finally, the high temperatures and pressures coupled with the short combustion time in the Diesel engine make its exhaust inherently high in nitrous oxides. It will be extremely difficult to reduce the nitrous oxide

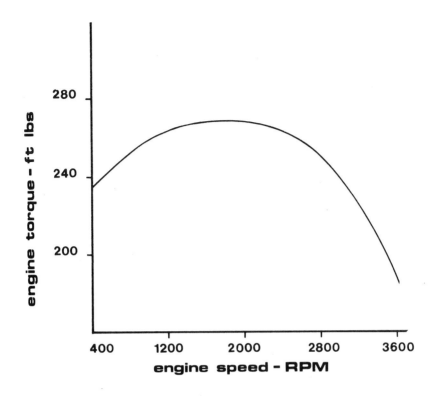

Figure 9-10. Torque-Speed Curve for an Otto Cycle Engine

concentrations in the Diesel exhaust because of the nature of the combustion process.

Weighed against these problems are two very important advantages. First, the Diesel has the highest efficiency across a broad range of speeds and loads of any vehicle engine yet developed. In other words it is the most parsimonious of our fuel supply, an attribute that has long endeared it to fleet operators. Second, it is a rugged machine with fairly long life and low maintenance requirements.

External Combustion Engines

External combustion engines utilize a continuous combustion process outside of the engine proper to burn the fuel. The already heated gas is then expanded in the engine proper to obtain mechanical work. Gas turbines and steam engines are typical of well known external combustion engines.

The Gas Turbine. The basic gas turbine process is somewhat akin to a

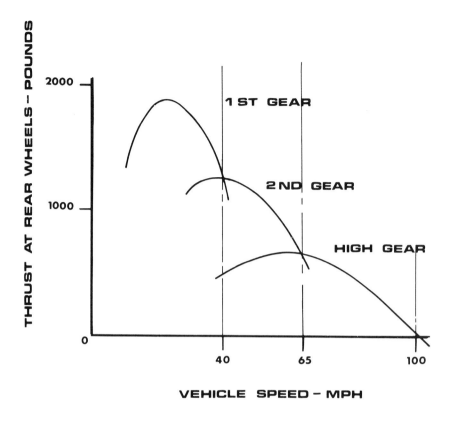

Figure 9-11. Use of Gears to Get a High Starting Thrust for an Automobile

windmill spinning in a man made hurricane. An inexpensive fuel such as kerosene is burned to raise the pressure and temperature of outside air pumped into the engine by an axial flow compressor. The resulting high energy air drives the power turbine much like the wind drives a windmill. Power may then be extracted from the turbine shaft. A turbine of this simple type, a single shaft turbine, is shown schematically in Figure 9-12a. Outside air is compressed and pumped to the combustion chamber. Power for the compressor is tapped directly from the turbine output shaft. Because turbine and compressor are driven by a common shaft it is difficult to optimize turbine inlet conditions (pressure, temperature, and air flow rate) for various speeds. This makes a turbine of this type unsuitable for variable speed applications in buses and trucks.

The above limitation can be overcome by the free turbine engine. In this configuration there is no mechanical connection between the compressor and the output shafts, permitting a wide range in output speeds. Power to drive the compressor is provided by a separate compressor turbine that is

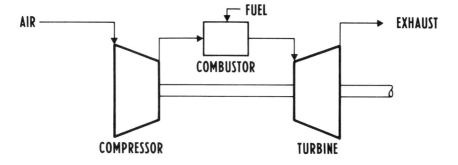

(a) Simple Gas Turbine

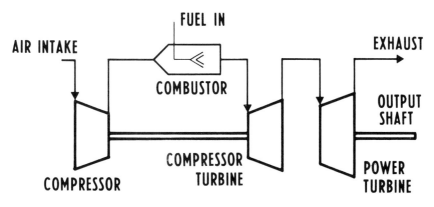

(b) Free Turbine Engine

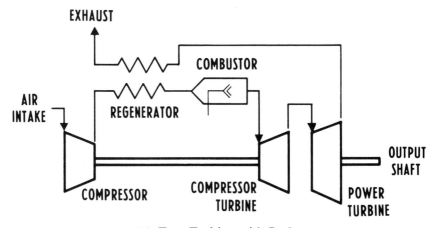

(c) Free Turbine with Preheat

Figure 9-12. Types of Gas Turbine Engines.

mechanically coupled to the compressor and runs at nearly constant speed. The power turbine is connected to the load. This physical arrangement is well suited to variable speed applications. Gas turbines under serious consideration for bus or truck application are invariably of the free turbine design (Figure 9-12b).

The major problem that a free turbine faces is poor fuel economy. One way to improve fuel economy is to use hot exhaust gases to heat intake air from the compressor. This reduces the fuel required in the combustion zone to heat the air to the power turbine inlet temperature. The improvement is dramatic—fuel economy is typically doubled by this technique. If heat transfer is accomplished using rotating discs, the heat exchanger is termed a regenerator. If a conventional stationary heat exchanger is used, it is termed a recuperator. Figure 9-12c shows a schematic of a regenerative free turbine engine. Another advantage of the regenerator is that it reduces exhaust temperatures from 1200°F to below 500°F, or less than that of a typical diesel engine exhaust. Even with regenerative techniques, the turbine suffers from poor part-load fuel economy compared with the internal combustion engine, so researchers have come up with two different approaches to further increase economy.

One approach uses variable power turbine nozzles. In the conventional gas turbine, nozzles are used to direct high energy air from the combustor against the power turbine blades. However, for different load conditions, the correct nozzle angle to obtain maximum thrust varies. Hence an obvious improvement would result from matching the nozzle angle to the load conditions. The disadvantage is the considerable mechanical complexity introduced.

Another approach has been taken by General Motors in the development of its Detroit Diesel 0404 Gas turbine engine. The power turbine is coupled to the compressor shaft through a variable-slip mechanical clutch. At part load a fraction of the output power is contributed by the compressor turbine. This serves to maintain the desired high inlet temperature under part load operating conditions. In effect, it permits the GM turbine to run as a simple single shaft turbine, a free turbine, or with any operating characteristics lying between these two extremes. Developments of this type have made the gas turbine a viable competitor with the Diesel for large load constant speed missions such as intercity bus runs or over the road trucking.

For stop and go driving as is characteristic of the urban transit mission, the diesel remains superior in terms of fuel economy. Nevertheless, the lower pollution inherent in the gas turbine engine, might yet make it a preferred choice for the urban mission. Gas turbines run with very lean combustion (400-500 percent excess air) to keep turbine inlet temperature down. Accordingly, emissions, except for oxides of nitrogen, are much less than for IC engines. NO_x emissions depend strongly on combustion chamber design and can be made quite low.

Fewer moving parts and the absence of reciprocating motion contribute to the gas turbine's greater reliability and reduced maintenance requirements. An important practical advantage of gas turbines is the absence of engine cooling requirements, except for lubrication oil, which is air cooled. Figure 9-13 shows the torque-speed curve for a gas turbine engine. Because its torque does increase at low speeds, it may require fewer gear changes to properly match a gas turbine to its load. The gas turbine may burn a wide variety of fuels from diesel oil to natural gas. Generally used are the lower cost, low volatility petroleum distillates like kerosene.

Rankine Cycle Engines. The Rankine cycle engine,[a] using water as a working fluid, is the familiar "steam engine." Organic fluids (such as the freon refrigerants) and liquid metals may also be used as working fluids. Water is attractive because of its thermal and chemical stability; however, freezing and the need for separate lubricants can be problems. Organic fluids do not have freezing and lubrication problems, but, because of thermal instability, must use a relatively low vapor generator temperature which in turn yields relatively low efficiency. Liquid metals have the disadvantage of being highly toxic.

The basic Rankine cycle consists of: (a) heat addition at constant pressure to vaporize and superheat the working fluid; (b) adiabatic expansion of the vapor to produce shaft power, either in a positive displacement expander (reciprocating or rotary) or in a turbine; (c) cooling and condensing of the working fluid at constant pressure in a condenser (usually air-cooled); (d) pumping of the condensate up to boiler pressure. The expander is the basic work-producing unit of the Rankine cycle. There are three types of expanders: reciprocating, turbine, and rotary positive-displacement. Reciprocating expanders are nearly always used in water systems of automotive size; steam turbines, which are quite feasible in large electric generating stations (another application of the Rankine cycle), are simply not practical in the range of 100 horsepower (too many stages and/or too high a rotating speed). The higher molecular weight of most organic fluids permits their use with vapor turbine expanders of practical proportions. Rotary positive-displacement expanders (e.g., vane motors, Roote's expanders) are practical for all working fluids.

Positive-displacement Rankine expanders are well suited for vehicles using mechanical drive trains. A negative sloping torque characteristic

---

[a] This section was contributed by W.E. Fraize based on his work in "A Survey of Propulsion Systems for Low Emission Urban Vehicles," W.E. Fraize, R.K. Lay, the MITRE Corp., M70-45, McLean, Va. September 1970.

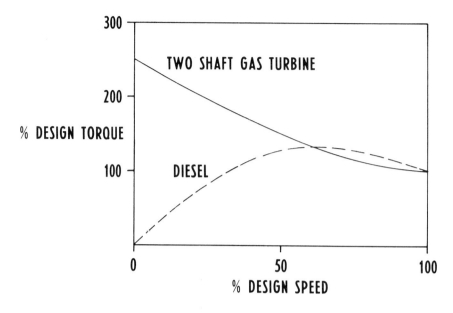

Figure 9-13. Torque-Speed Curve for a Gas Turbine Engine Compared with an Internal Combustion Engine

from stall to maximum speed is well matched to vehicle propulsion requirements to the extent that transmission and clutch are not required (i.e., direct connection to the wheels is possible). Reverse motion is obtained by reversing the rotation of the expander.

Because of the availability of high torque at low speed, the maximum power rating for a Rankine reciprocator is substantially less than that of a conventional IC engine required for a given vehicle. Because the direct connected expander does not idle, accessories must be powered either by battery or by a separate small Rankine expander.

Relative to IC engines, the reciprocating steam engine is less efficient and bulkier. Offsetting these disadvantages are the low exhaust pollution, low noise, and excellent torque-speed characteristic.

Stirling Cycle Engines. The Stirling cycle engine[b] runs on a closed cycle using gaseous hydrogen or helium as a typical working fluid. There are two basic engine types: the *displacer* type, using a displacer piston and a power piston acting together in a common cylinder; the *Rider* type, using two separate cylinders and two power pistons. Most of the published work on Stirling engines relates to displacer types for which this discussion may be

[b] This section was contributed by W.E. Fraize based on his work in "A Survey of Propulsion Systems for Low Emission Urban Vehicles," W.E. Fraize, R.K. Lay, the MITRE Corp., M70-45, McLean, Va. September 1970.

assumed to apply; this type is schematically illustrated in Figure 9-14. The basic Stirling cycle consists of: (a) heat addition at constant temperature as the hot working fluid expands against the power piston, doing useful work; (b) cooling of the fluid at constant volume as the power piston remains stationary and the displacer piston moves the fluid through a regenerator from the hot zone to the cool zone; (c) heat rejection at constant temperature as the fluid now in the cool region, is worked on by the returning power piston; (d) heating of the fluid at constant volume as the power piston remains stationary and the displacer piston moves the fluid back through the regenerator from the cool zone to the hot zone.

The major attractions of the Stirling engine are low emissions, low noise (there are no valves), and high efficiency. The high efficiency (35-40 percent) is attained through the use of a regenerator through which the working fluid passes when moving between the hot and cold regions of the engine; the regenerator recovers heat that would otherwise be dumped into the cooling system.

Drawbacks to the Stirling engine are: high cost, weight, and bulk. In commercial vehicles, weight and bulk penalties might be acceptable. The less acceptable high cost results from large radiator surfaces and complex heat exchanger geometries, items that are inherent in the basic engine.

Because of leakage past the power piston, torque drops off sharply at lower speeds; thus, the inferior torque-speed characteristic (compared to that of the Rankine positive-displacement expander) precludes direct connection, so that a clutch and transmission are required.

Energy Storage Devices

This section[c] reviews components that store energy on board the vehicle; these may be mechanical, thermal, or electrochemical. Several examples are illustrated in Table 9-2. In practice, the most common energy storage device is the secondary cell (rechargeable battery). Much of this section is devoted to batteries because of the extensive range of development activity. However, using the energy stored in a flywheel or in a thermal process is a practical, if less often considered, technique.

Secondary Batteries (Electrochemical Energy Storage)

Battery characteristics are commonly quoted in terms of energy density (watt-hours per pound) and power density (watts per pound). These

[c]This section was contributed by R.K. Lay and W.E. Fraize based on their work in "A Survey of Propulsion Systems for Low Emission Urban Vehicles," the MITRE Corp., M70-45, McLean, Virginia, September 1970.

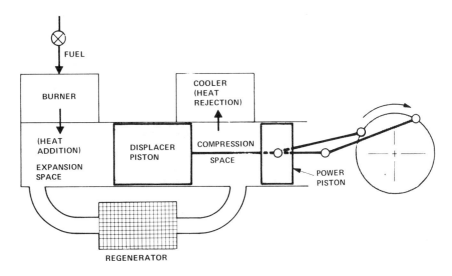

Source: Reprinted from "A Survey of Propulsion Systems for Low Emission Urban Vehicles." W.E. Fraize and R.K. Lay, MITRE Corp., M70-45, McLean, Virginia, September 1970, page 39.

Figure 9-14. Schematic of a Stirling Cycle Engine

Table 9-2
Vehicle Propulsion System Components: Energy Storage

	Specified Weight (pounds/ horsepower-hour)	Specified Volume (feet³/ horsepower-hour)	Specified Costs (dollars/ horsepower-hour)	Efficiency
Mechanical				
Flywheel	100	0.8	100	0.9
Compressed Gas	500	8.0		0.8
Electrical (batteries)				
Lead-Acid	50-75	0.45	40	0.50*
Nickel-Iron	50-75	0.45	140	
Nickel-Cadmium	35-50	0.45	240	0.95
Silver-Cadmium	30	1.05	310	
Silver-Zinc	12-15	0.65	350	0.91
Zinc-Air	10-15	0.55		

$$*\text{For batteries, efficiency} = \frac{\text{Delivered Energy at 1 Hour Discharge Rate}}{\text{Delivered Energy at Very Slow Discharge Rate}}$$

Source: "A Survey of Propulsion Systems for Low Emission Urban Vehicles," W.E. Fraize, R.K. Lay, MITRE Corp., M70-45, McLean, Virginia, September 1970.

properties are interdependent as a function of the rate at which the battery is charged and discharged (Figure 9-15). When comparison is made of

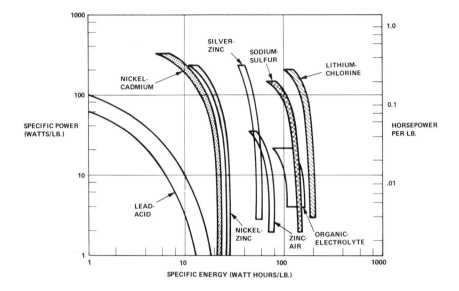

Source: Reprinted from "A Survey of Propulsion Systems for Low Emission Urban Vehicles," W.E. Fraize and R.K. Lay, MITRE Corp., M70-45, McLean, Virginia, September 1970, page 460.

Figure 9-15. Specific Power versus Specific Energy for Batteries

battery characteristics for a vehicle power supply, it is helpful to relate the energy density to the vehicle range per charge and the power density to the vehicle performance (i.e., acceleration, cruise speed, etc.).

The most familiar secondary battery is the lead-acid battery. The power density is sufficient to accelerate small urban vehicles in mixed traffic conditions; it is reliable, rugged and moderately priced. Nevertheless, typical energy densities (10-15 watt-hours per pound) are insufficient to give the vehicle an adequate range. Further, the life of a lead-acid battery, measured in charge/discharge cycles, is marginal for this type of severe use.

The addition of cobalt salts to the electrolyte will allow an increased energy density. Short period power densities of 30 watts per pound are delivered by existing batteries, other developments with "pile-type" construction offer improvements in power density to around 60 watts per pound.

The nickel-iron system has a lifetime measured in decades but poor charge retention. Nickel-cadmium batteries are up to five times more expensive than the lead-acid battery while having the same low energy density range. The "bi-polar" nickel-cadmium battery can achieve power densities of 300 watts per pound, which makes it attractive in combination with a high energy density battery for an all electric system.

Silver-zinc batteries have been used in demonstration vehicles; both energy and power densities are excellent. The cycle life, however, seldom exceeds 100 cycles and the scarcity of silver makes this system costly and impractical. Silver-cadmium batteries offer longer life but lower energy density. Because they need five to six pounds of silver per kilowatt of stored energy they are used only for experimentation.

The major rechargeable metal-air system under investigation is the zinc-air battery. Projected characteristics are 50-80 watt-hours per pound and 30-40 watts per pound. As a class, metal-air systems are power limited. When developed, it would seem logical to combine the zinc-air with the "bi-polar" nickel-cadmium battery to produce a high-energy (Zn-Air), high-power (NiCad) system. However, commercial examples of the zinc-air battery are still in the future.

Figure 9-15 includes sodium-sulphur and lithium-chlorine cells, which have a long-term development potential to provide greatly increased storage. The liquid sodium and molten lithium-chloride electrolytes present problems of sealing and safe containment at high temperatures in both cells. The constituents are relatively inexpensive and the theoretical specific energy and power values are most attractive. Such a battery could provide an electric vehicle with the performance of a modern private automobile.

Recent developments show high promise for lithium/metal sulfide batteries being developed at the Energy Research and Development Administration's Argonne National Laboratory. The cells consist of positive electrodes of iron sulfide, negative electrodes of a solid lithium-aluminum alloy, and an electrolyte of a molten mixture of lithium chloride and potassium chloride. To keep the salt molten, operating temperatures of 700°F are required. Test cells have produced as much as 70 watt-hours of energy per pound with a lifetime of 130 charge-discharge cycles. Ultimate lifetime is projected at 1000-1500 charge and discharge cycles. Costs are projected at 20-30 dollars per kilowatt-hour compared with 60 dollars per kilowatt hour for high performance lead-acid batteries.

Mechanical Energy Storage

Mechanical schemes for storing energy include the more obvious: elastic energy in a compressed spring, internal energy in an adiabatically compressed gas, and kinetic energy in an accelerated flywheel.

Only flywheel storage and compressed gas systems are considered in Table 9-2, from which it is seen that mechanical energy storage is relatively costly and bulky, compared to thermal systems, and roughly equivalent to electrical systems. Of the two mechanical devices, the flywheel system is nearly an order of magnitude better than compressed gas, in terms of energy density.

The compressed gas and spring systems have not appeared as working prototypes. Paper studies have shown compressed steel springs to be excessively heavy (10,000 pounds mass per horsepower-hour) and that the use of elastomerics (rubber-like substances) will be necessary. The questions of spring life and energy recovery efficiency will require considerable development. The compressed gas system has also been studied on paper only. The values in Table 9-2 apply for a hydraulic accumulator system wherein hydraulic fluid is pumped into or forced out of a spherical storage tank in which the fluid and the compressed gas are separated by a flexible diaphragm.

Flywheel systems, on the other hand, do exist as working prototypes. The Oerlikon Electrogyro bus (no longer produced) has operated in Europe and Africa. The bus uses wayside electricity, from frequently spaced connectors, to accelerate a large flywheel, the energy in which is used to propel the vehicle to the next charging location. A more modern flywheel system is the Gyreacta transmission in which a built-in flywheel augments the performance of an otherwise conventional mechanical drive train. In addition, Lockheed is presently working on a flywheel system for a trolly bus and Garrett Corporation has demonstrated a flywheel system on subway cars in New York City.

Flywheel systems appear to have the potential for matching the performance of battery systems and ought to be given more serious consideration. Relative to batteries, flywheels offer the advantages of long life and high energy recovery, tempered by a slight noise penalty.

Power Collector Systems

Three types of power supply have been used in rapid transit systems: DC (600-3000 volts), single phase AC (6.25-50 kilovolts, 16 2/3-60 hertz), and 3 phase AC (up to 6.6 kilovolts, 60 hertz.) Most rapid transit systems now use DC in the range of 600 to 1200 volts. Single phase AC has been extensively used for mainline railroads and for rapid transit systems operating partly on mainline trackage. Three phase AC systems are less extensively utilized.[22] The most notable are the demonstration by BART at its Diablo Test track (4160 volts, 60 hertz, 3 phase, speeds to 80 mph)[23] and the Westinghouse "Skybus" program at South Park (565 volts, 60 hertz, 3 phase, speeds to 50 mph).[24] In addition all four personal rapid transit systems demonstrated at

TRANSPO 72,[d] the Morgantown PRT; and the people mover at Dallas-Fort Worth Airport use 3 phase power at speeds to 30 mph.

Three types of collectors are generally used: pantograph/catenary, third rail, or pantograph/stiff-rail. Catenary systems are used for power transfer at high voltages. Since it has in the past been difficult to step down DC voltages, pantograph systems frequently use single phase AC in voltages to 50 kilovolts. The high voltages reduce line losses. Cable vibration sets an upper limit of 200 mph for catenary systems.[25] A good example of a single phase catenary system is Japan's New Tokaido line, which operates successfully at 210 kilometers/hour.[26]

Third rail systems are limited to low voltages of about 1000 volts because of the personnel hazard of the track mounted system and the inability adequately to insulate higher voltages.[27] Such applications lend themselves to DC systems because this voltage is suitable for driving the DC traction motors generally used for electric vehicle service. Collector bounce places an upper limit of 130 mph on these systems.[28]

Three phase systems have had less acceptance in the past because of the additional complexity of collecting from a three wire system. Three phase systems often use a pantograph mechanism holding collector brushes to pick up power from a set of four rigid rails. This is called a pantograph/stiff-rail system and is similar to that used for electric hoists. Recently the Garrett Corporation, under contract to the Federal Railroad Administration (FRA), successfully tested a 3 phase power collection system at a speed of 313 mph while carrying over 1000 amperes.[29] The Aerotrain in France uses an 1100 volt 3 phase AC system drawing 1000 amperes at speeds up to 110 mph.[30] The BART and Skybus demonstrations have already been mentioned. In principle the 3 phase system, aside from the complexity of three or four pickups instead of only one, is no different from a single wire system.

All rapid transit systems in the United States and Canada use DC systems of 600-1000 volts. Most use third rail pickup although some overhead systems are in use.

Rubber-Tired Systems

Electric power pickup is also common for rubber-tired vehicles. Trolley buses have operated successfully for many years. The Paris, Montreal, and Mexico City subways all pick up DC from a third rail and fourth rail system while running on rubber tires. The Westinghouse Skybus, which picked up 3 phase power at speeds to 50 mph, was also a rubber-tired system. The

---

[d] These systems were the Ford ACT, Bendix Dashaveyor, Rohr Monocab, and Otis/Transportation Technology Incorporated people movers which carried passengers as a demonstration throughout the TRANSPO exposition.

Alweg monorail is another operational rubber-tired system that picks up DC power from two contact rails on the side of the beamway. In Seattle such a system operates at speeds between 50 and 60 miles per hour. The 600 volt DC rails are supported by insulators spaced approximately 8 feet apart.[31] The Safege monorail, a suspended rubber-tired system with 60,000 pound vehicles, also picks up 600 volts DC power from two contact rails on the side of the beamway. It has operated at speeds up to 62 mph.[32]

Analytical Aspects

Figure 9-16 shows a schematic of a 3 phase pantograph operating on a stiff rail. Dynamic inputs to the pantograph come from two sources.

1. Collector bounce caused by undulation of the power rail
2. Movement of the vehicle with respect to the power rail

Vehicle movements of concern include vertical and lateral. For a side mounted system as shown in Figure 9-16 vertical movements will cause brush/power rail misalignment. To minimize such excursions, the pantograph should be mounted to the vehicle unsprung mass. It will experience its maximum excursion at low frequencies because guideway irregularity amplitude is generally proportional to some power of the wavelength. At low frequencies, the tires transmit the input amplitude essentially unchanged directly to the collector. Thus the worst case vertical excursion is essentially equal to the tolerance with which the guiderail can be aligned with the guideway. Rail brush overlap can be designed to accommodate this variation. Lateral vehicle movements will cause an unloading or overloading of the pantograph mechanism. Assuming a 1.5 hertz lateral resonance, the stiffness of the lateral suspension of a 10,000 pound vehicle would be 2500 pounds per inch. Assuming maximum side loads of 1/2 g, the expected lateral excursion would never exceed 2 inches. The pantograph spring mechanism should thus approach a constant force characteristic for deflections of a couple of inches. This should not pose any serious design problems.

Collector bounce caused by waviness in the power rail itself determines the required contact force. The criterion applied to prevent collector bounce is that the contact force must never become zero. This implies that the collector preload should equal the collector weight times the peak acceleration input from the power rail expressed in g's. The equation for required collector preload F in pounds of force is:

$$F = 0.05 \ W(a/x^2)v^2 \tag{9.51}$$

v = vehicle speed—feet/second

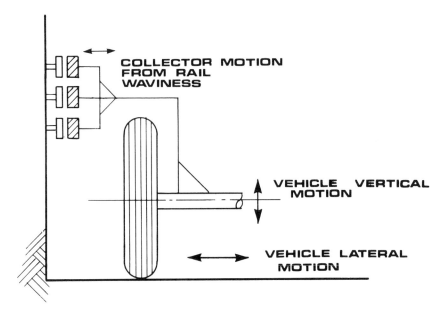

Figure 9-16. Sources of Collector Bounce

a = peak to peak amplitude of rail waviness—inches

x = wavelength of rail waviness—feet

W = collector weight—pounds

Figure 9-17 plots required collector preload as a function of rail waviness for a vehicle speed of 60 mph. A typical collector preload would be 20 pounds for a waviness of 1/2 inch peak to peak in 10 feet.

Matching the Motor to the Mission

We have spent some time considering the loads imposed on a transit vehicle by its mission. These loads include inertial forces, hill climbing forces, friction forces, and aerodynamic forces. We have also studied the torque versus speed characteristics of various types of motors and engines. The next step is to match the motor to the mission.

Total Propulsive Force Requirement

The total propulsive force required by a transit vehicle is given by:

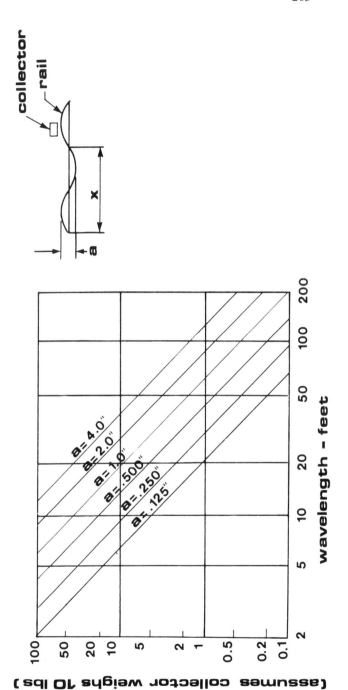

Figure 9-17. Collector Preload to Prevent Collector Bounce at 60 MPH

$$F_t = F_i + F_g + F_a + F_r + F_c \qquad (9.52)$$

F_t = total force required at the driving point—pounds

F_i = inertial force—pounds

F_g = grade force—pounds

F_a = aerodynamic drag force—pounds

F_r = frictional force associated with support and guidance system—pounds

F_c = additional frictional force associated with support and guidance system in the presence of side loads on the vehicle—pounds

For an air cushion vehicle, the air cushions are assumed to require no propulsive thrust. The horsepower required by the cushions *is* computed and added to the vehicle propulsion power requirement. The horsepower required *at the driving point* is simply the product of the thrust times the velocity:

$$P_{dp} = F_t v / 550 \qquad (9.53)$$

P_{dp} = horsepower required at the driving point

v = vehicle speed—feet per second

If the motor is a linear induction motor this thrust and power requirement can be directly related to the thrust-speed characteristic of the motor. Ordinarily, however, the motor or engine will not be located at the driving point—and, since it generally imparts rotary motion, its performance will be given in terms of torque versus engine speed.

The revolutions per minute delivered by the engine or motor is related to the vehicle speed by the equation:

$$n = 60v\zeta_m / 2\pi r \qquad (9.54)$$

n = motor or engine speed—revolutions per minute

v = vehicle speed—feet per second

ζ_m = reduction ratio between the engine or motor output shaft and the driving wheels

r = driving wheel radius at point of guideway contact—feet

The torque delivered by the engine or motor is related to the force at the driving point by the expression:

$$T_t = F_t r / \zeta_m \eta \qquad \text{(foot-pounds)} \qquad (9.55)$$

η = drive train efficiency expressed as a decimal fraction

Notice that the motor torque must be increased to compensate for losses in the drive train.

The motor or engine horsepower must be adequate to overcome all vehicle drag forces including inertia, and must also overcome drive train losses and provide any power required by motor driven accessories. Assuming an accessory power of P_a horsepower:

$$P'_{out} = F_t v/550\eta + P_a \qquad (9.56)$$

P'_{out} = power required by engine or motor—horsepower

(If air cushion power is provided by the propulsion system, it may be included as part of P_a).

For consideration of electric motors, P'_{out} may be converted to watts by multiplying it by 746.

In terms of torque and engine speed:

$$P'_{out} = 1.904 \times 10^{-4} T_t n + P_a \qquad (9.57)$$

Notice that T_t does *not* include the torque required by the motor to handle accessory power. Including this torque we have:

$$T'_t = T_t + 5252 P_a/n \qquad (9.58)$$

T'_t = total engine torque required including accessories—foot-pounds

With these relationships we are now in a position to compare directly the capability of a motor against the mission requirements. Figure 9-18 shows a typical motor torque-speed curve. The motor delivers a constant torque of 200 foot-pounds up to a speed of 1000 revolutions per minute. Above this speed it delivers a constant horsepower. We will consider its performance in accelerating a vehicle on a straight and level road with no head or tailwinds. The vehicle to be powered weighs 4000 pounds and has rubber tires with a rolling friction given approximately by 2 percent of the vehicle weight or eighty pounds. Frontal area is twenty square feet and the vehicle has a drag coefficient of 0.5. The aerodynamic drag is therefore:

$$F_a = 0.012 v^2 \qquad (9.59)$$

The motor drives two foot diameter wheels through a three to one gear reduction. Drive train efficiency is 85 percent. Since we are on a level road the grade forces are zero. Since the road is straight the curve forces are also zero. F_t is therefore:

$$F_t = 80 + 0.012 v^2 + 130.4 a \qquad (9.60)$$

a = vehicle acceleration—feet per second^2

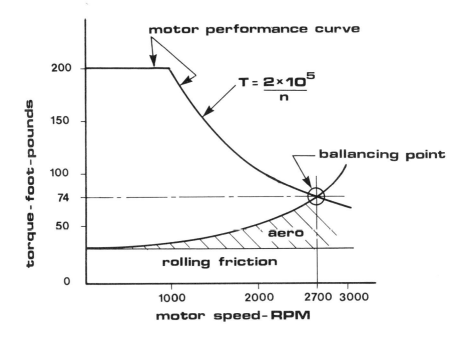

Figure 9-18. Matching the Motor to the Mission

(Equation 9.60 assumes a 5 percent mass ratio.)

The torque required at the motor output shaft if we assume a negligible accessory load is given by equation 9.55 or:

$$T_t = F_t \times 1/(3 \times 0.85) = 31.4 + 0.0047v^2 + 51.14a \qquad (9.61)$$

Substituting for v from equation 9.54:

$$T_t = 31.4 + 5.73 \times 10^{-6}n^2 + 51.14a \qquad (9.62)$$

The first two terms of equation 9.62 have been plotted on the motor performance curve of Figure 9-18. The difference between this curve, which represents the torque to overcome rolling drag and aerodynamic drag, and the torque available from the motor represents the available acceleration torque. In other words, by equating motor torque T with required torque T_t we obtain:

$$a = \frac{T - 31.4 - 5.734 \times 10^{-6}n^2}{51.14} \qquad (9.63)$$

From zero to 1000 revolutions per minute or for vehicle speeds from zero to

34.9 feet per second, the motor delivers a constant torque of 200 foot pounds so that:

$$a = 3.3 - 0.112 \times 10^{-6}n^2 \qquad (9.64)$$

The acceleration available thus varies from 3.3 feet per second² at zero revolutions per minute to 3.19 feet per second² at 1000 revolutions per minute.

Above 1000 revolutions per minute the motor provides a constant horsepower. Thus:

$$T = \frac{2 \times 10^5}{n} \qquad (9.65)$$

As torque decreases with speed the acceleration will continue to decrease until we reach the speed at which motor output just balances rolling friction and aerodynamic drag. This is called the balancing speed. From equations 9.63 and 9.65, the acceleration is zero when:

$$\frac{2 \times 10^5}{n} = 31.4 + 5.734 \times 10^{-6}n^2 \qquad (9.66)$$

The balancing speed can be found by trial and error to occur at approximately 2700 revolutions per minute or a vehicle speed of 94.2 feet per second (about 64 miles per hour). This represents the vehicle's maximum speed on a straight and level road with no wind—or the balancing speed. As is evident in Figure 9-18, the balancing speed is the intersection point of the drag curve (exclusive of inertial forces) and the motor performance curve.

It is of course quite possible to compare motor performance against a mission including a grade requirement and curves. One would ordinarily specify either the acceleration capability required on a grade, or the time required to accelerate from rest to a given speed. If performance is required against an adverse headwind, this too can be included and the analysis executed along the same lines.

To determine the time to accelerate to a given speed, one must remember that the acceleration capability of the vehicle, if it is limited by available motor torque, is continually changing. Acceleration can not be computed from a simple expression such as velocity equals acceleration times time. To illustrate the approach, consider the time to accelerate from zero to 30 feet per second on straight and level pavement for the previous example. From equation 9.64:

$$a = \frac{dv}{dt} = 3.3 - 0.112 \times 10^{-6}n^2 = 3.3 - 91.91 \times 10^{-6}v^2 \qquad (9.67)$$

separating variables and simplifying:

$$t = 10881 \int_0^{30} \frac{dv}{(189.5)^2 - v^2} \qquad (9.68)$$

This is a standard integral which may be looked up in any mathematical handbook:

$$t = 28.71 \left.\right|_0^{30} \ln \frac{189.5 + v}{189.5 - v} \qquad (9.69)$$

Substituting the limits one finds it takes about 9.2 seconds to accelerate to 30 feet per second.

Notes

1. *Principles of Direct Current Machines*, Alexander S. Langsdorf, 6th edition, McGraw-Hill Book Company, New York, 1959, pages 14-21.

2. *Electric Machinery*, Michael Liwschitz-Garik, Vol. I, 5th edition, D. Van Nostrand, New York, 1946, page 143.

3. *Electric Machinery*, A.E. Fitzgerald and C. Kingsley, McGraw-Hill Book Company, New York, 1952, pages 46-48.

4. Ibid.

5. *Switching Relay Design*, R.L. Peak and H.N. Wagar, D. Van Nostrand, New York, 1955, page 300.

6. *Electric Machinery and Control*, Irving L. Kosow, Prentice Hall, Englewood Cliffs, New Jersey, 1964, pages 24-26.

7. Ibid.

8. *Basic Electrical Engineering*, A.E. Fitzgerald and D.E. Higginbotham, McGraw-Hill Book Company, New York, 1957, page 262.

9. *Standard Handbook for Electrical Engineers*, 10th edition, D.G. Fink and J.M. Carroll, McGraw-Hill Book Company, New York, 1968, page 18-2.

10. *Electromagnetic and Electromechanical Machines*, L.W. Matsch, Intext Educational Pub., Scranton, Pennsylvania, 1972, pages 192-193.

11. Ibid.

12. *Rotating Machinery*, Harold J. Herbein, Rinehart Press, San Francisco, 1971, pages 98-99.

13. Ibid.

14. *Evaluation of Transportation Equipment Technology for Use in the Baltimore Region Rapid Transit System*, Daniel, Mann, Johnson, and Mendenhall and Kaiser Engineers, PB 180093, Baltimore, June 1968.

15. *San Francisco Bay Area Rapid Transit District Demonstration*

Project, Technical Report No. 4, Vol. II, Rapid Transit Propulsion Systems, Parsons, Brinckoff, Tudor, and Bechtel, San Francisco, September 1968.

16. *Electric Machinery and Control*, page 289.

17. *Basic Electrical Engineering*, pages 290-293.

18. Ibid.

19. *Electric Machinery and Control*, pages 310-313.

20. *Basic Electrical Engineering*, page 297.

21. Ibid.

22. "Frontiers of Technology," Vol. III. *Implementation*, M.A. Sulkin, T.R. Parsons, and D.I. Sinozer, PB 178272, North American Rockwell, Los Angeles, January 5, 1968, page 313.

23. "San Francisco Bay Area Rapid Transit District Demonstration Project Technical Report No. 7, Traction Power Collection," Parsons, Brinckerhoff, Tudor, Bechtel, San Francisco, 1965, especially pages 1 and 2.

24. "Transit Expressway Report," MPC Corporation, Pittsburgh, February 20, 1967, pages 172-180, page 130, pages 191-195, and pages 215-216.

25. *Mechanical Engineering*, New York, January 1973, page 75; and "The Current Collection System: The Key to Electric Propulsion of HSGT Vehicles," Richard Uher, TRI-3, *High Speed Ground Transportation*, Carnegie Mellon University, Pittsburgh, pages 117-139.

26. "Extension of the New Tokaido Line," Makoto Kato, preprint 1519, Joint ASCE ASME Transportation Meeting, Seattle, July 26-30, 1971.

27. "The Current Collection System."

28. Ibid.

29. *Mechanical Engineering*, January 1973, page 75.

30. "Suspended Vehicle Systems," Vol. 1, P.Y. Pei, TRW Systems, PB 202607, Redondo Beach, California, June 1971, pages 133-134.

31. "Alweg Monorail Technical Data," Wedgematic Corporation, 1962, pages 15-16, 21; and *Monorails*, Derek Harvey, GP Putnam's Sons, New York, 1965, pages 69-85.

32. "General Electric Aerial Transport System; A Baseline Definition," APL/JHU TCR002, Johns Hopkins University Applied Physics Laboratory, May 1970.

10 Braking and Traction

Propelling the vehicle is important, but it is even more critical to be able to stop safely. The ability to operate at close headways depends almost entirely upon reliable braking systems and adequate traction. This chapter addresses these facets of vehicle operation.

Braking

In chapter 9 we found that the thrust required at the driving point was equal to the sum of the inertial force, the grade force, the aerodynamic drag force, and the frictional forces associated with the support and guidance system.

The same equation is equally valid for stopping. In this case, however, the inertial force is trying to keep the vehicle going, while the frictional drag forces are helping the brakes stop the vehicle. Ordinarily the aerodynamic drag also helps to stop the vehicle. However with a strong tailwind, the aerodynamic forces at low vehicle speeds can actually be pushing the vehicle forward. Gravity will be slowing the vehicle down on uphill gradients and speeding it up on downhill gradients. The total brake thrust required is therefore:

$$F_b = -F_t = -F_i - F_g - F_a - F_r - F_c \qquad (10.1)$$

$F_i = $ inertial force, taken as positive with vehicle accelerating—pounds

$F_g = $ hill climbing force, taken as positive for an uphill gradient—pounds

$F_a = $ aerodynamic drag force

$F_r = $ frictional force associated with support and guidance system—pounds

$F_c = $ additional friction force associated with support and guidance system in the presence of side loads on the vehicle—pounds

$F_b = $ total braking force required—pounds

Consider the force required to decelerate a 4000 pound automobile at

0.3 g from a speed of 45 mph. Assume a mass factor of 1.05 and a rolling friction of 2 percent of the vehicle weight. The vehicle is stopping on a 5 percent straight downhill grade. The aerodynamic drag coefficient is 0.5, frontal area 20 square feet, and there is a 30 mph tailwind. Equation 10.1 becomes:

$$F_b = 1.05(4000)(0.3) + 4000(0.05)$$
$$- 0.5(20)(0.0012)(v - 44)|v - 44| - 0.02(4000)$$
$$= 1140 - 0.012(v - 44)|v - 44| \tag{10.2}$$

(The absolute value of $(v - 44)$ is required so that tailwinds will produce a positive value when they exceed the vehicle speed)

Table 10-1 indicates the braking force required at 45 mph, 30 mph, 15 mph, and 0 mph (just before the vehicle stops). Notice that the maximum braking force is required at the lowest speed, since wind resistance is then at a minimum. In fact for the high tailwind in this example, the wind is actually moving the vehicle forward.

Wheeled vehicles are usually stopped by applying a frictional force to brake pads or linings on the wheel. If the driving wheel radius at the point of contact is r, the force applied at the brake pad or lining will be given by (see Figure 10-1):

$$F_{br} = F_b r/nr_b \tag{10.3}$$

r_b = radius from center of wheel to brake pad or lining—feet

n = number of wheels being braked

F_{br} = force required at brake on each wheel—pounds

For the 4000 pound automobile example cited, we may assume disc brakes at all four wheels, with the average radius to the lining equal to half the radius of the tire measured at the point of guideway contact. In that case F_{br} is 582 pounds per brake disc. If the brake linings have a coefficient of friction of 0.6, this means the normal force pushing the pads against the disc must be 970 pounds. If the hydraulic piston has a one inch diameter the pressure required will be 1235 pounds per square inch.

The most important factor in sizing friction brakes is the need to dissipate the kinetic energy of the vehicle as heat. The instantaneous power being dissipated by the brakes is given by:

$$P_b = 3600F_b v/778 = 4.63F_b v \tag{10.4}$$

F_b = total braking force required—pounds

v = vehicle speed—feet per second

Table 10-1
Braking Force for a 4000 Pound Car Stopping at 0.3 G on a 5 Percent Downgrade

Vehicle Speed—mph	Braking Force—pounds
45	1134
30	1140
15	1146
0	1163

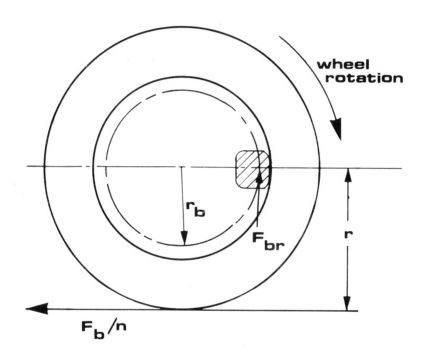

Figure 10-1. Forces on a Braked Wheel

P_b = total brake heat dissipation—BTU/hour

With four disc brakes each brake must dissipate a quarter of this heat. The total heat dissipated by the brakes on a particular mission is given by:

$$H = \int_0^t P_b \, dt = 4.63 \int_0^s F_b \, ds \qquad (10.5)$$

ds = incremental distance traveled—feet

F_b = the total braking force (a function of the distance, which must be kept inside the integral)

H = heat dissipated—BTU

If the retarding effects of aerodynamic and frictional forces are ignored, the heat that must be dissipated to stop a vehicle on a straight and level guideway is equal to its kinetic energy. For this special case:

$$H = \frac{3600 \ (GVW)v^2}{778 \times 2 \times 32.2} = 0.072(GVW)v^2 \tag{10.6}$$

The temperature of the brake linings may be estimated by noting that the heat generated by friction is equal to the heat lost to the air plus the heat stored in the mass of the brake disc or drum. (Such a relationship assumes that heat lost by conduction is not significant.) Thus:

$$P_b = hA\theta + mc_p \frac{d\theta}{dt} \tag{10.7}$$

h = heat transfer coefficient to air—BTU/hour feet^2-degree Fahrenheit

A = total area available for heat transfer—feet^2

m = brake mass available for heat absorption—pounds

c_p = specific heat of brake mass—BTU/pound mass-degree Fahrenheit

θ = temperature rise of brake above ambient—degrees Fahrenheit

t = time—hours

Notice that m is in pounds mass, *not* slugs.

If the rate of heat generation by friction is assumed to be constant, which is true for a vehicle maintaining a constant speed down a steep hill by applying the brakes, the temperature rise from equation 10.7 is given by:

$$\theta = (P_b/hA)(1 - e^{-hAt/mc_p}) \tag{10.8}$$

Another case of interest is the temperature rise caused by stopping at a constant rate of deceleration. Assuming the variation in aerodynamic drag with speed may be ignored we can assume the brake force is also constant. Then:

$$P_b = 4.63F_b \ (v_0 - 3600Dt) = hA\theta + mc_p \frac{d\theta}{dt} \tag{10.9}$$

v_0 = initial velocity—feet per second

D = vehicle deceleration—feet per second²

This yields the second order differential equation:

$$\frac{-4.63 \times 3600 F_b D}{hA} = \frac{d\theta}{dt} + \frac{mc_p}{hA}\frac{d^2\theta}{dt^2} \qquad (10.10)$$

The solution of this equation gives the following expression for the brake temperature rise:

$$\theta = 4.63 F_b\left[B - (B + A)e^{-A/B}\right] \qquad (10.11)$$

where $B = 3600 D mc_p/(hA)^2$

$A = v_0/hA$

Equation 10.8 may be simplified by noting that for continuous duty operation ($t = \infty$):

$$\theta = P_b/hA \qquad (10.12)$$

The term $1 - \exp(-hAt/mc_p)$ may thus be taken to be indicative of the duty cycle. In other words the heat dissipation capacity of a brake may be estimated as:

$$P_b = KhA\theta \qquad (10.13)$$

The factor K is proportional to the duty cycle, being 1 for continuous operation and perhaps 2 or 3 for intermittent operation.

The permissible temperature rise of a brake varies. For automobiles it is usually around 500 degrees Fahrenheit.[1]

Traction

If a vehicle is supported on wheels, then invariably it is propelled by driving all or a portion of the wheels. For example, the usual automobile is powered by the rear wheels only. Jeeps, on the other hand, have all four wheels powered. Subway cars also usually have all wheels powered. Such wheel powered vehicles obtain their thrust from the frictional force generated between the driving wheels and the guideway. We are all well aware that when the roads are icy, it is difficult to obtain sufficient traction to operate our automobiles. When the propulsive thrust requirement is high, as when negotiating a steep hill, the reduced traction available in ice and snow becomes more serious, and we are likely to "get stuck." The traction available will be equal to the product of a friction factor times the weight on the driving wheels. Assuming the same friction factor, a passenger car with two driven wheels will have only about half the weight on the driving wheels, while a jeep will have all of its weight supported by driving wheels. The jeep thus has about twice as much traction capability as the ordinary car. In formal terms:

$$F^* = f_0 W_w \tag{10.14}$$

$F^* =$ traction force available—pounds

$f_0 =$ friction factor

$W_w =$ total weight supported by all driving wheels—pounds

Because station wagons have more weight over the rear wheels they often perform better in snow. Similarly cars such as the Volkswagon, Saab, or Oldsmobile Toronado, which have the engine located over the driving wheels, are also excellent snow performers.

The friction factor in equation 10.14 represents the available coefficient of friction between the driving wheels and the guideway. In the railroad industry the tractive capability of a train or locomotive is referred to as "adhesion," while in the world of rubber tired vehicles it is called "traction." Either way it refers to the same thing—the level of thrust that can be transmitted by the rotation of a wheel against a running surface.

Do not confuse f_0 with the rolling drag coefficient f, which measures not the available traction, but the losses inherent in rolling a wheel on a surface. The available friction factor f_0 is much larger than the rolling friction coefficient. Otherwise we would be unable to use wheels to push vehicles up steep hills and to accelerate heavy loads.

A wheel is able to transmit thrust to the running surface only because there is some relative motion between the wheel and the running surface. This relative motion is measured by the slip[a] ratio, which represents the difference between the linear speed of the tire at the point of contact with the guideway and the linear speed of the vehicle. In other words:

$$s = 1 - v/r\omega \tag{10.15}$$

$s =$ wheel slip ratio

$\omega =$ wheel angular velocity—radians per second

$r =$ radius from wheel center to running surface—feet

$v =$ vehicle speed—feet per second

Although much of the discussion thus far has concerned propulsive traction, the traction required for braking will often be more critical. When the vehicle is accelerating or cruising, the driving wheels must rotate slightly faster than the vehicle actually is moving and the slip is given by

---

[a] In railroad usage "slip" is called "creep."

equation 10.15. When the vehicle is braking, on the other hand, the wheels must turn slightly slower than the vehicle is moving in order to transmit a braking thrust to the guideway. The slip for braking is therefore given by the expression:

$$s = 1 - r\omega/v \qquad (10.16)$$

If the wheels lock when the vehicle is being braked, ω becomes zero and the slip is unity.

The friction factor available for transmission of thrust is a function of the wheel slip. With no wheel slip the friction factor is zero. As wheel slip increases the friction factor increases until it reaches a maximum value known as the "maximum friction factor."[b] The slip at this point is called the "critical slip." The critical slip is not a constant, depending upon the guideway surface and the condition of the tire, but it typically occurs at a slip of from 5 to 20 percent. Since tractive force decreases for slip greater than the critical value, any attempt to increase the braking force above the maximum will cause the wheels to lock up. Two points are worth noting. First, since the friction factor at critical slip is typically 50-100 percent higher than at lock-up, the greatest deceleration of a vehicle is not obtained when the wheels are locked. Second, control is lost when the wheels lock. For these reasons automatic brake control systems have been developed whose task is to keep the wheels operating in the vicinity of critical slip. This is also the reason drivers "pump the brakes" when stopping on slick roads.

Figure 10-2 shows a typical friction factor curve. The locked wheel friction factor, although less than the maximum, is the largest friction factor that can be guaranteed, regardless of the force applied to the brakes. For this reason it is usually the basis for specifying highway surfaces. A common method of measuring the locked wheel friction factor has been standardized in ASTM Method E274.[2] In this test, a standard test tire, (itself defined by ASTM Standard E249) is installed on the wheel or wheels of a single or two wheeled trailer. The trailer is towed at a speed of 40 mph over dry pavement and water is applied in front of the test wheel according to a set procedure. The test wheel is locked up by a suitable brake and the force or torque produced by the skidding tire is measured. The "skid number" is defined as:

$$SN = 100F/L \qquad (10.17)$$

SN = skid number as obtained from ASTM Method E274

F = force produced by skidding tire—pounds

L = load on tire—pounds

---

[b] Also called the "impending" or "incipient" friction.

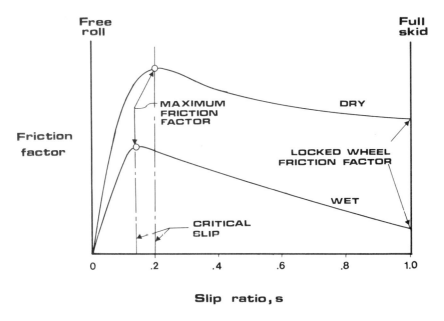

Figure 10-2. Typical Variation in Friction Factor with Slip Ratio

It will be evident that the skid number is nothing but the locked wheel friction factor. It is obtained, however, using a specific tire and according to a rigidly specified technique. For this reason the term "skid number" should only be used to refer to friction factors obtained by the ASTM Method E274.

Factors Affecting the Friction Factor

The actual value of the friction factor is dependent upon a number of complex interactions, including:[3]

1. Surface characteristics, of which surface texture and type and amount of lubricant are the most important
2. Rubber characteristics, of which the elastic and damping properties are the most important
3. Operational parameters—that is the load or pressure acting on the tire, the sliding speed, and the temperature of both surface and rubber

The usual "lubricant" referred to above is nothing but water. The presence of water on the road can significantly reduce the available friction. Studies have shown that in eastern and central United States the pavements are wet at least 15 percent of the time, and that wet pavement accident rates are

Table 10-2
Typical Skid Numbers for Rubber Tires on Portland Cement

		Skid Number
Dry pavement	10-40 mph	70-80
Wet pavement	10 mph	65
	40 mph	35-41
Ice at 32° F		5-9
Packed snow		10-30

Source: "Evaluation of Transportation Equipment Technology for Use in the Baltimore Region Rapid Transit System," Daniel Mann, Johnson and Mendenhall, Kaiser Engineers, Baltimore, Md., June 1968.

twice as high as those for dry pavements.[4] The effect of water on pavement friction is serious and can not be ignored. Ice and snow are also excellent "lubricants" and can deteriorate available friction to an even greater degree. Table 10-2 lists typical skid numbers for pavements under wet, dry, and icy conditions. Undoubtedly the primary operational parameter is vehicle speed. When the pavement is wet, the locked wheel friction factor decreases dramatically as speed is increased.

Figure 10-3 summarizes the important effects of speed and water upon the skid number. Although skid number tends to remain nearly constant with speed for dry surfaces, it decreases significantly with wet surfaces.

Forces Producing Tire-Pavement Traction

There are two basic phenomena that produce forces between a tire and a pavement. These are called "adhesion" and "hysteresis." Adhesion is analogous to the force developed when a hand slides over the smooth surface of a table. It refers to the inherent shearing resistance to sliding motion between the two surfaces. Hysteresis, on the other hand, represents the energy required to deform the tire to conform to surface irregularities in the pavement (e.g., projections caused by semi-exposed aggregate particles).

With a railroad wheel on a track, the surface is very smooth and there is essentially no hysteresis effect. Rail traction may thus be attributed entirely to the adhesion effect.

Surface Material and Texture

Surface material and texture do not have any significant effect on the

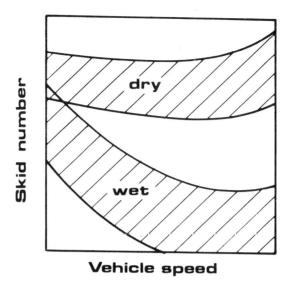

Source: "Tentative Skid-Resistance Requirements for Main Rural Highways," National Cooperative Highway Research Program Report 37, Highway Research Board, National Academy of Sciences, Washington, D.C., 1967, page 5. Reprinted with permission.

Figure 10-3. Effect of Wet Surface and Speed on Tire-Pavement Friction

friction factor of dry pavements. But when the guideway is wet, the effect of surface condition on friction factor is considerable. Two basic types of surface texture must be considered.[5]

1. Large or macro-texture—This depends on the sizes and proportions of the aggregates used. Macro-texture may be roughly estimated by eye. Alternatively, a measure of the average surface texture depth may be obtained by working a known volume of sand or grease into the surface voids until a smooth finish is obtained. The average texture depth is then the ratio of the volume of grease or sand used to the surface area covered.

2. Small or micro-texture—This is the texture of the individual stones and particles of which the surface is composed. It is the finish which one "feels" by passing the finger tips over a surface and noting whether it feels "rough" or "smooth." Micro-texture can be significantly altered by the effects of surface wear and polishing.

Figure 10-4 shows four idealized surfaces which illustrate the various combinations of texture. Figure 10-5 indicates the variation in friction factor with speed for wet surfaces of these types.

SURFACE		Scale of Texture	
		MACRO (LARGE)	MICRO (FINE)
I	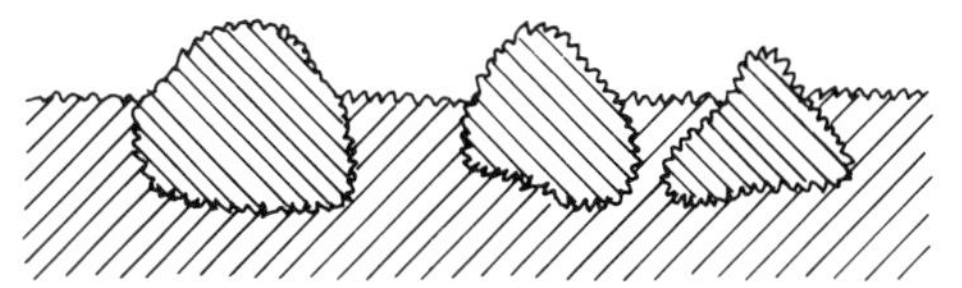	OPEN	HARSH
II	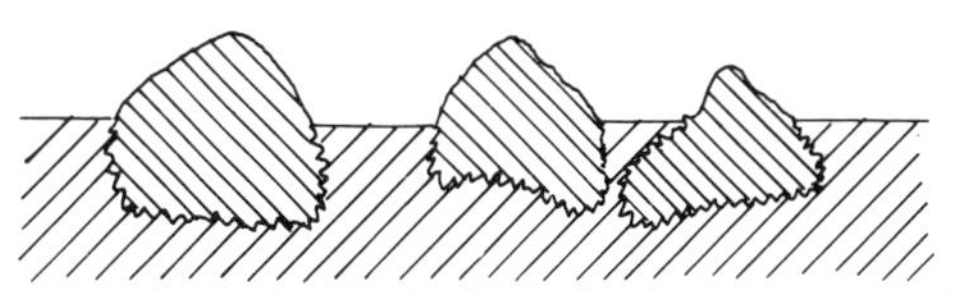	OPEN	SMOOTH OR POLISH-ED
III	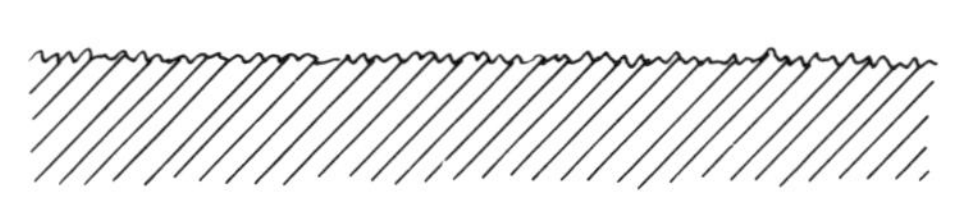	CLOSED	HARSH
IV	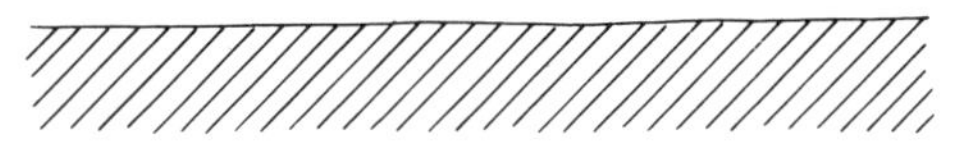	CLOSED	SMOOTH OR POLISH-ED

Source: Based upon the Classifications Proposed by the Engineering Sciences Data Unit in "Frictional and Retarding Focus on Aircraft Tyres," *Part 1, Introduction*, ESDI 71025, Engineering Sciences Data Unit, London, England, August 1972.

Figure 10-4. Idealized Pavement Surfaces

Surface I. Surface I has a large average texture depth (macro-texture) and a micro-texture that feels harsh to the touch. This would be characteristic of a properly finished portland cement concrete surface when new. The large macro-texture provides good water drainage at all speeds and braking is increased by the tire deformation caused by the rough road surface. The harsh micro-texture breaks through any film of water remaining and assures that dry contact is obtained between tire and pavement at all speeds. As a result, this is the ideal surface for maintaining good traction on both wet and dry pavements.

Surface II. Surface II retains the large macro-texture, but has a smooth micro-texture. This surface is characteristic of a heavily traveled portland cement concrete pavement where the traffic has had a polishing effect in

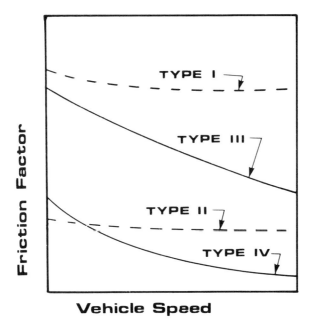

Source: "Frictional and Retarding Forces on Aircraft Tyres," *Part I, Introduction*, ESDI 71025, Engineering Science Data Unit, London, England, August 1972, page 29. Reprinted with permission.

Figure 10-5. Typical Wet Pavement Friction Factor versus Speed Curves for Various Types of Pavement

wearing down the originally harsh micro-texture. The smooth micro-texture means that it is difficult for the tire to break through the residual film of water on a well drained, but wet, pavement to establish dry contact between tire and pavement. As a result the wet pavement friction factor for this surface is significantly poorer than for surface I.

Surface II is common for many heavily traveled sections of urban freeways. A major problem in pavement design is to prevent traffic polishing from changing a type I surface into a type II surface.

Surface III. Surface III has a small average texture depth (macro-texture) and a micro-texture that feels harsh to the touch. It is typical of many lightly brushed concrete or small aggregate asphalt surfaces. The small macro-texture provides poor drainage so that, at high speeds, there is insufficient time to eject fluid from the tire pavement contact area. As a result, this surface has a wet guideway friction factor that decreases with speed.

Surface IV. Surface IV has a small macro-texture and a smooth micro-texture. In terms of traction, this is the worst possible combination. The lack of bulk fluid drainage channels and of small scale asperities to penetrate the residual fluid film, results in very low friction factors which decrease to practically zero at higher speeds. In practice, this surface is only likely to occur as a result of the polishing or wearing smooth of a type III surface—or because there is a film of ice on the road surface.

Effect of Tire Tread Design

On highly skid resistant surfaces such as type I, tread design is a secondary factor and a smooth tire will produce as good or often higher skid resistance as one with a good tread.[6] However, on smooth surfaces with small macro-texture, the tire grooves and ribs provide channels for the ejection of fluid from the tire-pavement contact area and significantly improve the friction factor.

The Effect of Water on Surface Friction

We have seen that the presence of water on the guideway can cause a significant decrease in the friction factor. Let us consider the mechanism by which this occurs. Consider the situation on surfaces that appear smooth to the eye, such as surfaces III and IV. The tire-pavement contact area may be divided into three regions or zones as illustrated in Figure 10-6.

In zone 1, fluid inertial forces build up sufficient pressure to completely support the tire with no dry contact between tire and pavement. Throughout this zone, the tire is supported by an unbroken layer of fluid and no traction force is developed. To minimize the size of zone 1, a large macro-texture is required to permit ejection of fluid from the tire pavement interface and prevent the buildup of high fluid pressure.

Zone 2 is a transition region in which the flow of fluid is governed by viscous, rather than inertial forces. A thin film (of the order of a few thousandths of an inch thick) is maintained between the tire and pavement by viscous forces. This film begins to break down at points where the local bearing pressure is high—i.e., at sharp surface asperities. This region is thus reduced by having a harsh micro-texture to establish dry contact through the viscous water film.

In zone 3, predominantly dry contact is achieved and the major component of the traction force is developed. The presence of zones 1 and 2 means that the total area of dry contact is less than on a dry surface—and that only a portion of the total vehicle weight is supported by this portion of the tire-pavement contact area.

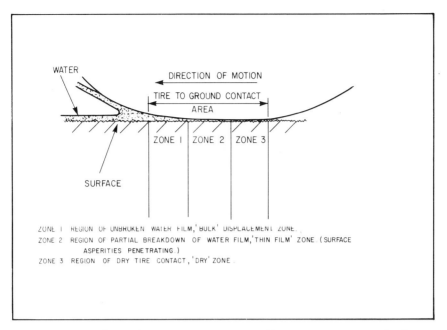

ZONE 1 REGION OF UNBROKEN WATER FILM,'BULK' DISPLACEMENT ZONE.
ZONE 2 REGION OF PARTIAL BREAKDOWN OF WATER FILM,'THIN FILM' ZONE.(SURFACE
ASPERITIES PENETRATING.)
ZONE 3 REGION OF DRY TIRE CONTACT,'DRY' ZONE.

Note: Description of Zones based upon theory presented in "Frictional and Retarding Forces on Aircraft Tyres," *Part 1, Introduction*, ESDI 71025, Engineering Science Data Unit, London, England, August 1972.

Figure 10-6   Zones of Tire Contact on a Wet Pavement

The friction factor thus depends on the relative extent of zones 1, 2 and 3. These are determined in large measure by the fluid depth, the vehicle speed, the tire pressure, the tire tread, and the surface texture.

An increase in vehicle speed increases the inertial forces of the fluid and decreases the time available to eject water from the tire-pavement contact area. As a result, the relative size of zones 1 and 2 increase with vehicle speed until no zone 3, and eventually, no zone 2 exist. In this condition the tire is completely floating on a film of water and no traction force is developed. The tire is said to be hydroplaning.

Dynamic Hydroplaning

With no traction between tire and pavement the brakes will lock and the wheel will "spin down" to zero revolutions per minute. The tire then "skates" or hydroplanes on the water surface and no braking or directional control is possible.

For dynamic hydroplaning of this type to occur, fluid must be present in sufficient depth that surface irregularities and tire tread are inadequate to eject fluid from the tire pavement interface. The speed at which dynamic hydroplaning occurs may be estimated by equating the tire normal load to the lift force developed by the fluid.[7]

$$F_n = (1/2)CA\rho v_c^2 \qquad (10.18)$$

F_n = tire normal load—pounds

C = tire lift coefficient

ρ = fluid density—slugs/foot^3

v_c = vehicle speed for hydroplaning—feet per second

A = tire contact area—square feet

Solution gives the critical speed v_c as:

$$v_c = \sqrt{2P/\rho C} \qquad (10.19)$$

$P = F_n/A$ = tire pressure—pounds per square foot

Using a typical value of $C = 0.7$, substituting ρ for water, 1.94 slugs/foot^3, and converting pressure to pounds per square inch, we obtain:

$$v_c = 14.6 \sqrt{P} \qquad (10.20)$$

v_c = critical planing speed—feet/second

P = tire pressure—pounds per square inch gauge.

The planing speed increases as the square root of the tire pressure. For a typical automobile tire, the critical planing speed is about 75 feet per second or about 50 miles per hour. Hydroplaning can clearly be serious in emergency stops from freeway speeds.

Although there is a critical speed for the onset of hydroplaning it *does not* follow that reduction of the speed below this value will cause planing to cease. Once planing has begun it can be sustained at speeds considerably below v_c.

Viscous Hydroplaning

The term viscous hydroplaning is used to describe the wide range of low friction conditions where the fluid depth or vehicle speed are insufficient to cause dynamic hydroplaning.[8] The pressures that support the planing tire are generated by viscous forces in a thin film of fluid. Pure viscous planing is obtained on very smooth surfaces with very shallow fluid depths. Being caused by viscous effects, it can not be remedied by improving the water drainage with tire or pavement grooving. Instead it is necessary to provide a harsher micro-texture to break down the viscous film. In most practical situations hydroplaning develops as a combination of both viscous and inertial forces.

Steering and Cornering Traction

The cornering force of a tire increases with slip angle α. Eventually the slip angle reaches a critical value beyond which an increase in slip angle no longer produces an increase in cornering force (for small slip angles the cornering force is linear with slip angle, justifying the assumptions made in chapter 8.) Figure 10-7 plots cornering friction factor versus slip angle for wet and dry pavements. The cornering friction factor is defined as the ratio of the available cornering force to the vehicle weight. Above the critical slip angle, the vehicle goes into a cornering skid and directional control is lost.

Combined Cornering and Braking

The required friction factor for combined cornering and braking of a rubber tired vehicle is equal to the vector sum of the friction factor required for braking and that required for cornering.[9] This is readily shown by taking the vector sum of the traction and cornering forces:

$$\mathbf{F}_t = \mathbf{F}_\alpha + \mathbf{F}_b \tag{10.21}$$

For small cornering angles, the cornering force and braking force are approximately perpendicular. Therefore:

$$F_t = \sqrt{F_\alpha^2 + F_b^2} \tag{10.22}$$

Substituting and assuming all wheels are braked:

$$F_b = f_0 W \tag{10.23}$$

$$F_\alpha = c\alpha W \tag{10.24}$$

f_0 = braking friction factor

c = cornering coefficient—pounds/pound degree slip

W = vehicle weight—pounds

α = slip angle—degrees

$$f_t = F_t/W = \sqrt{f_0^2 + c^2\alpha^2} \tag{10.25}$$

f_t = friction factor required for combined braking and cornering

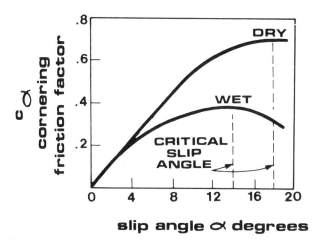

Source: "Tentative Skid-Resistance Requirements for Main Rural Highways," National Cooperative Highway Research Program Report 37, Highway Research Board, National Academy of Sciences, Washington, D. C., 1967, page 13. Reprinted with permission.

Figure 10-7. Cornering Coefficient versus Slip Angle for an Automobile Tire

If f_t exceeds the locked wheel friction factor as obtained from a braking friction factor curve, it may be assumed the vehicle may skid.

Traction for Steel Wheel on Rail Systems

Since hysteresis does not contribute to traction for steel wheel on rail systems, traction is commonly referred to as adhesion. The limiting value of adhesion is usually about 25 percent of the total weight on the wheels but can vary from as low as 10 percent to as high as 35 percent.[10] For braking, a value no greater than 15 percent is usually assumed. Adhesion can be greatly reduced by lubricants that are placed on the sides of the rails to reduce noise on curves and work their way onto the running surface.

Automated rail transit systems have experienced difficulty in maintaining adhesion levels high enough to prevent the wheels from sliding when the rails are wet. Wheel lock on a rail vehicle not only causes a rather piercing "screeching" noise, but produces flats on the steel wheels which cause the familiar "clackety clack" sound. This in turn leads to increased maintenance costs for wheel grinding.

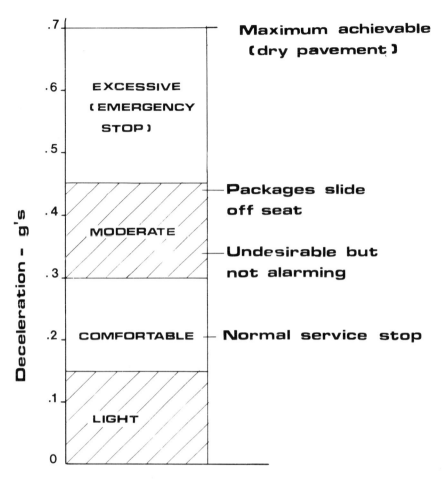

Source: Based on data from "Skid Resistance—National Cooperative Highway Research Program Synthesis of Highway Practice," Report 14, Highway Research Board, Washington D.C., 1972. Also, "Tentative Skid Resistance Requirements for Main Rural Highways," Report 37, National Cooperative Highway Research Program, Highway Research Board, Washington, D.C., 1967. Also, *Traffic Engineering Handbook*, 3rd edition, edited by John E. Baerwald, Institute of Traffic Engineers, Washington, D.C., 1965, pages 26-27.

Figure 10-8. Typical Deceleration Levels for Automobile Braking

Comfort Levels for Braking and Cornering

Even if adequate traction is available, it may be desirable to limit braking and cornering forces to avoid discomfort to the passengers. Table 10-3 summarizes longitudinal acceleration and braking levels commonly encountered in transit vehicles. Figure 10-8 characterizes the nature of

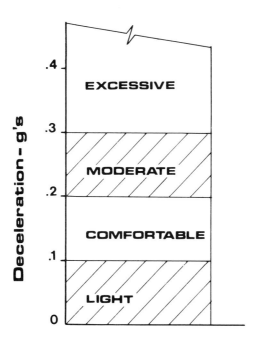

Source: Based on data from "Tentative Skid Resistance Requirements for Main Rural Highways," National Cooperative Highway Research Program Report 37, Highway Research Board, National Academy of Sciences, Washington, D.C. 1967.

Figure 10-9. Typical Lateral Acceleration Levels for Cornering in an Automobile

various deceleration levels in an automobile. Ordinarily drivers stop at less than 0.3 g and stops over 0.45 g may be classified as emergency or panic stops. Auto deceleration levels are below 0.5 g 99.8 percent of the time.[11]

Figure 10-9 characterizes automobile lateral accelerations. For seated persons, lateral accelerations up to 0.2 g appear satisfactory—although highway curves are usually designed to no more than 0.12 g. For vehicles with standing passengers, lateral accelerations are usually kept below 0.12 g. Conservative limits on acceleration and jerk are required for vehicles with standees—especially because of the difficulty which elderly people have in maintaining their balance. The major cause of all accidental deaths over age 65 is from falls.[12]

Table 10-3
Summary of Acceleration and Jerk Levels for Some Transportation Systems

System	Service Braking g	Emergency Braking g	Acceleration g	Jerk g/second
Frankfurt Subway[a]	0.175	0.365	0.145	
Montreal Metro[a]	0.113	0.138	0.113	
London Underground[a]	0.16	0.16	0.09	0.045
Penn Central Commuter[a]	0.103	0.113	0.103	
Munich Subway[a]	0.102	0.143	0.102	
Swiss Rapid Transit[a]	0.075		0.088	
NY Subway Car[b]	0.068-0.137	0.137	0.114	
BART Car[c]	0.124		0.137	0.068
Typical Rail Transit[d]	0.12-0.14	0.14-0.3	0.137	
Seattle Monorail[e]	0.150	0.260	0.114	
PCC Street Car[e]	0.143-0.165	0.273-0.320	0.165 average 0.196 maximum	
Trolley Coach[e]	0.171-0.205	0.593-0.615	0.137-0.177 average 0.158-0.217 maximum	
Motor Bus[e]	0.046-0.158	0.320-0.683	0.022-0.09 average 0.185-0.252 maximum	
Elevators (vertical)[f]	0.1-0.2 average 0.3 limit	2.5		
Aircraft-takeoff[f]			0.5	
Automobile[g]	0.25-0.3	0.43-0.7		

[a] "High Speed Rail Systems," TRW, Systems Group, Redondo Beach, Cal., PB 192506, February 1970.

[b] *Standard Handbook for Mechanical Engineers*, 7th Edition, T. Baumeister and L.S. Marks, McGraw-Hill Book Co., New York, 1967.

[c] "Personal Rapid Transit Station Design," R. Nathenson, Massachusetts Institute of Technology, Cambridge, Massachusetts, June 1972.

[d] "Acceleration and Comfort in Public Ground Transportation," J.W. Gebhard TPR002, John Hopkins University, Applied Physics Laboratory, Silver Spring, Md., February 1970.

[e] "Human Factors in High Speed Ground Transportation with Special Reference to Passenger Comfort and Safety," Ross A. McFarland, *High Speed Ground Transportation*, TRI-3, Carnegie-Mellon University, Pittsburgh, Pennsylvania, 1969.

[f] *Shock and Vibration Handbook*, Vol. III, C.M. Harris and C.E. Crede, McGraw-Hill Book Company, New York, 1961, pages 44-49.

[g] "Skid Resistance," National Cooperative Highway Research Program Synthesis of Highway Practice, Report 14 (1972) and "Tentative Skid Resistance Requirements for Main Rural Highways," NCHRP Report 37, (1967) Highway Research Board, National Academy of Sciences, Washington, D.C.; *Traffic Engineering Handbook*, edited by John E. Baerwald, 3rd Edition, Institute of Traffic Engineers, Washington, D.C., 1965, pages 26-27; and "Deceleration Distance for High Speed Vehicles," E.E. Wilson, Proceedings of Highway Research Board, Washington, D.C., 1940, pages 393-398.

Notes

1. *Machine Design*, 3rd edition, V.L. Maleev and J.B. Hartman, International Textbook Company, 1954, Scranton, Pennsylvania, page 365.

2. "Skid Resistance"—National Cooperative Highway Research Program Synthesis of Highway Practices Report 14, Highway Research Board, Washington, D.C., 1972.

3. "Tentative Skid-Resistance Requirements for Main Rural Highways," National Cooperative Highway Research Program Report 37, Highway Research Board, National Academy of Sciences, Washington, D.C., 1967.

4. See note 2.

5. See note 3.

6. See note 3.

7. "Frictional and Retarding Forces on Aircraft Tyres," Part III, Planing, ESDI 72008, Engineering Sciences Data Unit, London, August, 1972.

8. Ibid.

9. See note 3.

10. *Standard Handbook for Mechanical Engineers*, 7th edition, T. Baumeister and L.S. Marks, McGraw-Hill Book Company, New York, 1967, page 11-31.

11. "Hard Braking is More Common than You Might Think," Rudolf G. Mortimer, *Automotive Engineering*, New York, August 1971, page 32.

12. "Human Factors in High Speed Ground Transportation with Special Reference to Passenger Comfort and Safety," Ross A. McFarland, *High Speed Ground Transportation* TRI-3, Carnegie-Mellon University, Pittsburgh, 1969.

11 Ride Quality

Ride quality refers to how smooth and comfortable it is to ride in a transportation conveyance. It is a measure of the quality of the guideway surface and the performance of the vehicle suspension in isolating passengers from road vibrations. If the guideway condition is allowed to deteriorate, no vehicle will be able to deliver a good ride. Similarly with a poor suspension, the best guideway can not produce a comfortable ride.

When budgets are squeezed, the first area to be cut back is often guideway maintenance so that in these days of mounting deficits, poor ride quality is far from unusual.

There is more than comfort at stake in a smooth ride, although comfort is certainly a major objective. A rough ride subjects the steering mechanism, electronics, and all other vehicle parts to a severe environment. Fatigue life is shortened, nuts and screws are shaken loose, and solder joints fail.

In sum, total vehicle reliability and service life suffer from poor ride control.

Terminology

Figure 11-1 shows the terminology generally used to describe ride quality.[1] Vertical vibration is perhaps the most obvious and is caused by bumps or undulations in the guideway. Vertical vibration is frequently refered to as "heave." Since the vehicle often is supported at two points along its longitudinal axis it can oscillate like a see-saw as well as just up and down. This see-saw motion is called "pitch." Lateral or sideways vibration can be caused by rail misalignment or by irregularities in the lateral guiding surface. Lateral vibration for an automobile or bus is almost entirely caused by vehicle response to steering wheel inputs (e.g., centrifugal forces), and by wind gusts. Longitudinal vibrations may be caused by the hunting characteristics of automatic propulsion and braking control systems. Finally the vehicle can "roll" about a longitudinal axis or it can "yaw" about a vertical axis through its center of gravity.

This gives a total of 6 degrees of freedom for the cab of the vehicle. But this is just the beginning! The cab is usually supported by wheels connected to the cab through a variety of springs and bushings. Associated with the

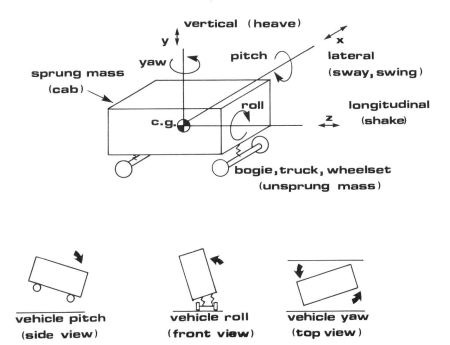

Figure 11-1. Vehicle Ride Terminology

wheels and "unsprung" weight may be axle housings, axles, brakes, and sometimes propulsion gear. This combination of unsprung weight is called a "bogie" or "truck" on a railroad car and a wheelset on an automobile.

Obviously the truck or bogie is free to oscillate independent of the vehicle chassis—thus we have another 6 degrees of freedom associated with each wheelset. So far we have 18 degrees of freedom. But why stop there? The vehicle chassis itself is not really a rigid body. We may want to consider its bending and torsional vibration modes. The problem can rapidly become complicated—although today's standard computer programs for dynamic analysis can routinely handle the most complex of these systems.

Analysis of Suspension Dynamics

What we seek in this book, however, is insight into the nature of the suspension problem—and this is perhaps facilitated by simplifying the problem. Let us consider first a simple single degree of freedom analysis as shown by Figure 11-2. The assumptions are:

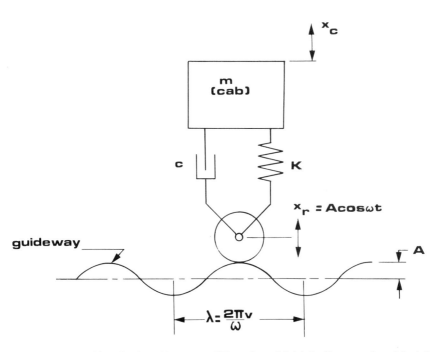

Figure 11-2. Simple One Degree of Freedom Vehicle Suspension Model

1. Only the heave response is of concern.
2. The unsprung weight is negligible.

Since heave usually has the lowest frequency response, this simple analysis can give valuable insight into the nature of a damped suspension system. As can be seen in Figure 11-2 the spring constant is K and the damping constant c. If the vehicle has a spring and shock absorber at each wheel for a total of n wheels:

$$K = nK_1 \tag{11.1}$$

$$c = nc_1 \tag{11.2}$$

$K_1 =$ spring constant for one wheel

$c_1 =$ damping constant for one wheel

The equation of motion for this simple system is given by:

$$\frac{m\,d^2x_c}{dt^2} = \frac{-c\,d(x_c - x_r)}{dt} - K(x_c - x_r) \tag{11.3}$$

substituting:

$$x_r = A \cos \omega t \tag{11.4}$$

$$\frac{dx_r}{dt} = -A\omega \sin \omega t \tag{11.5}$$

$$\frac{m\, d^2x_c}{dt^2} + \frac{c\, dx_c}{dt} + Kx_c = KA \cos \omega t - cA\omega \sin \omega t \tag{11.6}$$

The solution of this differential equation has two parts. The general solution is obtained by setting the left hand side of the expression equal to zero. It gives the transient response of the system. The general solution of equation 11.6 is of the form:

$$x_c = K_1 e^{P_1 t} + K_2 e^{P_2 t} \tag{11.7}$$

where

$$P_1 = \frac{c}{2m} + \sqrt{\left(\frac{c}{2m}\right)^2 - \frac{K}{m}} \tag{11.8}$$

$$P_2 = \frac{c}{2m} - \sqrt{\left(\frac{c}{2m}\right)^2 - \frac{K}{m}} \tag{11.9}$$

In order to get a sinusoidal oscillation, P_1 and P_2 must contain imaginary terms. Since $c/2m$ is always real this means the expression under the square root determines the frequency of oscillation. The system will oscillate at a rate ω_d providing that:

$$\omega_d^2 \equiv [K/m - (c/2m)^2] > 0 \tag{11.10}$$

When ω_d equals zero, the system has just enough damping to prevent any oscillating transient response. Such a system, if displaced, will return to its equilibrium position and come to rest. The response is shown in Figure 11-3a. The system is said to be critically damped if $\omega_d = 0$. The critical damping constant c_c may be found to be:

$$c_c = 2m\sqrt{K/m} = 2\sqrt{Km} \tag{11.11}$$

If c_c is zero, the system will theoretically oscillate forever if it is disturbed. The undamped natural frequency ω_n expressed in radians per second, is obtained by setting c equal to zero in equation 11.10:

$$\omega_n = \sqrt{K/m} \tag{11.12}$$

The response is shown in Figure 11-3b. Any real vehicle suspension will have a damping constant between 0 and c_c, and its response will be a damped sinusoid as shown in Figure 11-3c.

The particular solution to equation 11.6 represents the steady state response to a guideway disturbance $x_r = A \cos \omega t$. It will be of the form:

$$x_c = B \cos (\omega t + \phi) \tag{11.13}$$

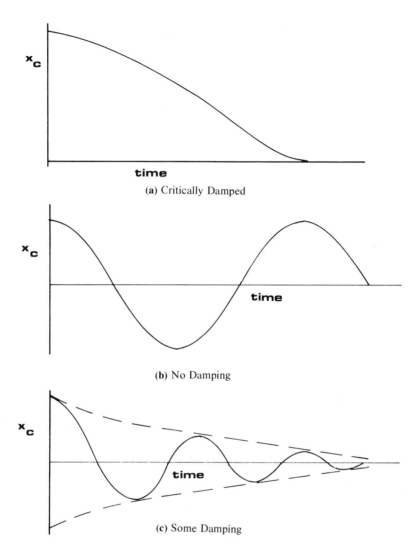

Figure 11-3. Transient Response of a Suspension

Substitution of equation 11.13 into equation 11.6 yields after some simplification:[2]

$$\frac{B}{A} = \sqrt{\frac{1 + (2\mu z)^2}{(2\mu z)^2 + (1 - z^2)^2}} \tag{11.14}$$

$z = \omega/\omega_n$ = ratio of forcing frequency to undamped natural frequency

$\mu = c/c_c =$ percent of critical damping (expressed as a decimal fraction)

The ratio B/A is defined as the "transmissibility" and gives the amount of guideway vibration transmitted from the road to the vehicle. Notice that the maximum amplitude of the vibration velocity and acceleration relate directly to A and B:

$$\frac{\text{maximum vehicle vibration displacement}}{\text{maximum guideway vibration displacement}} = \frac{B}{A} \qquad (11.15)$$

$$\frac{\text{maximum vehicle vibration velocity}}{\text{maximum guideway vibration velocity}} = \frac{\omega B}{\omega A} = \frac{B}{A} \qquad (11.16)$$

$$\frac{\text{maximum vehicle acceleration}}{\text{maximum guideway acceleration}} = \frac{\omega^2 B}{\omega^2 A} = \frac{B}{A} \qquad (11.17)$$

Thus the transmissibility is identical whether the stimulus is an acceleration, a velocity, or a displacement. Figure 11-4 shows the transmissibility versus frequency ratio for various damping ratios. Notice that regardless of damping ratio the transmissibility will be unity at $\sqrt{2}$ times the undamped natural frequency. Below this value the transmissibility is always greater than one, meaning that the suspension *amplifies*, rather than isolating, disturbances below $\sqrt{2}$ times the natural frequency.

The transmissibility is a maximum at the damped natural frequency, which can be readily shown to occur at:

$$z_d = \sqrt{1 - \mu^2} \qquad (11.18)$$

$z_d = \omega_d/\omega_n =$ frequency ratio for maximum transmissibility

Below the damped natural frequency, the transmissibility decreases again, reaching a value of unity when the frequency becomes zero.

If there is no damping, ($\mu = 0$), the transmissibility relationship simplifies to:

$$B/A = 1/|1 - z^2| \qquad (11.19)$$

In this case the transmissibility at the natural frequency, ($z = 1$), is infinite. As damping is added to the system, the transmissibility at resonance is decreased—but at the expense of increasing the transmissibility for values of z above $\sqrt{2}$. In short, stiff shock absorbers improve the low frequency response but make the high frequency ride harsher. The response at the higher frequencies may be estimated by expanding the denominator of equation 11.14:

$$\frac{B}{A} = \sqrt{\frac{1 + (2\mu z)^2}{(2\mu z)^2 + 1 - 2z^2 + z^4}} \qquad (11.20)$$

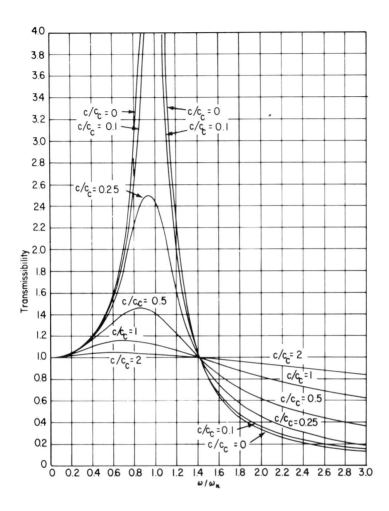

Source: *Mechanical Vibrations*, Austin H. Church, John Wiley and Sons, New York, 1957, page 89. Reprinted with permission.

Figure 11-4. Transmissibility for a Damped Single Degree of Freedom System

Assuming $z \gg 1$ and $z \gg 1/2\mu$, which is valid for most damping ratios of interest, equation 11.20 simplifies to:

$$B/A = \sqrt{2\mu}/z \qquad (11.21)$$

Thus the high frequency response is assymptotic to zero and inversely proportional to frequency. To summarize:

1. No reduction in road disturbance is possible below 1.414 times the undamped natural frequency of the suspension. To the contrary the signal is amplified.

2. Adding damping reduces the transmitted amplitude below 1.414 times the natural frequency but increases it above 1.414 times the natural frequency.

3. The higher the frequency, the less signal is transmittted by the suspension to the vehicle.

One might think that it would be desirable to have a suspension with as low a natural frequency as possible in order to minimize the transmitted vibration. In practice, however, this causes problems. Assuming the suspension must absorb 0.5 g vehicle dynamic loads without bottoming, the maximum deflection is given by:

$$0.5mg = Kx \qquad (11.22)$$

m = vehicle mass—slugs

g = gravity constant—feet/second^2

K = spring constant—pounds/inch

x = deflection—inches

Substituting for K/m in terms of the suspension undamped natural frequency yields:

$$x = 4.888/f_n^2 \qquad (11.23)$$

$f_n = 2\pi\omega_n$ = undamped natural frequency—hertz

In other words, if the undamped natural frequency is one hertz, a maximum excursion of almost five inches is required. Space constraints thus limit how low a resonance is feasible. In addition, a low resonance will cause the vehicle to roll excessively on curves producing poor road holding characteristics.

Another reason to avoid suspension resonances too much below 1 hertz is motion sickness. Motion sickness in automobiles, ships, and planes appears to be caused by very low frequency but high amplitude vibrations. Alexander et al. report on having observed motion sickness with 13 cycles per minute (0.2 Hz) vibrations with an amplitude of $\pm$ 0.2 g's. For these reasons, the practical lower limit on suspension resonance is about 1 hertz.

Handling More Than One Driving Function

The equation for the damped single degree of freedom system was written for a single sinusoidal driving function. If there are more than one sinusoidal driving functions, the equation is unchanged. Since the system is linear, the principle of superposition may be used. The transmissibility is thus valid for any driving function that can be represented by a Fourier series.

Chassis Stiffness

It is important that the frame or chassis be sufficiently stiff that its resonance is well above the suspension natural frequency, so it is not excited by transmitted road vibrations. The first resonance of a simply supported beam is given by:[3]

$$f = 1.57 \sqrt{gEI/wL^4} \qquad (11.24)$$

g = gravity constant—inches/second^2

E = modulus of elasticity—pounds per square inch

I = moment of inertia—inches^4

w = weight of vehicle —pounds/inch

L = length of vehicle—inches

The static deflection of such a beam under its own weight is given by:[4]

$$\delta = 5wL^4/384EI \qquad (11.25)$$

δ = static deflection at midpoint of vehicle—inches

From substitution of 11.24 into 11.25 we obtain:

$$f = 3.5/\sqrt{\delta} \qquad (11.26)$$

In other words, the natural frequency of the vehicle is inversely proportional to the square root of its deflection.[5] To provide adequate isolation, assume the transmissibility at the resonant frequency of the chassis should be no more than 10 percent. In that case from equation 11.21 and assuming 50 percent of critical damping:

$$z = \sqrt{2 \times 0.5}/0.1 = 10 \qquad (11.27)$$

This means the chassis resonance should be 10 times the suspension resonance. For a suspension resonance of 1 hertz, equation 11.26 indicates the midspan static deflection should be less than 1/8 inch. A similar approach may be used to determine the torsional rigidity requirement.

Effect of Unsprung Mass

Thus far we have ignored the effect of unsprung weight. To get some idea of the effect of the primary suspension stiffness and unsprung weight on ride characteristics, it is worthwhile to consider a simple two degree of freedom analysis. Figure 11.5 shows the model to be analyzed. As before, we ignore pitch and roll and consider only the heave mode of vibration. For simplicity in this case we also have ignored the effects of damping. With these assumptions the governing differential equations are:

$$m_w \, d^2x_w/dt^2 + K_w(x_w - A\cos\omega t) + K(x_w - x_c) = 0 \qquad (11.28)$$

$$m \, d^2x_c/dt^2 - K(x_w - x_c) = 0 \qquad (11.29)$$

x_w = deflection of unsprung mass—feet

x_c = deflection of vehicle chassis or sprung mass—feet

K_w = primary suspension stiffness—pounds/foot

K = secondary suspension stiffness—pounds/foot

m_w = unsprung mass—slugs

m = sprung mass—slugs

As an example, the primary suspension corresponds to the tires on an automobile. The unsprung mass consists of the tires, wheels, brake assemblies, and, depending on the design of the suspension, the rear axles and housings and the differential. The sprung mass is the vehicle chassis and body including the engine and transmission. The secondary suspension is composed usually of coil or leaf springs.

If there is no damping, the masses vibrate either in phase or 180° out of phase, so the solution is of the form:

$$x_c = B\cos\omega t \qquad (11.30)$$

$$x_w = C\cos\omega t \qquad (11.31)$$

Substituting in equations 11.28 and 11.29:

$$\begin{vmatrix} K + K_w - m_w\omega^2 & -K \\ -K & K - m\omega^2 \end{vmatrix} \begin{vmatrix} C \\ B \end{vmatrix} = \begin{vmatrix} K_wA \\ 0 \end{vmatrix} \qquad (11.32)$$

To find the resonances, it is sufficient to set the determinant of the left hand matrix equal to zero:

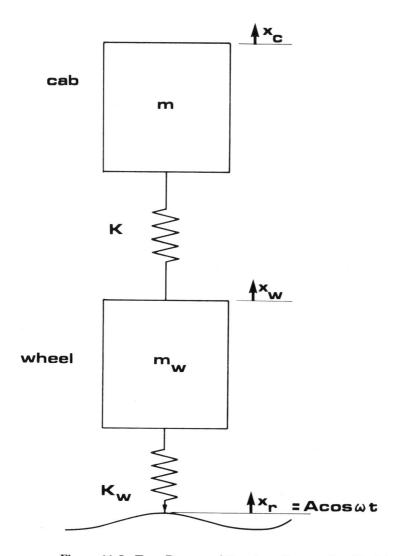

Figure 11-5. Two Degree of Freedom Suspension Model

$$\omega^4 - \left(\frac{K + K_w}{m_w} + \frac{K}{m}\right)\omega^2 + \frac{KK_w}{mm_w} = 0 \qquad (11.33)$$

Therefore:

$$\omega^2 = \frac{K + K_w}{2m_w} + \frac{K}{2m} \pm \sqrt{\left(\frac{K + K_w}{2m_w} + \frac{K}{2m}\right)^2 - \frac{KK_w}{mm_w}} \quad (11.34)$$

Equation 11.34 gives the exact solution for the two natural frequencies of the system. It is too complex, however, to offer much physical insight. To simplify it we multiply both sides by m_w/K_w to obtain:

$$\frac{m_w\omega^2}{K_w} = \frac{K + K_w}{2K_w} + \frac{Km_w}{2mK_w} \pm \sqrt{\left(\frac{K + K_w}{2K_w} + \frac{Km_w}{2mK_w}\right)^2 - \frac{m_wK}{mK_w}} \quad (11.35)$$

Usually, the primary suspension is much stiffer than the secondary suspension and the unsprung mass is much less than the sprung mass. Thus:

$$Km_w/K_wm << 1 = \varepsilon \quad (11.36)$$

Substituting $Km_w/K_wm = \varepsilon$ in equation 11.35 one obtains after some simplification:

$$\omega_1^2 \approx \frac{KK_w}{m(K + K_w)} \quad (11.37)$$

and:

$$\omega_2^2 \approx \frac{K + K_w}{m_w} \quad (11.38)$$

Therefore the first two resonant frequencies are:

$$f_1 \approx \frac{1}{2\pi} \sqrt{\frac{KK_w}{m(K + K_w)}} \quad (11.39)$$

$$f_2 \approx \frac{1}{2\pi} \sqrt{\frac{K + K_w}{m_w}} \quad (11.40)$$

Notice that if $K << K_w$, we can still further simplify these expressions to:

$$f_1 \approx \frac{1}{2\pi} \sqrt{\frac{K}{m}} \quad (11.41)$$

$$f_2 \approx \frac{1}{2\pi} \sqrt{\frac{K_w}{m_w}} \quad (11.42)$$

We can now see the nature of the two resonant frequencies. The first is associated with the secondary suspension. It is approximately the same as the undamped natural frequency of a single degree of freedom system. The second is associated with the primary suspension stiffness and unsprung weight. Figure 11-6 plots the response for an undamped system. In a real system with damping the resonances will be attenuated as indicated by the dotted line. Typically the secondary suspension produces the first resonance at 1-2 hertz and the primary suspension produces its resonance at about 10-15 hertz (for a rubber tired vehicle).

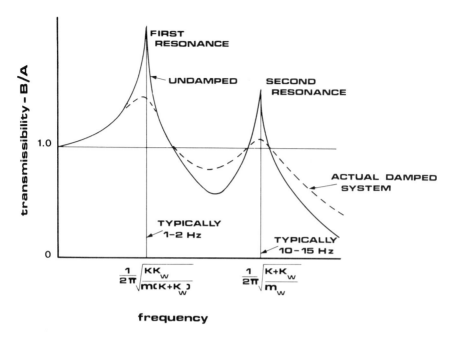

Figure 11-6. Transmissibility of a Two Degree of Freedom Suspension

Wheel Hop

Wheel hop occurs when the wheel loses contact with the guideway. Under such conditions, traction is lost. Wheel hop is therefore not only uncomfortable but dangerous. To prevent wheel hop, the force between the pavement and the ground must always be positive. Therefore the acceleration of the unsprung mass should never exceed 1 g.

Effect of Vehicle Speed on Forcing Frequency

A guideway with surface irregularities of period λ will impart a frequency $f = v/\lambda$ to the vehicle suspension, if the vehicle is travelling at a speed v.

When the vehicle speeds up, the wave length of the forcing function at a given frequency is increased. Since the amplitude of a road irregularity tends to be proportional to its wave length, this means that the input disturbance at a given frequency increases with vehicle speed. It thus becomes increasingly difficult to maintain satisfactory ride quality as vehicle speed is increased.

Computing Natural Frequencies for a Vehicle

The computation of the secondary suspension natural frequency for mechanical springs is quite straightforward. K for the vehicle is simply the sum of the spring constants of all the springs supporting the vehicle weight. Computation of the spring constant is obtained for standard spring shapes and designs from any engineering handbook.

The analysis of the spring constant for automobile tires and for air springs is more interesting and will be treated here.

Air Springs

Figure 11-7 shows a schematic of an air spring consisting of a piston in an enclosed volume V_1. An increase in force ΔF causes a decrease in volume ΔV. From the perfect gas equations for adiabatic compression:

$$P_2 = \left(\frac{V_1}{V_1 - \Delta V} \right)^{\gamma} P_1 \qquad (11.43)$$

$P_2, P_1 =$ initial and final absolute pressures

$\gamma =$ ratio of specific heats

Therefore:

$$\Delta F = (P_2 - P_1)A = \left[\left(\frac{V_1}{V_1 - \Delta V} \right)^{\gamma} - 1 \right] P_1 A \qquad (11.44)$$

$A =$ cross sectional area of piston

For small values of ΔV:

$$\Delta F = \left[\left(1 + \frac{\Delta V}{V_1} \right)^{\gamma} - 1 \right] P_1 A \approx \frac{\gamma \Delta V P_1 A}{V_1} \qquad (11.45)$$

Since the deflection Δx is equal to $\Delta V / A$:

$$\frac{\Delta F}{\Delta x} = K = \frac{\gamma P_1 A^2}{V_1} \qquad (11.46)$$

Equation 11.46 gives the stiffness of an airbag in terms of its volume, pressure and area.[6] Notice that because the perfect gas law was used in deriving equation 11.46, it is necessary to use the *absolute* rather than the gauge pressure in the expression (thus if the airbag pressure is 10 psi above atmospheric, P_1 should be 24.7 psia $\times$ 144 = 3567 pounds/square foot absolute). Notice also that the units of equation 11.46 are pounds, feet, and seconds.

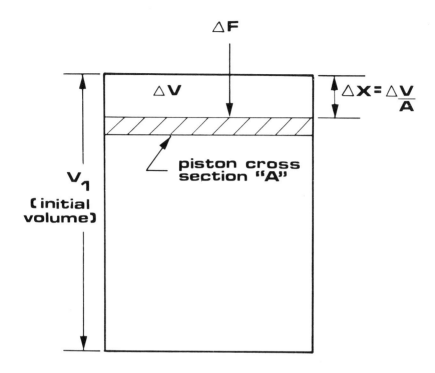

Figure 11-7. Schematic of Airspring

Equation 11.46 not only gives the spring constant for airbags, but it is sometimes used to estimate the spring constant for air cushions.[7] In this case V_1 is the plenum chamber volume and A the cushion area. P_1 again is the *absolute* cushion pressure in *pounds per square foot*.

Tire Stiffness Estimation

Unlike the air spring, the primary factor influencing the increase in load carrying capacity for a tire is not an increase in the tire pressure, but rather a change in the footprint area. The tire pressure hardly changes at all from no load to full load—it is the footprint area that changes. Thus we can approximate the tire stiffness by assuming the pressure stays constant. Figure 11-8 shows a tire in contact with the ground. The load supported by the tire is given by:

$$F = P_g A \qquad (11.47)$$

P_g = tire pressure above atmospheric—pounds/square foot

A = footprint area—feet

Notice in this case the pressure is *not* absolute. From Figure 11-8, the relation between deflection and footprint area is given by the Pythagorean theorem:

$$(R - x)^2 = R^2 - (A/2t)^2 \qquad (11.48)$$

R = radius of undeflected tire—feet

t = width of tire footprint—feet

For small values of x compared to R this simplifies to:

$$A^2 = 8Rt^2x \qquad (11.49)$$

Accordingly:

$$\frac{dA}{dx} = \frac{4Rt^2}{A} \qquad (11.50)$$

The spring constant, assuming a constant pressure is then:

$$K = \frac{dF}{dx} = \frac{P_g\,dA}{dx} = \frac{4P_gRt^2}{A} \qquad (11.51)$$

Equation 11.51 may be used to compute tire stiffness. Consider a 4000 pound car with four tires inflated to 24 pounds/inch² gauge. The footprint area of each tire is given by:

$$A = \frac{GVW}{nP_g} = \frac{4000}{4 \times 24 \times 144} = 0.29 \text{ feet}^2$$

GVW = vehicle gross weight—pounds

P_g = tire pressure—pounds/foot²

n = number of tires

Assume the tread width is 6 inches and the tire diameter is 24 inches. Then substituting directly in equation 11.51 we obtain K equals 11,917 pounds per foot or 993 pounds per inch. Assuming a total unsprung weight of 5 percent of the vehicle weight, the tire resonant frequency will be about 14 hertz.

Janeway Ride Comfort Theory

In 1948, R.N. Janeway proposed an empirically derived theory relating

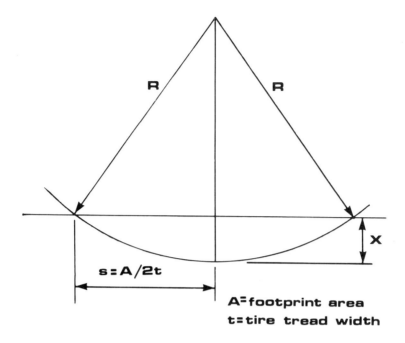

Figure 11-8. Geometric Relationship between Tire Radius, Tire Deflection, and Tire Footprint

vibration levels to passenger comfort.[8] Despite its inadequacies, it is still the accepted theory today and has been the basis for virtually every vehicle procurement specification written in recent years. The International Standards Organization has proposed vibration tolerance standards which continue to follow in the main Janeway's approach.[9]

Janeway reviewed vibration data collected by others. In general this data had been obtained by vibrating seated subjects on a shake table at a single pure tone sinusoidal frequency. The vibration amplitude was gradually increased and the subjective reaction of the person under test noted. Janeway claimed that the data he examined justified the division of vibration tolerance into three specific zones. Between 1 and 6 hertz, he found the acceptable amplitude for vertical[a] vibration to be given by:

$$A = 480/\omega^3 \approx 2/f^3 \qquad (11.52)$$

A = half amplitude of the sinusoidal excitation—*inches* (i.e., $x = A \sin \omega t$)

---

[a] Vertical vibration means in a direction parallel to the spiral cord.

From 6 to 20 hertz, he found the acceptable amplitude for vertical vibration to be given by:

$$A = 12.72/\omega^2 \approx 1/3f^2 \qquad (11.53)$$

Above 20 hertz the acceptable amplitude for vertical vibration was limited by the relationship:

$$A = 0.105/\omega \approx 1/60f \qquad (11.54)$$

Thus at 1 hertz, the allowable deflection was 2 inches, at 10 hertz, 0.003 inches, and at 30 hertz, 0.0005 inches. Figure 11-9 is a plot of Janeway's data showing the three zones. Present practice is usually to plot allowable peak acceleration rather than deflection as was done by Janeway. In terms of acceleration:

$$g_{max} = \omega^2 A/386 \qquad (11.55)$$

g_{max} = allowable acceleration—g's

ω = frequency—radians/second

A = allowable amplitude—inches

Janeway's theory may be stated in terms of acceleration as follows

$$1\text{-}6 \text{ Hz}: g_{max} = 0.20/f \qquad (11.56)$$

$$6\text{-}20 \text{ Hz}: g_{max} = 0.034 \qquad (11.57)$$

$$>20 \text{ Hz}: g_{max} = 0.0017f \qquad (11.58)$$

Figure 11-10 plots relationships 11.56 through 11.58 on log-log paper. This is the way in which ride quality data is usually presented today.

Notice that equation 11.56 is equivalent to specifying a constant jerk limit of 1.257 g/second. Equation 11.57 specifies a constant acceleration limit of 0.034 g's. And equation 11.58 is equivalent to specifying a maximum disturbance velocity of 0.0087 feet/second. Janeway spoke of jerk governing from 1-6 hertz, acceleration from 6-20 hertz, and disturbance velocity above 20 hertz.

On a log-log plot such as Figure 11-10, the constant jerk plots as a negative sloping 45 degree line, while the constant acceleration is of course a straight line, and the constant disturbance velocity limitation a positive sloping 45 degree line.

Many other ride comfort standards are now used, but most follow the basic Janeway approach. For example, the Japanese performed research to determine ride quality for the New Tokaido high speed railroad line, which has perhaps the highest railroad speeds in the world. They developed a set of curves following Janeway's general concept identified numerically as:

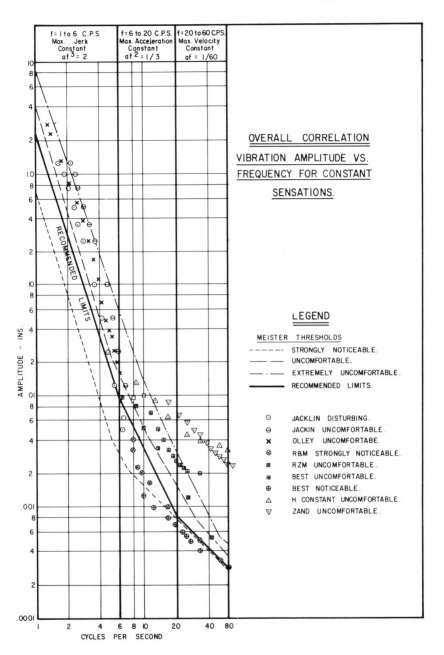

Source: "Vehicle Vibration Limits to Fit the Passenger," R.M. Janeway, Society of Automotive Engineers National Passenger Car and Production Meeting, March 3-5, Detroit, 1948, Report SAE SP-15, Figure 17. Reprinted with permission.

Figure 11-9. Janeway Ride Quality Data

Less than 1—excellent ride quality

1-1.5—good ride quality

1.5-2—not good ride quality

Above 2—bad ride quality

Figure 11-11 shows the Japanese ride quality curves. Like Janeway's, the slope is 45 degrees negative below 6 hertz and 45 degrees positive above 20 hertz.

ISO Proposed Ride Quality Standards

Figure 11-12 shows the ride quality standards for vertical vibration proposed by the International Organization for Standardization. The levels shown are the "reduced comfort boundary" related to difficulties in eating, reading, and writing that would normally govern in transportation situations[b]. Notice the level of vibration is related to the exposure time—higher levels being tolerable for shorter periods of time. The slope of the ISO curve at low frequencies is negative, but is not 45 degrees as specified by Janeway. Also the boundaries of the constant acceleration zone have been reduced to 4-8 hertz instead of Janeway's 6-20 hertz. Above 8 hertz the slope is 45 degrees upwards, following the Janeway theory.

Computing Ride Quality with More Than One Frequency

Ride tolerance curves are obtained by subjecting individuals to a single frequency vibration, increasing the amplitude by degrees, and recording the subject's reactions. What do we do when we have more than one frequency at once? What then is the subjective reaction? How do the different frequencies interact? It's impossible to collect data for every possible combination of frequencies and amplitudes. The truth is that we don't really have a completely satisfactory answer to this question. One approach, as proposed by the International Standards Organization,[10] is to assume the multiple frequency vibration is equivalent to a fictitious vibration at only a single frequency, the baseline or reference frequency. This reference frequency is usually chosen in the range of 4-8 hertz where

---

[b]To permit comparison with the Janeway theory, the ordinate is shown as peak acceleration—rather than rms acceleration as used in the ISO curves. This represents the peak acceleration of a single pure tone sinusoid—not the peak acceleration of a multiple frequency signal over some finite time period. Thus the ordinate may be converted to rms values as given in the referenced ISO standard by simply dividing by $\sqrt{2}$.

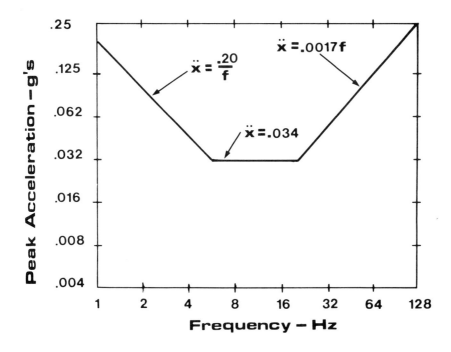

Figure 11-10. Janeway Ride Quality Curves Plotted in Terms of Acceleration

individuals have been found to have the lowest tolerance to vibration. The amplitude of each of the forcing frequencies is weighted by a number equal to the ratio of the tolerance to vibration at the baseline frequency divided by the tolerance to vibration at the forcing frequency. The amplitude of the single fictitious vibration is then equal to the square root of the sum of the squares of the weighted amplitudes at each frequency. In other words:

$$A_f^2 = \sum_{i=1}^{n} \left(\frac{C_f}{C_i} A_i \right)^2 \qquad (11.59)$$

A_f = amplitude of fictitious reference frequency

C_f = vibration tolerance from ride quality curve at reference frequency

C_i = vibration tolerance from ride quality curve at ith forcing frequency

A_i = amplitude of ith forcing frequency

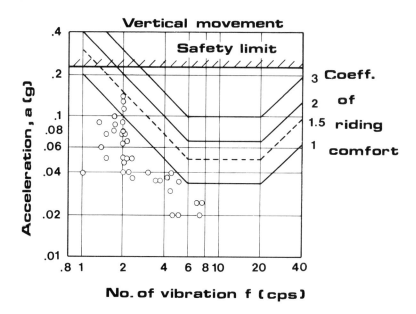

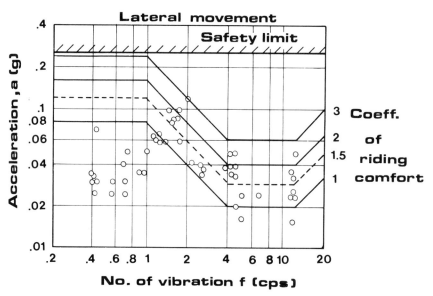

Source: Reprinted from "Survey of Technology for High Speed Transport," PB 168648, Massachusetts Institute of Technology, Cambridge, Massachusetts, June 15, 1965, page V-141.

Figure 11-11. Japanese Ride Quality Curves

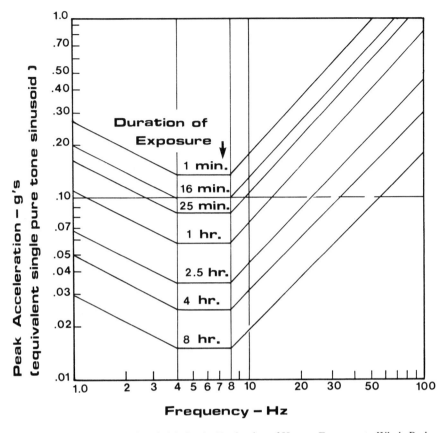

Source: Based upon curve in "Guide for the Evaluation of Human Exposure to Whole Body Vibration," Proposed International Standard ISO 2631, February 1974, page 10.

Figure 11-12. Ride Quality Standards Proposed by the International Organization for Standardization (vertical motion reduced comfort regime)

The value of A_f must not exceed the tolerance level C_f for an acceptable ride.

Consider an example in which the amplitudes of vibration transmitted through the suspension to the vehicle are given by:

$$A_1 = 0.02 \text{ g at } 1 \text{ Hz}$$

$$A_2 = 0.012 \text{ g at } 6 \text{ Hz}$$

Using the ride quality tolerances from Figure 11-12 for an 8 hour exposure, C_f equals C_2 equals 0.015 g, and C_1 equals 0.03 g. Thus:

$$A_f = \sqrt{(0.015 \times 0.02/0.03)^2 + (0.015 \times 0.012/0.015)^2}$$

$$= \quad 0.0156 \text{ g} \tag{11.60}$$

Thus the ride quality exceeds the permissible level, even though the acceleration at each frequency taken separately is within the allowable limit.

Another simpler method, also suggested by the International Standards Organization, simply requires that each separate vibration excitation be below the maximum permissible level at its frequency. This theory assumes that the effect of two vibrations at different frequencies is no different from the effects of each one acting by itself—which seems questionable. According to this theory the previous example with 0.02 g at 1 hertz and 0.012 g at 6 hertz *would* satisfy the ISO tolerance curves. It is clear that further research in this area is required to substantiate an appropriate technique for combining multiple frequency excitations.

Power Spectral Density

Thus far we have assumed the guideway irregularity to be composed of a discrete number of frequencies. An actual surface, of course, consists of all frequencies. Figure 11-13 shows a typical displacement versus distance plot for a guideway surface. If a vehicle travels on this surface at a speed v, the distance plot may be converted to a time plot by dividing it by the vehicle speed.

To convert this amplitude-time curve into an amplitude frequency curve, we pass this data through n perfect band pass filters[c], each of band width B_i. The band widths are chosen to cover the entire frequency range over which significant roughness is anticipated.

Having passed the surface roughness data through the bandpass filters, we now have n traces of roughness data. The mean square response for each of these traces is computed as:[11]

$$\sigma^2 = \frac{1}{T}\int_0^T (F_n(t))^2 \, dt \tag{11.61}$$

It is readily computed by squaring and numerically integrating the filtered data. The "Power Spectral Density" is defined as the limiting value of the mean square response of an ideal bandpass filter divided by the bandwidth B of the filter—as B approaches zero.[12]

For the filtered data we are considering, the *PSD* is approximately given by:

$$PSD = \sigma^2/B \tag{11.62}$$

---

[c] We assume the bandpass filter has unity gain within the frequency range and 0 gain outside of it.

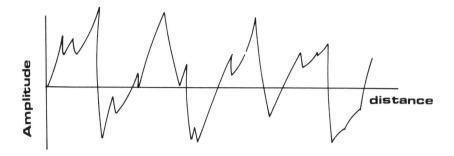

Figure 11-13. Typical Amplitude-Distance Plot for a Guideway Surface

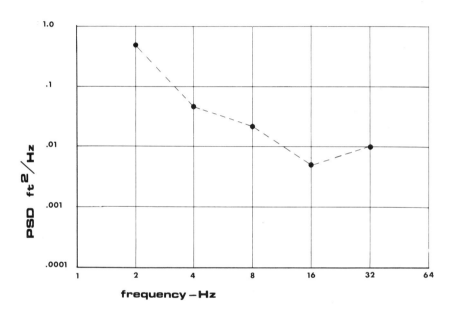

Figure 11-14. Typical Approximate Power Spectral Density Curve Obtained by Filtering and Processing Frequency Time Data

By plotting the *n* values for the *PSD* versus the frequency we obtain a power spectral density curve (Figure 11-14). This curve is only approximate since we did not use an infinite number of band pass filters.

Spatial PSDs

Power spectral density data is frequently obtained from an actual surface using the approach outlined. To eliminate the velocity at which the data was taken, the data is frequently plotted in spatial, rather than frequency terms. The relationship between frequency, wave length, and velocity is given by:

$$f = v/\lambda \tag{11.63}$$

To eliminate the effect of velocity, we define a new frequency f' as the "spatial frequency":

$$f' = \frac{1}{\lambda} \frac{\text{cycles}}{\text{foot}} = \frac{f}{v} \tag{11.64}$$

The spatial power spectral density is thus defined as:

$$PSD' = \sigma^2/B' = v\,PSD \tag{11.65}$$

B' = the band width—cycles per foot

PSD' = spatial power spectral density—feet^2/cycle/foot

σ = rms amplitude—feet

To convert a spatial power spectral density plot to the frequency domain, we simply multiply the abscissa by the vehicle speed in feet per second and divide the ordinate by the vehicle speed in feet per second.

Relationship between PSD and Peak Amplitudes

What should be the peak amplitude of n constant amplitude sinusoidal oscillations at the center band frequency of each of our filters, in order to obtain a response approximately equivalent to the original data? If the original signal was made up of n sinusoidal vibrations each at the center band frequency of the band pass filters, then the mean square response of each filter would have been:

$$F_i(t) = A_i \sin 2\pi f_i t \tag{11.66}$$

$$\sigma_i^2 = f_i \int_0^{1/f_i} A_i^2 \sin^2 (2\pi f_i t)\, dt = \frac{A_i^2}{2} \tag{11.67}$$

A sinusoidal function at the center band frequency f_i with a constant peak amplitude of $\sqrt{2}\sigma$ will thus have the same rms amplitude as the actual $F(t)$ which consists of all frequencies in the band width and has amplitudes varying randomly with time.

We can thus relate the power spectral density to the peak acceleration

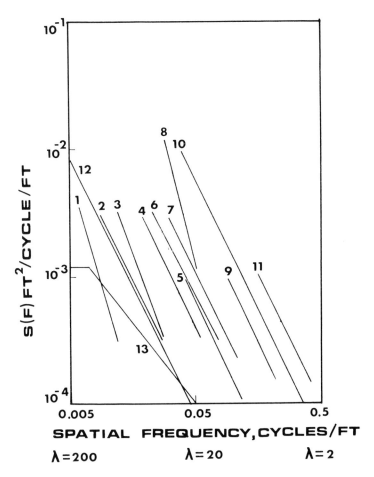

Source: Reprinted from "High Speed Rail Systems," TRW Systems Group, PB 192506, Redondo Beach, California, February 1970, Figure 6.4.7, page 4-15.

Figure 11-15. *PSD* Plots for Typical Guideway Surfaces (numbers relate to Table 11-1)

of a hypothetical constant amplitude vibration at the center band frequency:

$$PSD \equiv \sigma_i^2/B_i = A_i^2/2B_i \tag{11.68}$$

or

$$A_i = \sqrt{2B_i PSD} \tag{11.69}$$

Equations 11.68 and 11.69 permit us to relate peak amplitude and power spectral density requirements. This is most important since guideway

Table 11-1
Values for Relationship $PSD' = K/f'^n$

Plot Number (Figure 11-15)	Description	n	K
1	Runway	3.8	1.6×10^{-11}
2	Runway 3	2.0	2.2×10^{-7}
3	Runway 1	2.6	2.9×10^{-8}
4	Runway 35	2.1	7.7×10^{-7}
5	Smooth Highway	2.1	1.2×10^{-6}
6	Runway	1.9	2.3×10^{-6}
7	Runway 12	2.0	2.5×10^{-6}
8	Runway 4	4.1	5.3×10^{-9}
9	Smooth Runway	2.1	6.6×10^{-6}
10	Gravel Highway	2.1	1.1×10^{-5}
11	Rough Runway	2.1	2.3×10^{-5}
12	Site 3 Welded Track Vertical Waviness	2.0	2.0×10^{-7}
13	Site 3 Welded Track Cross Level	1.5	1.2×10^{-6}

Reprinted from "High Speed Rail Systems," TRW Systems, PB 192-506, Redondo Beach, California, February 1970.

roughness data is usually available in terms of power spectral density curves, while ride quality tolerances are given in terms of peak amplitudes of pure sinusoidal oscillations. To relate *PSD* data with ride quality data, the procedure is simply to:

1. Convert the spatial *PSD* to the frequency domain.
2. Convert the *PSD* data into peak amplitudes by dividing it into discrete frequencies and band widths and using equation 11.69.
3. Pass the amplitude data through the transmissibility function for the vehicle suspension.
4. Relate the $A_i s$ to the ride quality data using the techniques outlined by the International Standards Organization[13]

Guideway roughness power spectral density data is often given by an equation of the form:[14]

$$PSD' = K/f'^n \qquad (11.70)$$

Figure 11-15 and Table 11-1 list values of n and K for typical guideway surfaces.

As an example of how to use this data, consider surface number 7 whose power spectral density is given by:

$$PSD' = \frac{2.5 \times 10^{-6}}{f'^2} \qquad (11.71)$$

Converting to the frequency domain:

$$PSD = \frac{2.5 \times 10^{-6}v}{f^2} \qquad (11.72)$$

Next we divide the power spectral density data into m octal frequency bands so that:

$$B_i = 2^{(i-1)} \qquad (11.73)$$

$$f_i = 1.5B_i \qquad (11.74)$$

From equations 11.59 and 11.62:

$$A_i = \sqrt{2B_iPSD} = 1.48 \times 10^{-3}\sqrt{v/B_i} \qquad (11.75)$$

Assume the suspension may be characterized by a single degree of freedom system with a first resonance at 1 hertz and 50 percent of critical damping. The transmissibility is then:

$$T = \sqrt{\frac{1 + f^2}{1 - f^2 + f^4}} \qquad (11.76)$$

Multiplication of A_i by the transmissibility gives the magnitude of the disturbance transmitted to the vehicle in each frequency band.

Table 11-2 lists the disturbance amplitude in feet at the road and in the vehicle, and also the g's acceleration in the vehicle. To obtain acceleration, observe that $\ddot{x} = (2\pi f)^2 A_i$, and in g's the acceleration is thus $1.226f^2A_i$.

Table 11-2
Conversion of PSD Data to Ride Quality Data

Bandwidth hertz	Frequency hertz	A_i feet	T	A_iT feet	g's in Vehicle
1	1.5	0.0081	0.92	0.0074	0.0204
2	3	0.0057	0.37	0.0021	0.0232
4	6	0.0040	0.17	0.0007	0.0309
8	12	0.0029	0.08	0.00023	0.0406
16	24	0.0020	0.04	0.00008	0.0565
32	48	0.0014	0.02	0.00002	0.0565

Velocity—30 feet/second.

Table 11-3
Weighting Functions

Band	C_i	C_f/C_i	$(C_f/C_i)g$	$(C_f/C_i)^2g^2$
1-2	0.024	0.6	0.014	0.000196
2-4	0.017	0.88	0.020	0.000400
4-8	0.015	1.0	0.0309	0.000955
8-16	0.022	0.68	0.027	0.000729
16-32	0.043	0.35	0.020	0.000400
32-64	0.088	0.17	0.009	0.000081
				0.00276

Square root = 0.052 g

Table 11-2 was prepared for a vehicle speed of 30 feet/second. The values of the weighting function in each frequency range as obtained from Figure 11-12 are given in Table 11-3. From Figure 11-12, this vibration can be tolerated for over one hour.

Notes

1. "Passenger Psychological Dynamics," Kathleen M. Solomon, Richard J. Solomon, and Joseph S. Silien, American Society of Engineers, New York, June 1968, (Sources of Information on Urban Transportation—Report No.3).

2. *Mechanical Vibrations,* Austin H. Church, John Wiley and Sons, New York, 1957.

3. Ibid.

4. *Standard Handbook for Mechanical Engineers,* 7th edition, T. Baumeister and L.S. Marks, McGraw-Hill Book Company, New York, 1967.

5. "High Speed Rail Systems," TRW Systems Group, PB 192506. Redondo Beach, California, February, 1970, pages 6.1-6, 6.4-15 et seq.

6. *Mechanical Design and Systems Handbook,* H.A. Rothbart, McGraw-Hill Book Company, New York, 1964, pages 36-12.

7. "Study of the Potential of Hovair for High Speed Ground Transportation," Frederick Jindra, PB 177523, General Motors Laboratories, Warren, Michigan, March 1968, page 94.

8. "Vehicle Vibration Limits to Fit the Passenger," R.N. Janeway,

SAE paper SP-15, presented at Society of Automotive Engineers National Passenger Car and Production Meeting, Detroit, March 3-5, 1948.

9. "Guide for the Evaluation of Human Exposure to Whole Body Vibration," Proposed International Standard ISO 2631, International Organization for Standardization, Berlin, Germany, February 1974; "Guide for the Evaluation of Human Exposure to Whole Body Vibration," ISO/TC 108/WG7, December 1968, International Organization for Standardization, Technical Committee 108, Letter of Transmittal, January 9, 1969 (unpublished); "A Study for the Selection of an Intermediate Capacity Public Transit System," Ontario Department of Transportation and Communications, revised January 1972; and "Method of Evaluating Vehicle Ride Quality Acceleration Data," N. Rubinstein and W.C. Caywood, Engineering Memo EM4489, Johns Hopkins University Applied Physics Laboratory, Silver Spring, Maryland, December 14, 1972.

10. Ibid.

11. *Shock and Vibration Handbook,* C.M. Harris and C.E. Crede, Vols. 2 and 3, McGraw-Hill Book Company, New York, 1961.

12. Ibid.

13. See note 9.

14. See note 5.

12 Lateral Guidance and Switching

It is useful to categorize transportation vehicles in terms of the degrees of translational freedom of movement they possess. In this context the airplane may be said to possess three degrees of freedom. The automobile, and bus, although usually traveling on linear roadways, inherently have two degrees of freedom, since they are built to operate anywhere on a suitably paved planar surface. The rail vehicle, on the other hand, is a true one dimensional vehicle, lacking the ability to steer itself and being inherently constrained to follow the channel defined by the tracks on which it runs. Similarly new systems such as personal rapid transit are often designed as one dimensional systems.

The distinction of vehicles in terms of freedom of motion is an important one, not only in terms of defining their flexibility but also for determining their potential for automatic control. From the viewpoint of automatic control, the flexibility inherent in a two or three degree of freedom vehicle becomes a liability, as the two problems of controlling the motion of each vehicle and controlling the interactions between vehicles become enormously more complicated. Thus, excepting ballistic missiles and space vehicles, whose flight is essentially controlled to a specified channel by the laws of falling bodies, comparatively little progress has been made in remote control of aircraft. Electronic control of automobiles, on the other hand, has progressed to the test track stage. But with trains, where only the longitudinal motion and choice of directions at switch points require control, completely automatic systems are already carrying passengers. Similarly the elevator, consisting simply of a single vehicle constrained to a single shaft, was the first public conveyance to be successfully automated.

Many new systems being built are attempting to take the rubber tire, inherently designed to permit two degrees of movement, and mechanically constrain it to a single degree of freedom in order to simplify the control problem. Interaction between the lateral forces generated by tire slip and the lateral forces generated by mechanical constraint of the rubber tired vehicles, can induce high stresses in the suspension parts and cause rapid tire wear. It is necessary to be quite careful when adopting a rubber tired vehicle in this manner to be sure that its intrinsic principles of motion are not compromised.[1]

Steel Rail Guidance

The use of steel rails to guide vehicles is over 150 years old and dates back to horse drawn carriages. As a matter of fact, the 4′8½″ distance between track centers was originally dictated by the design of wagons. Steel rail systems have several advantages, foremost of which is their ability to support very high loads with low rolling drag and relatively low guideway costs. In addition, the railroad vehicle is easily switched and provides safe and reliable service. Speeds can be quite high. The Japanese New Tokaido Line operates a regularly scheduled operation at a speed of 125 mph and speeds up to 200 mph are believed feasible.[2] In addition, the one degree of freedom nature of the system makes it ideal for automated operation.

But the steel wheel on rail concept also has its deficiencies. A major limitation is wheel adhesion, or the ability to transmit tractive thrust between a steel wheel and rail. Automated transit systems have experienced difficulty in consistently maintaining acceleration and deceleration without wheel slip at levels barely over 0.1 g.[3]

Another serious problem is wheel screech. This is a high frequency piercing squeal caused by sliding of the steel wheel on the steel rail. It can occur as a result of loss of adhesion during acceleration or braking. In this case, the sliding of the wheel will produce a flat spot which results in the familiar railroad "clackety clack." Wheel grinding facilities to remove such flats dominate the operations of rail vehicle maintenance facilities. Wheel screech can also occur on turns when the wheel flange scrapes against the rail. Since flange contact is inevitable to react lateral forces on tight radius turns, some rail operations lubricate the sides of the rails in these turns to reduce wheel screech. However, it is often necessary to slow down on such turns, and migration of the grease to the rail head can cause loss of braking adhesion. Wheel screech from adhesion failure is thus aggravaged by the very procedure used to reduce wheel screech from flange contact. Further aggravating the problem of screech on turns is the fact that railroad trains use straight axles without a differential to permit different rotational speeds for wheels on the inside and outside of a turn. This means that on a tight turn, significant slip between the track running surface and the wheel is inevitable.

Wheel screech is a major reason why a survey of rapid transit properties in the United States and Canada concluded that noise was their most serious hardware related problem.[4] Noise and vibration are also inherent in the rigidity of the wheel rail interface. This rigidity makes both ride quality and noise extremely sensitive to proper maintenance of both the track and the steel wheels. Track surface should be free of corrugations, and alignment and offset tolerances rigidly controlled to prevent high noise and vibration levels. Maintenance can easily affect noise levels by 20 decibels.[5]

Unfortunately, the first areas to be cut back in the face of rising transit operating costs are inevitably track maintenance and wheel grinding schedules. The Federal Railroad Administration now specifies minimal standards for the condition of track from the viewpoint of safety (e.g., prevention of derailments).

A final deficiency inherent in the steel wheel on rail concept is "hunting" or track oscillation. Figure 12-1 shows a sketch of the steel wheel on rail guidance system. It is usual to taper the steel wheels as shown to prevent the almost constant rubbing of one or the other flange against the rail. The coning typically ranges from one part in twenty to one part in forty.[6] This is inadequate to generate significant lateral forces in curves where guidance is achieved almost entirely by the lateral forces exerted by the flanges. However, it does succeed in keeping the vehicle properly centered on straight track. The centering forces are generated by frictional forces at the wheel rail interface caused by the conical shape of the wheel.

If a rail vehicle with coned wheels is displaced laterally a small distance from the centerline of the track, there is a difference in the rolling radii of the left and right wheels. Because the wheels are mounted on a common axle and rotating at the same angular velocity, longitudinal creep forces are created. These forces in turn cause a yawing couple that generates lateral creep forces to steer the vehicle back towards the center position. Interaction between the longitudinal and lateral creep forces causes an oscillation of the wheel set from side to side that is known as "hunting." The hunting frequency at low speeds is given by:[7]

$$f = \frac{v}{2\pi}\sqrt{\frac{2\lambda}{lr_0}} \qquad (12.1)$$

$l =$ wheel track width—feet

$r_0 =$ wheel radius—feet

$\lambda =$ wheel conicity—feet per foot of width

$v =$ vehicle speed—feet per second

Interaction of suspension and inertial forces with the creep forces causes the hunting motion to become unstable above a critical speed. One of the reasons for the use of two sets of four wheeled bogies for rail system guidance is that the system has a much higher critical speed than a simple four wheeled vehicle. The bogie is generally designed with high lateral and yaw primary suspension stiffness and high critical speeds are obtained by providing a high yaw stiffness in the secondary suspension between the bogie frame and body.[8] The use of stiff lateral suspension to control hunting may be responsible for some of the annoying ride characteristics evident in trains—in particular—the susceptibility to rail misalignment.

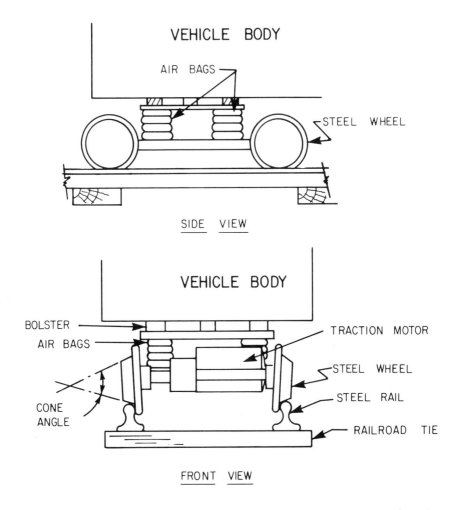

Figure 12-1. Railroad Truck or Bogie (typical of modern transit car)

Railroad Switches

Figure 12-2 shows the basic types of railroad switching functions. The "turnout" switch is designed to permit either merging or diverging from the mainline track. Since the mainline track is usually straight to permit higher speeds, it is referred to as the tangent track while the merge-diverge section is called the turnout track. As illustrated, the switch is a merge for traffic proceeding from the right and a diverge for traffic coming from the left. Notice that from the safety point of view the diverge condition is inherently

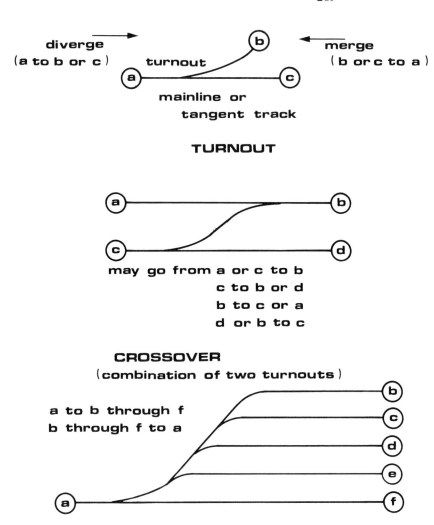

Figure 12-2. Railroad Switch Configurations

safe. Whichever direction the train goes, since traffic is being split, no traffic conflicts are possible.

In the merge condition where traffic is being combined, safety is a problem. Vehicles on the turnout and tangent track must share use of the switch so that conflicts do not occur. In addition, the position of the switch must be made to correspond to the track direction from which the train is coming. If the switch is set in the turnout direction and the train comes from the tangent direction it will "run the switch." While the switch is designed to be reasonably tolerant of such abuse there is an increased risk of derailment. Figure 12-2 also shows a crossover, where traffic may be routed from one track to another. The crossover consists of two turnout switches placed to create a diverge-merge combination. Notice that certain movements are not possible with the crossover. Thus for the crossover one can not go from c to a or from b to d without backing up.

Figure 12-2 also shows a "Ladder Track" arrangement used often in yards where many trains must be stored and rearranged. This is a series of diverge turnouts arranged in parallel form. Notice one can go from the mainline to any of the spurs but it is not possible to move from spur to spur without returning to the mainline and backing up.

Railroad systems also have an arrangement known as a crossing, which permits two different tracks to cross one another. It is *not* a switch since traffic on one track can not be routed to the other. As shown in Figure 12-3 the crossing permits movement from a to b or from c to d but does not permit movement from c to a or b or from b to c or d. Although not a switch, a crossing requires protection to prevent its use by more than one train at the same time.

Railroad Split Switch

The standard railroad turnout switch is known as the "split switch." It was developed over the years as a safe, reliable and economical means of switching trains. The split switch is shown in Figure 12-4. The large dotted lines indicate standard track rail and are not movable. They represent the "envelope" of the switch section. The point where the tangent and turnout track envelope intersects is called the "switch frog." Wing rails at the switch frog are designed to permit the vehicle to pass in either the tangent or turnout directions at the point of the switch. The active part of the switch consists of two parallel rails pivoted at one end (the heel) and moved by the switch actuator to align with either the turnout or tangent sides of the switch envelope. The ends of the switch that must fare into the envelope (the "toe" of the switch) are ground to a taper. When the switch is placed so that it aligns with the turnout side of the switch envelope, the wheels are blocked from entering the turnout and the train will take the straight direction. If the switch is aligned with the tangent side, it blocks the vehicle entrance into the tangent portion of the switch and diverts the train into the turnout. A vehicle proceeding into the switch at a merge will tend to force the switch in the proper direction even if it is improperly set—although the risk of derailment is increased if the switch position is incorrect. In recognition of its reliability and safety, the split switch is almost universally

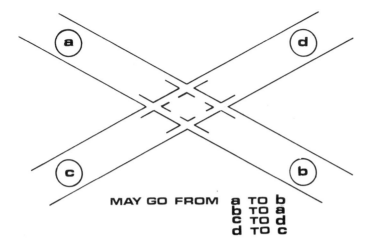

Crossings carry two tracks across each other at grade. Vehicles may not switch from one line to another. This is not a switch.

Figure 12-3. Rail Crossing

used on rail systems today. Because of the added complexity, split switch turnout sections are generally not superelevated. Thus, although speed need not be restricted on the tangent portion of the switch, speed limitations may be required on the turnout depending on its radius of curvature. Table 12-1 gives typical turnout speed limits for various radii turnouts.

Railroad Stub Switch

The stub switch has been largely superceded by the safer and more reliable split switch, but is still in use in yards and track sidings. The stub switch is not foolproof or safe for high speed operation. Figure 12-5 shows the details of the stub switch concept.

Rubber Tired Vehicle Steering

Standard automotive steering is based upon a modification of the simple parallelogram steering principle shown in Figure 12-6. Collapse of the parallelogram structure causes the wheels to turn. Most automobiles today

272

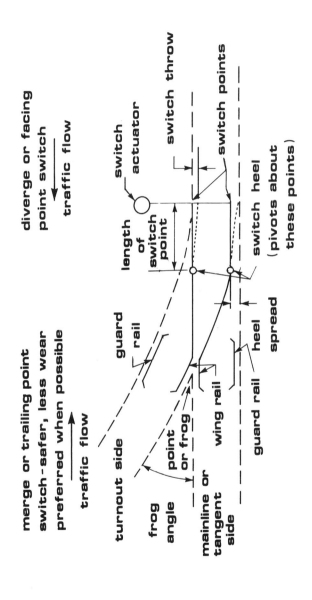

Figure 12-4. Railroad Split Switch

Table 12-1
Effect of Turnout Radius on Allowable Speed

Radius of Curve feet	Turnout Speed* mph
178	12
615	21
1581	28
3289	38

*Assumes lateral turnouts.

Source: *AREA Manual for Railway Engineering*, American Railway Engineering Association, Chicago, Illinois, 1948.

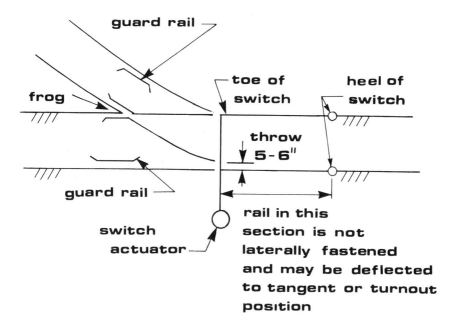

Figure 12-5. Railroad Stub Switch

use the Ackerman linkage, which is modified from the simple parallelogram to permit independent vertical motion of the front wheels.[9] As is clear from

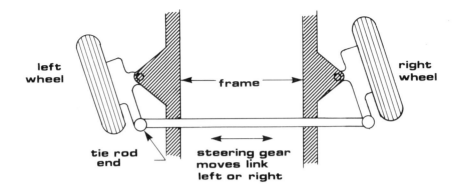

Figure 12-6. Simplified Parallelogram Type Steering Linkage

Figure 12-7, a simple parallelogram system would result in the inside and outside wheels turning about separate turn centers. In the Ackerman system, the geometry is arranged so that the inner wheel turns at a tighter radius than the outer wheel (see Figure 12-8). The relationship between turn radius and steering angle at zero vehicle speed is given by:

$$R \approx l/(2\sin\beta/2) \qquad (12.2)$$

R = turn radius—feet

l = wheelbase of vehicle—feet

β = steering angle—degrees

If the vehicle is turning at speed, a portion of the steering angle will be required to react centrifugal forces and the steering angle must be increased to negotiate the same turn radius.

Wagon Wheel Steering

Wagon wheel steering refers to a design where the axle is pivoted about its center. Figure 12-9 shows a vehicle with front and rear wagon wheel steering. Some new people mover concepts use steering of this type. At zero speed (with no slip angle effects) the turn radius is related to the steering angle by:

$$R = l/2\sin\beta \qquad (12.3)$$

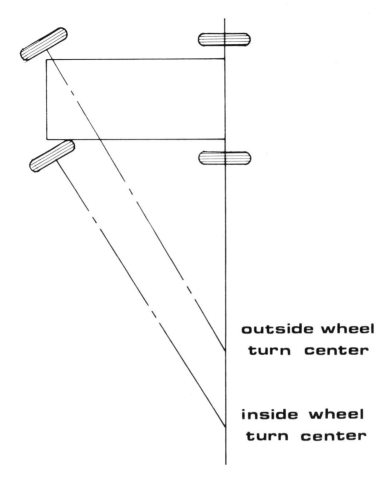

**outside wheel
turn center**

**inside wheel
turn center**

Figure 12-7. Parallelogram Linkage Has Different Turn Centers for Front
Wheels

Oversteer and Understeer

A rubber tired vehicle will tend to be stable or "understeer" if the forces
that result from perturbing it act to oppose the disturbing force. It will tend
to be unstable or "oversteer" if the forces that result from perturbing it act
to augment the disturbing force. While the actual dynamics of vehicle

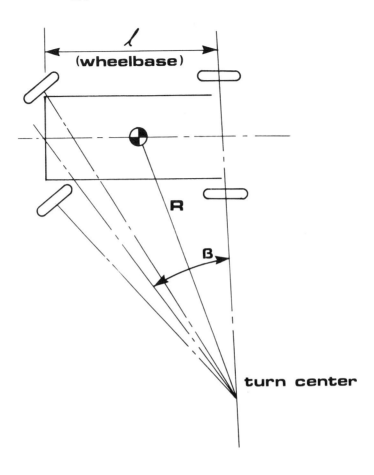

Figure 12-8. Ackerman Steering Geometry Produces Tighter Turn Radius for Inside Front Wheel So Both Front Wheels Have the Same Turn Center

stability are quite complicated, this principle may be illustrated by considering the effect of caster on vehicle stability. It is important to realize that caster is only one of many forces that are used to control vehicle understeer and oversteer.

Caster Effect. In the absence of other forces, a rubber tire will be stable or

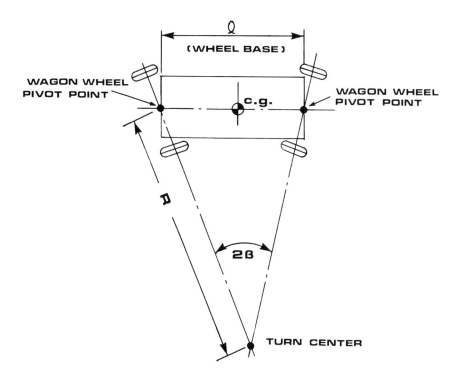

Figure 12-9. Wagon Wheel Steering

understeer if the intersection of the axis about which the wheel is pivoted (to steer the vehicle) with the ground plane is in *front* of the point on the tire at which resultant frictional drag forces act. It is unstable (oversteer) if this intersection is behind the point on the tire at which resultant frictional drag forces act. Figure 12-10 and 12-11 illustrate the situation.[10]

Assume the tire is rolling slightly misaligned with the vehicle direction of motion by an angle α. This angle is called the slip angle. Drag of the tire sidewise in the direction of vehicle motion will produce a thrust F on the tire. This thrust will produce a net torque Fx tending to align the wheel with the direction of vehicle motion, providing that the force F is behind the pivot axis intersection with the ground plane. The quantity Fx is called the "self-aligning" torque. As we have seen, caster is one means of producing self-aligning torque. The magnitude of F increases with slip angle until the limit of sliding is reached. At this point, the available force flattens out to

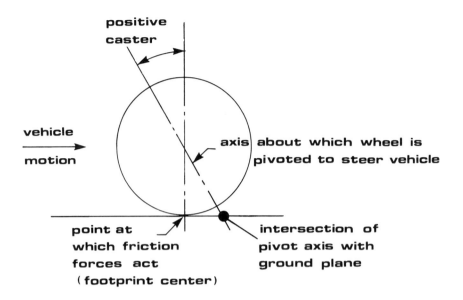

Figure 12-10. How Caster Generates a Self-Aligning Torque

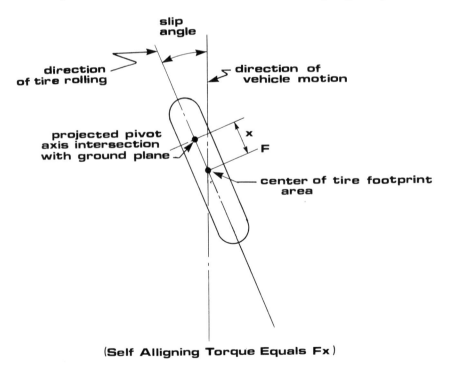

Figure 12-11. Generation of Self-Aligning Torque

the skid value. In a sharp turn the centrifugal force may overpower the available lateral force F (often called "cornering force") and result in a skid. If the cornering force were to act in front of the tire center of rotation it would turn the tire in the direction of the turn, tending to amplify any steering action. In this case a driver would have to apply a torque to prevent further turning instead of applying a torque to cause turning. This case of amplified steering action is called "oversteer."

A shopping cart wheel is a good illustration of the use of caster. So long as the wheels trail behind the pivot point (Figure 12-12) the vehicle will go wherever you push it. If the wheels are in front of the pivot point they will rotate swiftly around until they return to the stable trailing configuration. Caster is also used on motorcycles and bicycles as the primary means of obtaining understeer characteristics.

Camber and Toe-in. In addition to caster, camber and toe-in are also important geometric properties of rubber tired suspensions. Toe-in represents the angle at which the tires are "pigeon toed" inwards during normal straight-ahead driving (see Figure 12-13). The slip forces caused by toe-in provide a self-aligning torque to keep the vehicle traveling in a straight line without continual driver correction. Camber represents the difference in the track width between the wheels as measured at the top and bottom of the tire (see Figure 12-13). The tires usually are slanted inwards so that the track at the ground plane is narrower than that measured between the tops of the tires. Camber also affects the self-aligning torque.

Switches in Transit Systems

There is at present a great deal of research in the field of transit, which has produced a number of novel switching concepts. The ideal switching operation may be said to consist of the following sequence:

1. Switch unlock—if no vehicle conflicts are possible the switch is unlocked to permit it to respond to a command and power is applied to the switch actuation circuit.
2. Switch command—a signal is sent to change the position of the switch.
3. Switch actuation—the switch mechanism is permitted to respond and move the switch into the desired position.
4. Switch lock—the switch mechanism is locked so it can not respond to any future command to change its position and power is removed from the switch actuation circuit.
5. Switch position verification—independent verification of correct switch position is transmitted back to the source of the switch command.

This could be considered to be the ideal safe switching sequence. An

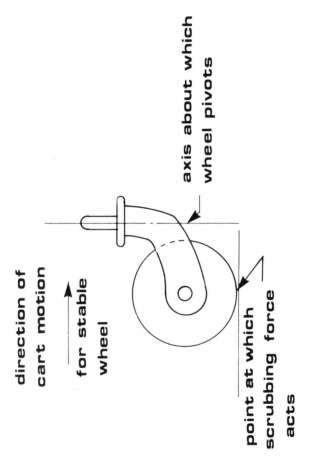

Figure 12-12. How Caster Affects a Shopping Cart Wheel

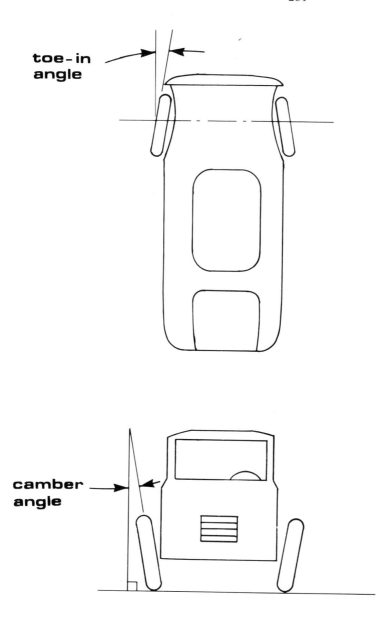

Figure 12-13. Camber and Toe-in Angles

independent switch lock prevents movement of the switch once it has been dedicated to the movement of a particular vehicle through the switch section. Switch movements are only permitted when vehicle safety cannot be affected by an incorrect switch movement. After the switch position is changed and relocked, the new position is verified by a system completely independent of the command and actuation functions.

In addition to this actuation sequence, the ideal switch will provide *positive* lateral guidance of the vehicle throughout the merge or diverge region. Positive lateral guidance means that vehicle lateral position is mechanically constrained to a unique path as opposed to relying upon frictional type forces.

It is important to realize that not all switching concepts have the attributes of this ideal switch—nor has it been proven that all of these attributes are necessary to have a safe switch. It can be shown, however, that possible failure modes are introduced if a switch departs from these ideal characteristics.

Types of Switches

Switches may be loosely classified into three categories:

1. Guideway switches
2. Vehicle switches
3. Guideway actuated vehicle switches

The railroad switch is a good example of a guideway switch. The automobile steering system, on the other hand, provides an excellent example of a vehicle switch. Guideway actuated vehicle switches are typical of some new automated transit systems. For example the Airtrans system at Dallas-Fort Worth Regional Airport uses this type of switch.

The guideway switch has several important advantages. Foremost, perhaps, is that it lends itself very nicely to the movement of mechanically coupled trains. Since all moving switch parts are in the guideway, there is no risk of one vehicle in the train trying to go in a different direction than its brothers. (This can be a serious problem for trained vehicles using a vehicle switching concept.) In addition, guideway switches can be placed as close together as is permitted by geometrical design considerations. This is because all switches can be set in advance *before* the vehicle arrives at the first switch. With a vehicle switch, it may be necessary to change the vehicle switch direction as one passes through a sequence of turnouts. The time required safely to accomplish such a movement sets a limitation on how close together switches can be placed. If complex station movements are required, the vehicle switch may provide less flexibility and require more real estate than the guideway switch. Finally, guideway switches have a long and successful history of application in the field of automated transit. They can be looked upon as safe and reliable.

The guideway switch, however, also has several serious deficiencies. First, since it is necessary to move a portion of the guideway, the guideway switch can be heavy and cumbersome. As a result it may have a slow actuation time.[a] With large numbers of guideway switches needed throughout the system, their relatively high cost becomes an important consideration. When close headway vehicle operation is required, the guideway switch may be deficient. The headway between vehicles must be increased by the time required to reposition the guideway switch in the event subsequent vehicles are following different routes. The increase in headway can be significant. Sufficient extra time must be provided not only for moving the switch, but for locking it and independently verifying correct position. For this reason close headway systems generally would not use guideway switching.

The vehicle switch is ideal for close headway operation since subsequent vehicles can be preset for different routes in advance of the actual diverge section of the guideway. The vehicle switch will also be much lighter so that it is both less expensive and tends to have a more rapid switching time. With a vehicle switch there are no moving parts in the guideway, reducing guideway costs and eliminating environmental problems such as freezing of switches in bad weather. On the negative side, it is difficult to assure that a train of vehicles will all be switched in the same direction. Problems can arise in verifying proper switch positioning, especially where multiple switch arms are involved. Finally, where multiple diverge switches are to be close together, as in a ladder switch arrangement, the vehicle switch is deficient. The spacing between "rungs on the ladder" must be large enough to permit repositioning, locking, and verifying the vehicle switch.

The guideway actuated vehicle switch is an attempt to get the best features of both types of switches. Guideway actuation is meant to assure that all vehicles in a mechanically coupled train position their switch mechanisms in the same direction. Having the actual switching function on the vehicle eliminates the heavy weight, high cost, and long actuation time inherent in many guideway switches. If it is not necessary to verify that the vehicle has correctly responded to the guideway actuation, then ladder switching arrangements may be spaced as close as desired. However, if it *is* necessary to verify that the vehicle mechanism has properly responded to the actuation input from the guideway, then the ladder spacing must be increased in the same way as for the vehicle switch. In addition, vehicle headways may have to be increased by the time required to move, lock, and verify the position of the actuator mechanism. Because of its lighter weight, this penalty can be less than that for a guideway switch.

---

[a] This is not *necessarily* true. Railroad switches have been built with actuation times of less than a second.

Guidance Characteristics of Vehicle and Guideway
Actuated Vehicle Switches

The major distinction between vehicle and guideway actuated vehicle switches is whether the switch is active on the vehicle, or whether it passively responds to the mechanical position of an actuating device on the guideway. Almost all vehicle and guideway actuated vehicle switches are based upon a curb following principal. The guideway is "U" shaped with vertical sidewalls. In a switch area the vehicle is constrained to follow either the left or right guideway sidewall, thereby selecting its switch direction.

The switch may be further characterized depending upon how it follows the guideway wall. If mechanical forces between the vehicle and the guideway walls literally force the vehicle to follow a particular direction the switch may be called a herd switch. A common type of herd switch employs lateral guidance wheels that literally grab on to the guideway sidewall in the direction of the turn. At the other extreme, the guideway may simply provide an input signal which is then used to turn a conventional auto steering mechanism. In this case the actual steering forces are developed through tire slip generating lateral tire scrubbing forces. Such an approach is called a "curb follower." In between the extremes of herd and curb follower guidance are combinations in which some of the force is provided by the walls and some by the tires. The analysis of just how the forces will distribute under these conditions is rather complicated and as a result many steering problems have been experienced with prototype designs attempting to use sidewall guidance with rubber tired vehicles.

A major objection to "curb follower" guidance is the dependence upon tire friction for vehicle control in the switch area. The presence of ice, brake lock up, flat tires, or other failures causing large yaw moments on the vehicle could cause it to go out of control, possibly impacting the guideway sidewall or the switch frog. A similar problem exists with "automated highway" concepts in which an automotive steering mechanism is steered by signals from cables buried in the guideway. In addition, the latter system is prone to communications and electrical failures in the guidance system.

Table 12-2 lists switches used in a number of new automated transit systems and characterizes them in the manner described in this chapter.

Vehicle Stability Analysis

A transit vehicle must not tip over when subjected to the worst case combination of centrifugal load, wind load, and dynamic load caused by guideway roughness. Side wind loads at 60 mph are roughly ten pounds per

Table 12-2
Switch Concepts

System	Switching/Lateral Guidance
Alden Switch Morgantown, W. Va. PRT	On vehicle—curb follower— Ackerman steering
Bendix Dashaveyor	Guideway switch
TTI Air Cushion PRT	On vehicle—herd guidance
Airtrans	Guideway actuated vehicle switch—herd and curb follower combination— parallelogram steering
Monocab	Guideway actuated vehicle switch—herd and curb follower— castered wagon wheel type steering
General Motors Dual Mode	On vehicle—buried cable lateral guidance—Ackerman steering
Ford ACT	On vehicle—herd and curb follower combination—wagon wheel steering

square foot of surface. Centrifugal loads are of course directly proportional to the square of the speed and inversely proportional to the turn radius. Dynamic load factors will vary depending upon the application and terrain. For automobiles, a rule of thumb is that stable operation will be possible provided that:[11]

1. The center of gravity is not more than 75 percent aft or forward.

2. Lateral acceleration of at least 1.5 g is possible without tipping.

For guided vehicles such as trains, a total wind, centrifugal, and dynamic lateral load of 1.5 times the vehicle weight would be unnecessarily stringent. Values of about half this would be more typical. This is because the guided vehicle can not be subjected to such sudden steering maneuvers on such unpredictable terrain as an automobile. Figure 12-14 shows a vehicle taking a superelevated turn in a sidewind. The equation for tipping stability for small superelevation angles is given by:

$$F_d(\bar{y} - \alpha T/2) - W(T/2 + \bar{y}\alpha) + F_w H < 0 \qquad (12.4)$$

F_d = centrifugal force plus dynamic load force—pounds

$\bar{y}$ = distance from guideway surface to vehicle center of gravity—feet

α = superelevation angle—radians

T = vehicle track width—feet

W = vehicle weight—pounds

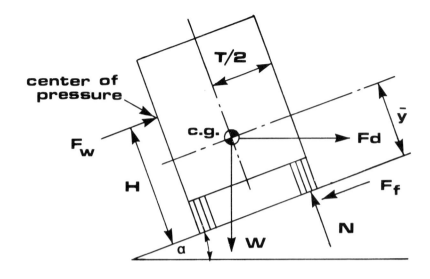

Figure 12-14. Vehicle Tipping Stability

F_w = sidewind load—pounds

H = distance from guideway surface to center of pressure of side of vehicle—feet

If the vehicle is stationary on the same incline with a sidewind blowing *down* the incline, the condition for stability becomes:

$$F_w H - W (T/2 - \bar{y}\alpha) < 0 \qquad (12.5)$$

To prevent tipping the most stringent of these conditions should be used. In general equation 12.4 will be found to govern.

Notes

1. *Post-Transpo Test Program—Summary Report,* Volume 1, R.T. Cusick and E.E. Mooring, editors, CP 029/TPR 026, Johns Hopkins University Applied Physics Laboratory, Silver Spring, Maryland, June 1973, page IV-113, et seq.

2. "High Speed Rail Systems," TRW Systems Group, PB 192506, Redondo Beach, California, February 1970.

3. "Research Requirements Survey of the Rapid Rail Industry," T.J. McGean, PB 204438, Mitre Corporation, McLean, Virginia, June 17, 1971.

4. Ibid.

5. "Comparison of Noise and Vibration Levels in Rapid Transit Vehicle Systems," Edward W. Davis et al., PB 184973, Operations Research Inc., Silver Spring, Maryland, April 1964.

6. "Recent Developments in the Lateral Dynamics of High Speed Railway Vehicles," A.H. Wickens, Monthly Bulletin of the International Railway Congress Association, December 1967.

7. "Vehicle Dynamics and Wheel Rail Interface Problems," Allen H. Wickens, TRI-3 High Speed Ground Transportation, Carnegie-Mellon University, Pittsburgh, 1969.

8. See note 6.

9. *Standard Handbook for Mechanical Engineers,* 7th edition, T. Baumeister and L.S. Marks, McGraw-Hill Book Company, New York, 1967, pages 11-13, et seq.

10. "Mechanics of Vehicles," J. Taborek, reprinted from *Machine Design,* Penton Publishing Company, Cleveland, Ohio, May 30, 1957 through December 26, 1957 issues inclusive.

11. "New Systems Implementation Study—Vol. II, Planning and Evaluation Methods—Study in New Systems of Urban Transportation," E.T. Canty et al., PB 178274, General Motors Research Laboratories, Warren, Michigan, February 1968.

Index

About the Author

Thomas McGean has been developing and teaching graduate level introductory courses in transportation technology at both George Washington University and Howard University. As a transportation systems engineer at the MITRE Corporation, he supported the Urban Mass Transportation Administration, Federal Rail Administration and Office of High Speed Ground Transportation on programs ranging from 300 mph tracked air cushion vehicles to improved subway cars. He has been on the conference committee for the 1973 and 1975 International Conference on Personal Rapid Transit, and is a member of the New Systems and Technology Committee of the Transportation Research Board and the Automated Guideway Transit Task Force of the American Public Transit Association. He also served on a task force evaluating automated transit systems for the Office of Technology Assessment at the request of the U.S. Senate. Mr. McGean has been a major contributor to alternative evaluations of transit modes in numerous cities including Denver, the Twin Cities, Los Angeles, Pittsburgh, and Santa Clara. He recently headed a federally sponsored study of light rail transit and is currently engaged in private practice as a transportation consultant.